POSTCARD HISTORY SERIES

Broome County

IN VINTAGE POSTCARDS

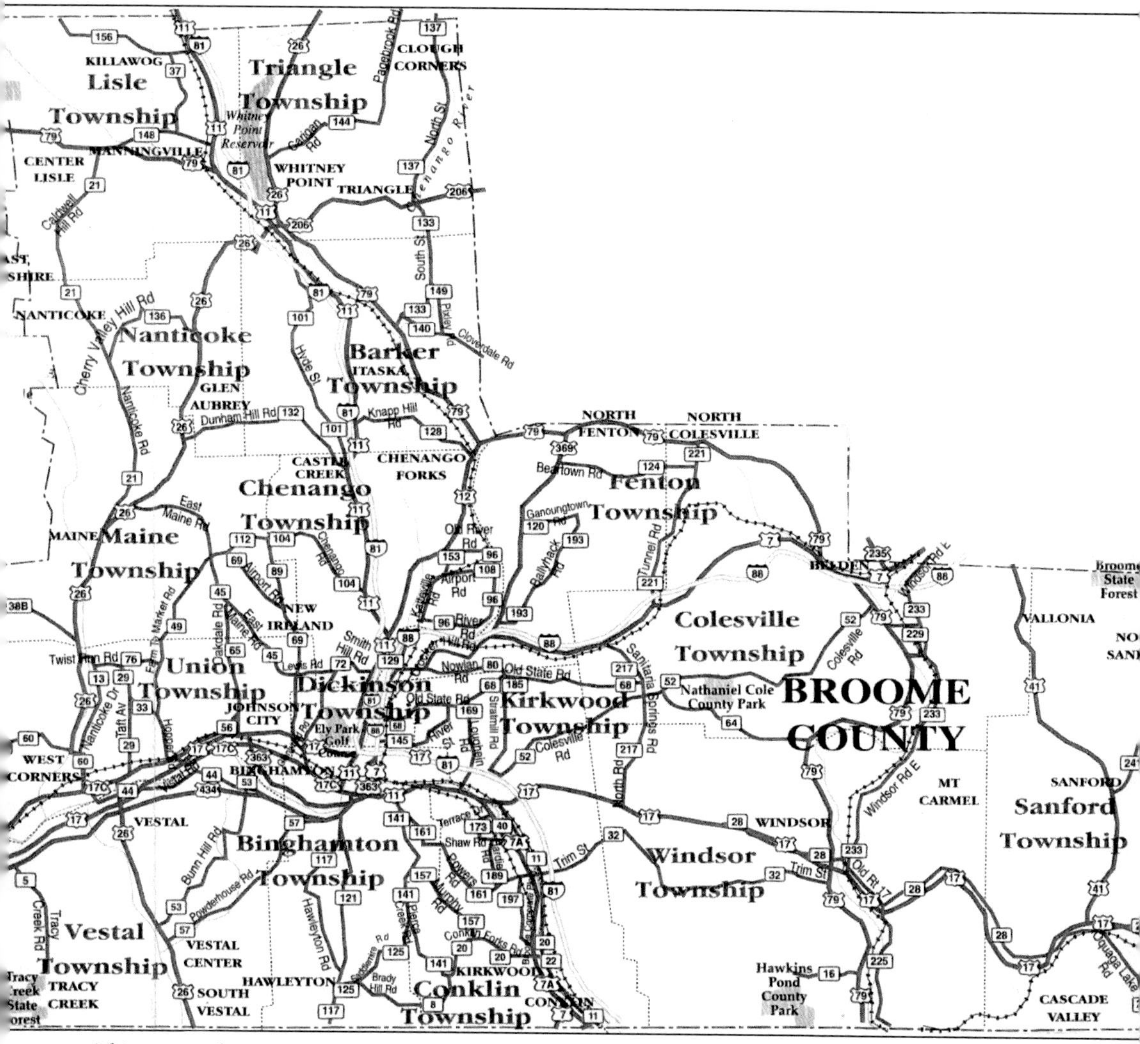

This map shows Broome County, which was established in 1806 when it separated from neighboring Tioga County.

POSTCARD HISTORY SERIES

Broome County

IN VINTAGE POSTCARDS

Ed Aswad and Suzanne M. Meredith

ARCADIA PUBLISHING

ISBN 978-0-7385-04447-6

Published by Arcadia Publishing
Charleston, South Carolina

Printed in the United States of America

Library of Congress Catalog Card Number: 00104044

For all general information contact Arcadia Publishing at:
Telephone 843-853-2070
Fax 843-853-0044
E-mail sales@arcadiapublishing.com
For customer service and orders:
Toll-Free 1-888-313-2665

Visit us on the Internet at www.arcadiapublishing.com

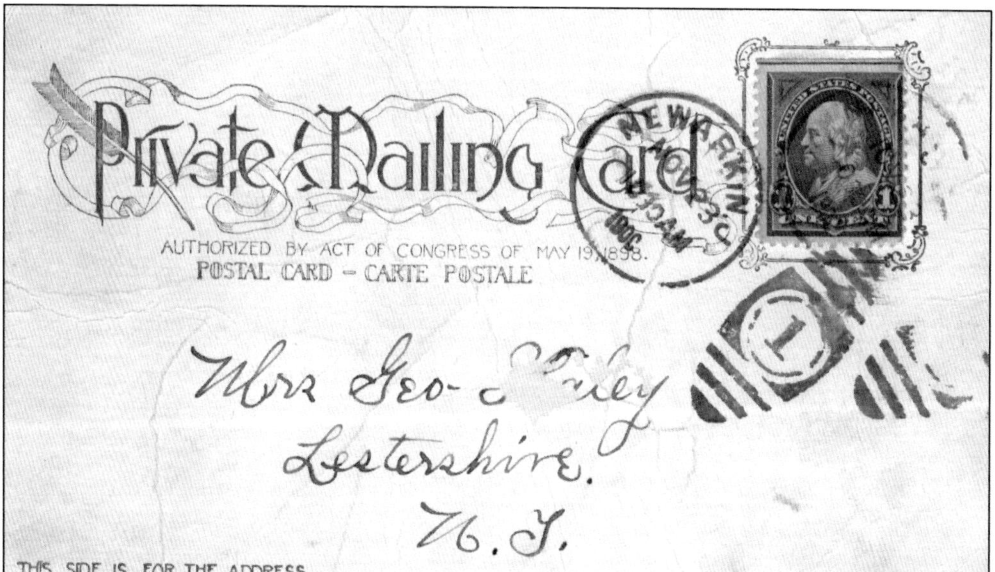

The private mailing card era is generally considered to be 1898 through 1901. By act of Congress in May 1898, private printers were given permission to produce postcards properly inscribed with the words "Private Mailing Card." Postage was 1¢. Writing was not permitted on the address side, but people often squeezed short notes around the picture on the front of the postcard. This postcard, mailed in 1900, is a fine example.

CONTENTS

ACKNOWLEDGMENTS

This volume is due in large measure to the historical awareness of Ed Aswad, who is well known for his dedication to collecting and preserving local history. At least 90 percent of the postcards included are from his vast collection. His willingness to share these rare images of Broome County make this a truly unique book. Furthermore, all of the new photo postcards and "after" images in Chapter Four were taken by him.

Special appreciation is expressed to Eloise Bower, Shirley Alig, the Amos Patterson Museum, Jan Mangan, and S. Meredith for allowing the use of postcards from their collections, and to Robert Struble for his expertise in identifying the year and make of the vintage automobiles.

This book is dedicated to

Marjory Hinman

in recognition of her example in

preserving our local heritage.

INTRODUCTION

From the legends of the Iroquois to modern high-tech corporations, the history of Broome County is the history of America. The picturesque city, towns, villages, and hamlets nestled in the twin river valley epitomize a way of life that our ancestors dreamed of achieving. Both Native Americans and immigrants from all over the world who settled in this area have contributed to a diverse and unique heritage.

In 1790, the land of Broome County was in part Montgomery County. A large area split off in 1791 as Tioga County, and at that time Chenango Point (Binghamton) was designated a half shire. Broome County was established in 1806, when it separated from Tioga. Broome now covers 710 square miles, including sixteen towns, two villages, and one city.

Over the decades, local history has been recorded in many forms. However, some of the truest images are preserved on postcards. Authorized by the U.S. Post Office in 1892, the first postcards printed as souvenirs were produced in 1893 at the Colombian Exposition in Chicago. When the U.S. government reduced the mailing card postage rate to a penny in 1898, they quickly became the greeting of choice. Fast, inexpensive, and fashionable, millions of miniature missives flooded the mailing system, conveying photographs, advertisements, humor, art, and history. The world fell in love with the visual mementos. Memories and messages could be sent around the world for 1¢. Collections of postcards became the rage, and in the process, a chronicle of life was preserved. Deltiology, or postcard collecting, is now the third largest hobby in America. There are as many categories of postcards as there are collectors; every subject has at one time been put in a postcard. After World War I, the increase in means of communication, the telephone, and radio, combined with higher postage rates, caused a drop in the number of postcards printed, thus ending the golden era of postcards.

Many of the vintage postcards presented here have never been published in book form. Each postcard is a tribute to the numerous anonymous photographers whose dedication and diligence preserved images of life. The real photo postcards offer a glimpse into the past that otherwise could have been lost. Everyday events were embedded in time through the photographer's lens.

The Broome County seat of Binghamton and the Triple Cities (Binghamton, Endicott, and Johnson City) are heavily showcased, as a great number of postcards were produced of this area. Every effort has been made to represent the entire region from approximately 1870 to the present day. A second volume is being planned, so search your attic and albums for messages from the past—postcards—and your find could be included in another *Broome County*.

Guest Introduction

The importance of picture postcards as historic documents cannot be overstressed. They are valuable records of the early days of our country. It was not until the local photography pioneer Ansco produced inexpensive cameras that families and the general public could afford to take their own pictures. Until that time, postcards were purchased from professional photographers so that images could be sent to friends and family.

Bird's-eye-view postcards, taken from hilltops, the dome of the courthouse, or a church tower are powerful tools for studying the early buildings and city layout. Many vintage postcards are the only records that exist of some significant subjects.

It is therefore good to see a comprehensive printing of a postcard book so that these historical images can be shared. We are indeed grateful to photographer Ed Aswad and writer-historian Suzanne Meredith for their collaboration on this important work. Ed Aswad has drawn on his collection of early postcards for the major portion of the book. His interest led to the creation of his own line of postcards, and we are indebted to him for continuing the photographic tradition, from the air as well as on the ground.

A Binghamton native, Ed has been snapping pictures since he was ten years old with his Ansco box camera. His professional career began as an army photographer at Fort Shafter in the Hawaiian Islands. From there, he served for 11 years as company photographer for General Electric in Westover, New York. His photography continued with Carriage House Photography, where he specializes in commercial, aerial, and industrial work, and is now sole owner of the business. He has a reputation as an outstanding photographer and an accomplished artist with a lens. He is also a recognized authority on cameos and a published co-author of the book *The Art and Mystique of Shell Cameos.*

Suzanne Meredith, also a Triple Cities native, has a passion for recording local history. She is the Town of Union historian and historical adviser to the Amos Patterson Museum. As a writer of note, her publications include *Images of America: Union,* a pictorial history of the Town of Union; *Gravely Interesting,* a book of unusual facts about cemeteries and mourning customs; and *Broome County: A Contemporary Portrait,* for which she wrote half the book containing business profiles. Her expertise in working with the crucial but often neglected oral history is evident in *Footsteps in Kindness,* a volume she coauthored with the subject, John H. Van Gorden, age 100. She has been president of the Association of Municipal Historians of New York State, a columnist for the local magazine *Tier Perceptions*, and continues as a freelance writer for numerous other publications.

—Marjory B. Hinman

One

The History of Postcards

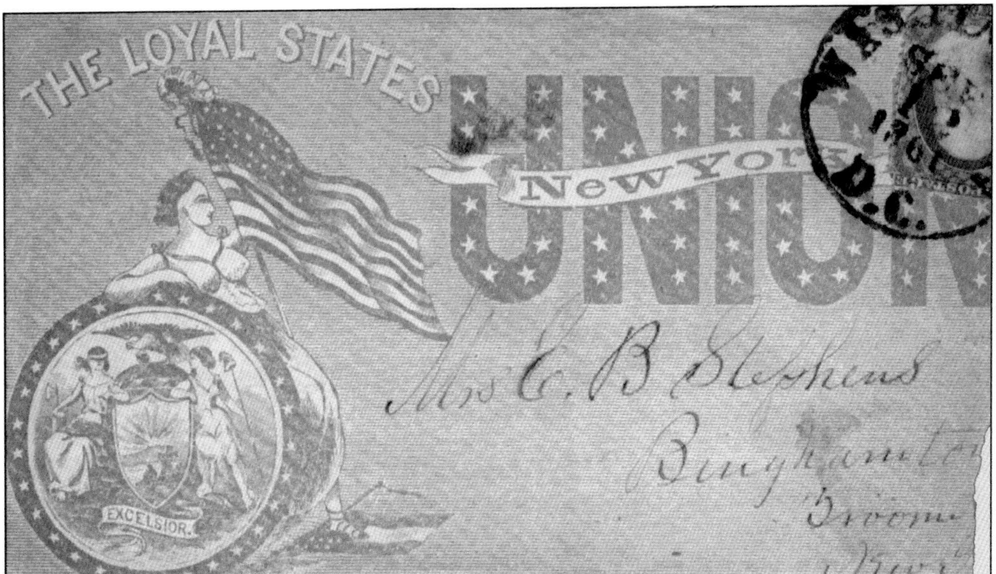

The direct ancestors of the postcard are envelopes printed with elaborate pictures. Thousands were produced during the Civil War era (1861 to 1865) and are now called Patriotic Covers. This envelope was mailed in 1861.

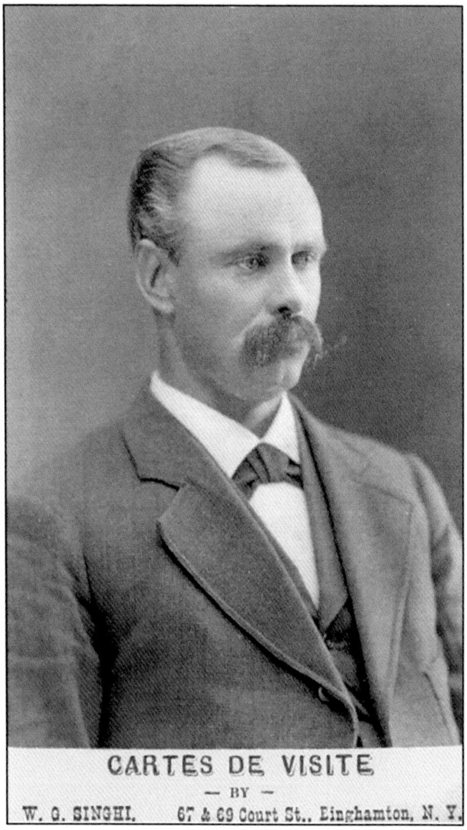

Another card influential in the creation of the postcard was the "Carte de Visite," usually printed in groups of from one to twenty for the client, and often mailed. This example is advertising the photographer's skill.

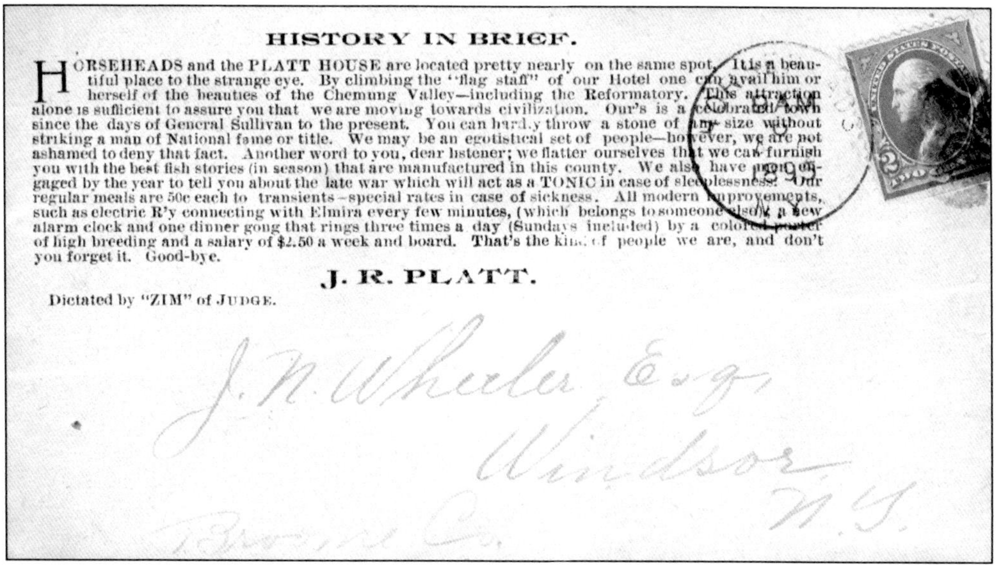

HISTORY IN BRIEF.

HORSEHEADS and the PLATT HOUSE are located pretty nearly on the same spot. It is a beautiful place to the strange eye. By climbing the "flag staff" of our Hotel one can avail him or herself of the beauties of the Chemung Valley—including the Reformatory. This attraction alone is sufficient to assure you that we are moving towards civilization. Our's is a celebrated town since the days of General Sullivan to the present. You can hardly throw a stone of any size without striking a man of National fame or title. We may be an egotistical set of people—however, we are not ashamed to deny that fact. Another word to you, dear listener; we flatter ourselves that we can furnish you with the best fish stories (in season) that are manufactured in this county. We also have men engaged by the year to tell you about the late war which will act as a TONIC in case of sleeplessness! Our regular meals are 50c each to transients—special rates in case of sickness. All modern improvements, such as electric R'y connecting with Elmira every few minutes, (which belongs to someone else), a new alarm clock and one dinner gong that rings three times a day (Sundays included) by a colored porter of high breeding and a salary of $2.50 a week and board. That's the kind of people we are, and don't you forget it. Good-bye.

J. R. PLATT.

Dictated by "ZIM" of JUDGE.

J. N. Wheeler Esq,
Windsor
N.Y.
Broome Co.

A letter sent to a Broome County resident in 1895 is also a forerunner of the postcard. This one includes details about a boardinghouse. The Platt House advertisement wants readers to understand that it is run by good people who "pay a colored porter, of high breeding, a salary of $2.50 a week and board, and that is the kind of people we are and don't you forget it. Good-bye."

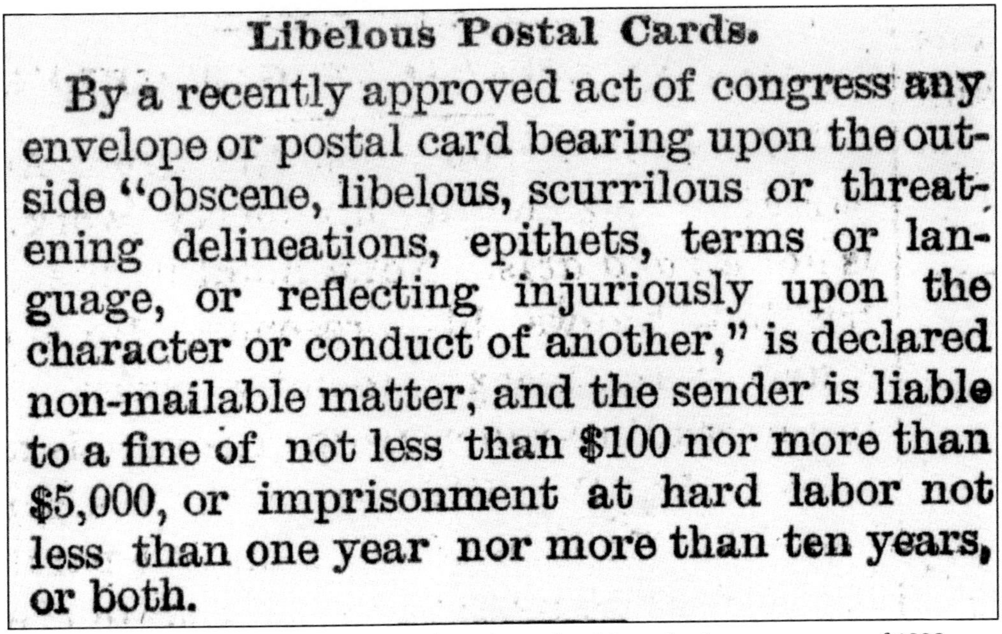

Libelous Postal Cards.

By a recently approved act of congress any envelope or postal card bearing upon the outside "obscene, libelous, scurrilous or threatening delineations, epithets, terms or language, or reflecting injuriously upon the character or conduct of another," is declared non-mailable matter, and the sender is liable to a fine of not less than $100 nor more than $5,000, or imprisonment at hard labor not less than one year nor more than ten years, or both.

Postcards were not always easily accepted, as shown by this notice in a newspaper of 1888.

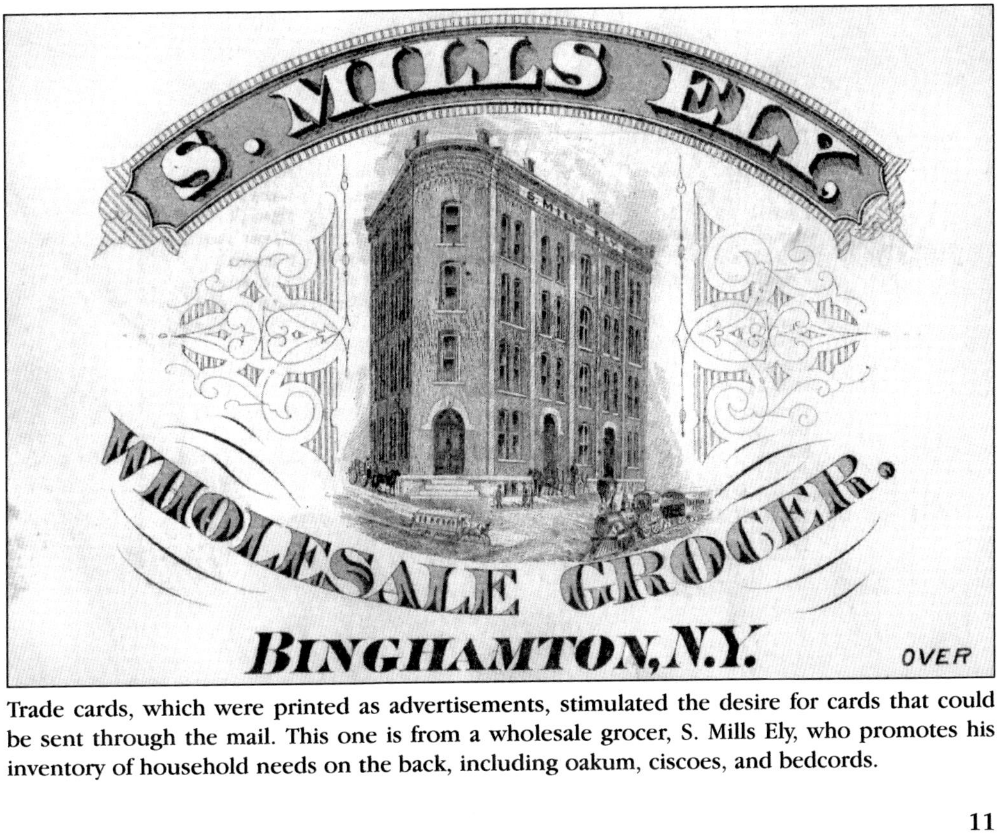

Trade cards, which were printed as advertisements, stimulated the desire for cards that could be sent through the mail. This one is from a wholesale grocer, S. Mills Ely, who promotes his inventory of household needs on the back, including oakum, ciscoes, and bedcords.

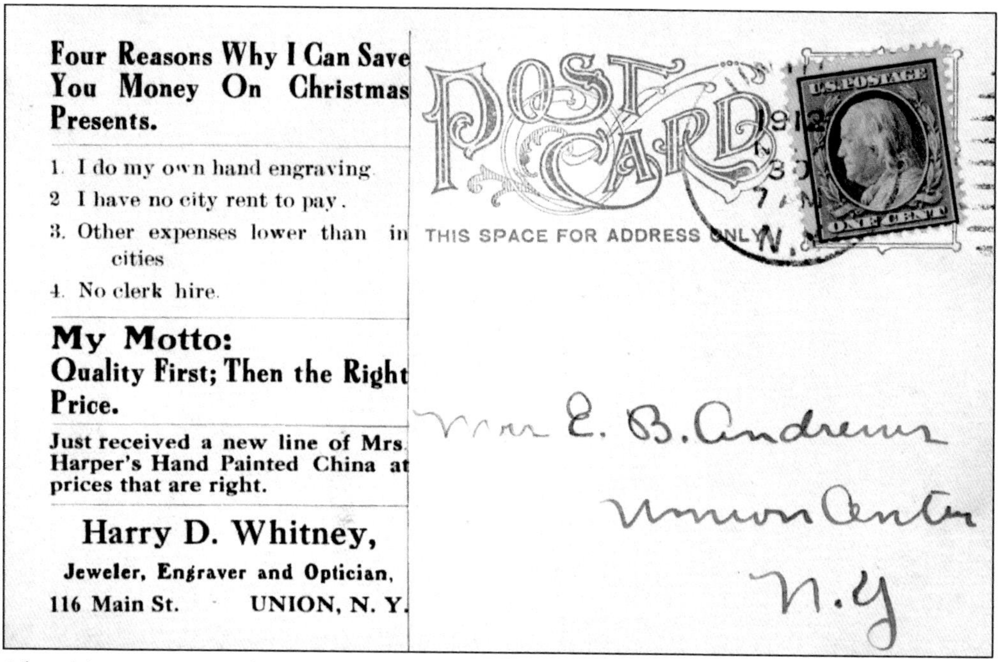

Advertising on postcards was considered a sound one-cent investment in the early 1900s. The postcards became a 3-by-5-inch sales force, showing an attractive photograph of the store location on the front, and giving product details on the back.

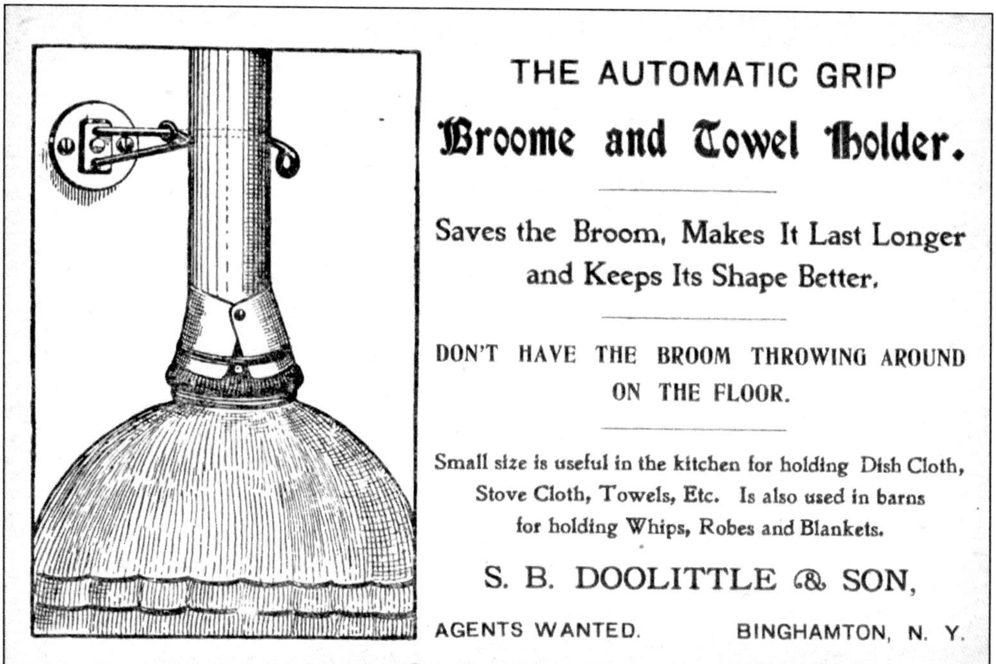

This is a very early card, sent to advertise the benefits of using a handy gadget called the Broome and Towel Holder, taking advantage of the spelling of Broome County to attract customers.

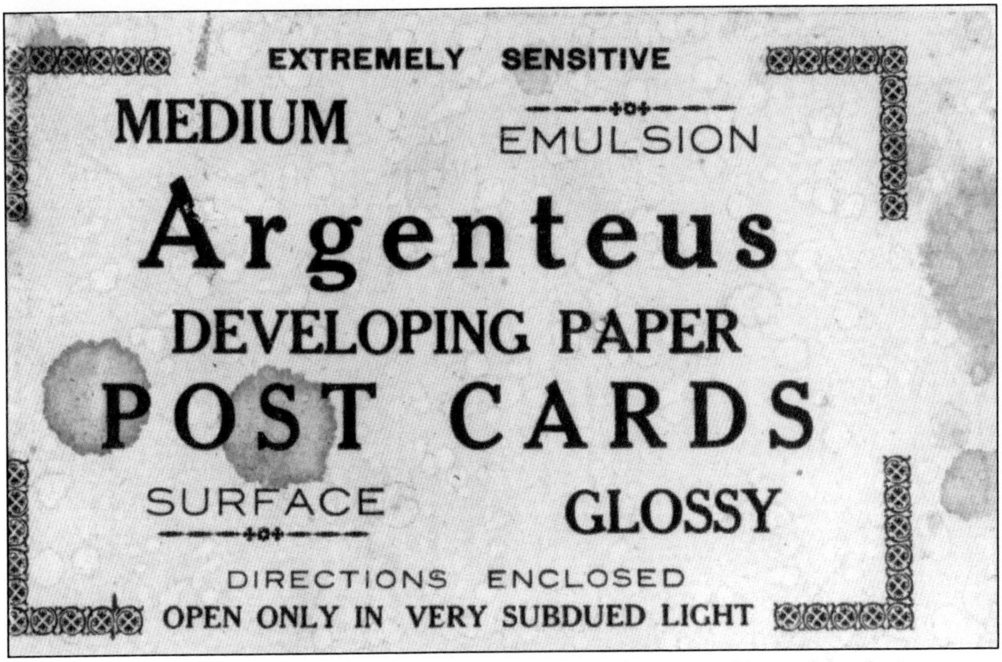

Real photo postcards were made from card stock, such as this original box of developing paper that already has the words "post card" imprinted on the back. If a card is left in the light, it turns a bright violet, making it unusable for photographs.

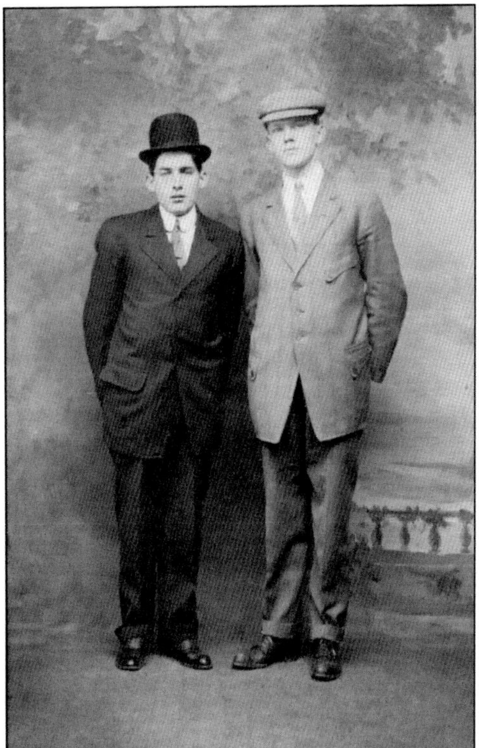

Real photo postcards are first-generation photographs printed directly on postcard blanks, as opposed to the commercially produced postcards made through a printing process. Some collectors believe a photo postcard should not be considered a postcard unless it has been legitimized by mailing. (The unknown gentlemen on this postcard might be a local comedy team.)

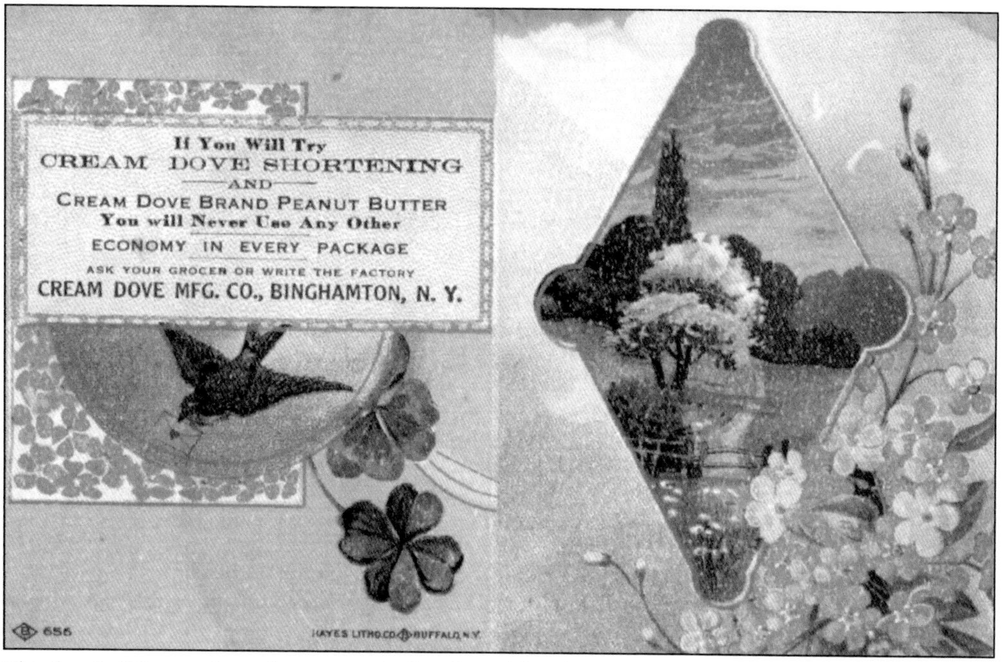

This lovely lithograph trade postcard, distributed by the Cream Dove Manufacturing Company, was produced to entice customers. The color lithograph process, a type of printing that made possible the making of high-quality postcards with many bright colors, increased the demand for promotional postcards. This postcard is dated 1914.

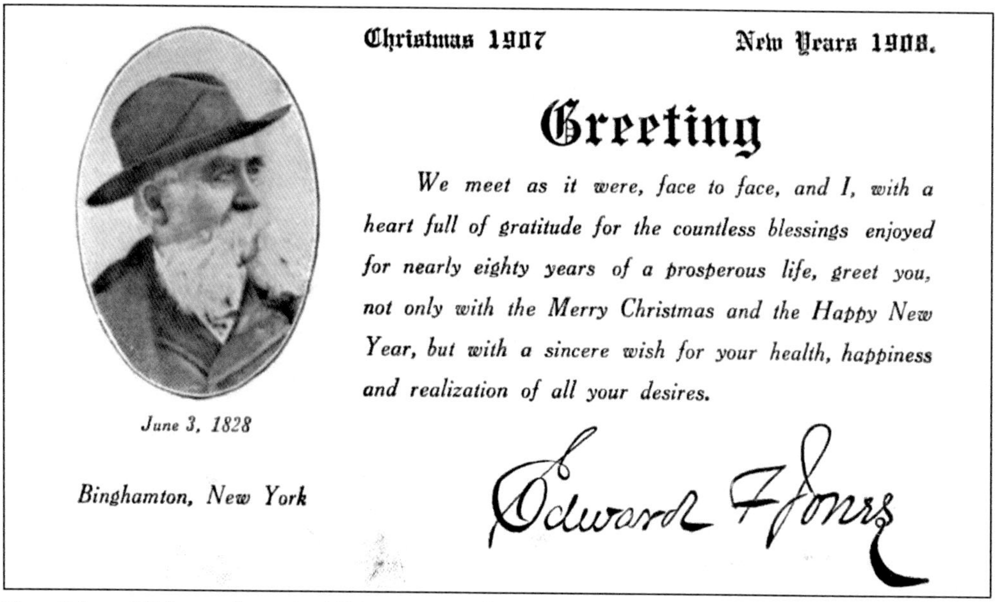

Gen. Edward F. Jones, born in 1828, was a Civil War veteran, a lieutenant governor of New York State, and an author. He may be best known for establishing a scales manufacturing company in 1865, putting Broome County on the map with his novel style of advertising. "Jones, he pays the freight," was a slogan that came to be recognized around the world, making the name Jones synonymous with scales.

Two

The Broome County Seat: Binghamton

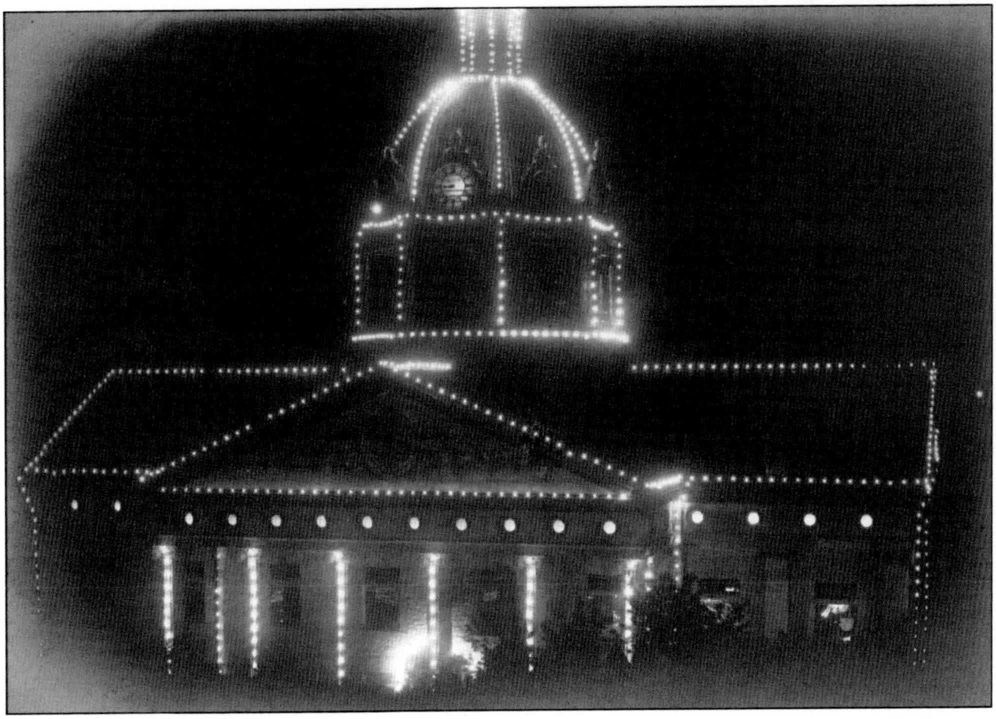

The first Broome County Courthouse was built in the early 1800s near what came to be known Court House Hill. The structure contained two log cells, used as the jail, as well as court facilities. This postcard shows the fourth courthouse, decorated in festive lights for the 1906 Broome County centennial.

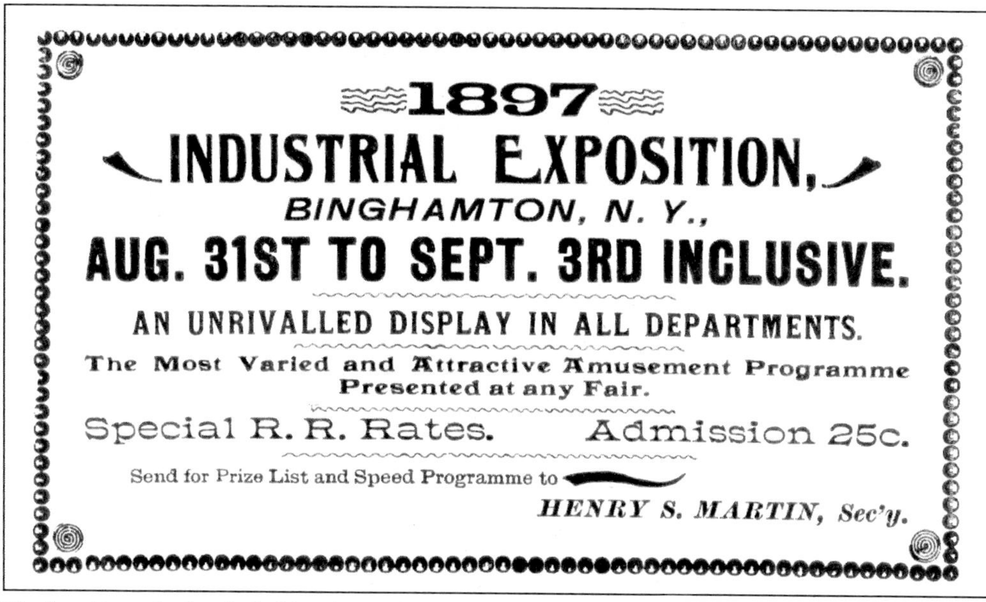

The local board of trade held industrial expositions and fairs almost yearly, beginning in 1887, to extol the advantages of commerce in Broome County. This postcard advertises the entertainment programs available at the 1897 fair. By 1900, the local newspaper headlines had proclaimed, "Prosperity indicated by crowds with money to spend at the Exposition!" and "This McKinley, Republican, good times sort of fair is a success!"

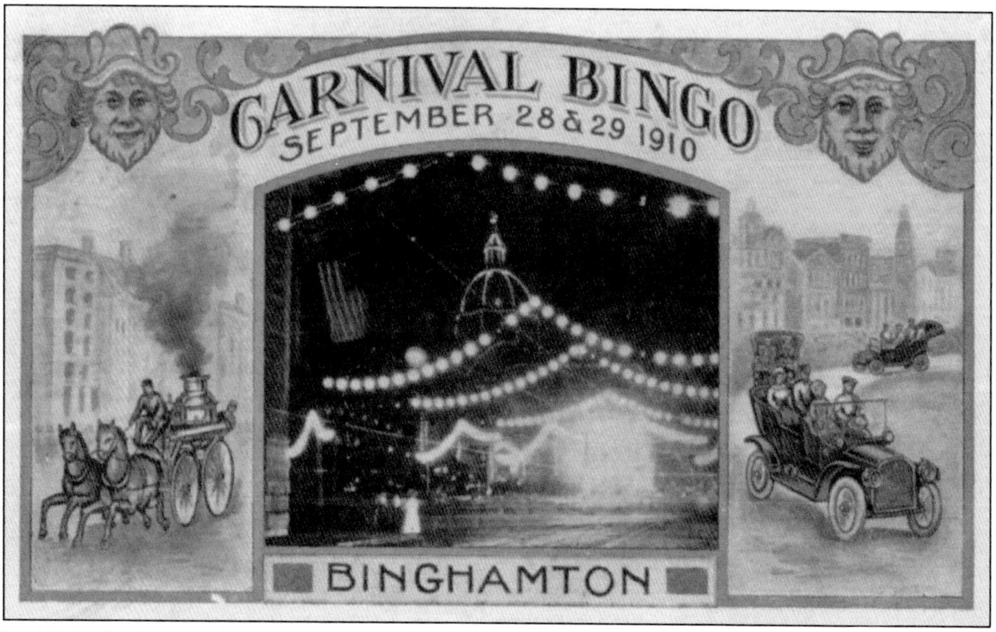

In 1905, the board of trade and the chamber of commerce combined to promote the industrial excellence in the area through Carnival Bingo. Festivities were held at the Stow Flats Fairgrounds in Binghamton. The invitation on the back is to visit a business display at the fair, signed, "Bingo Yours, the Morgan Company."

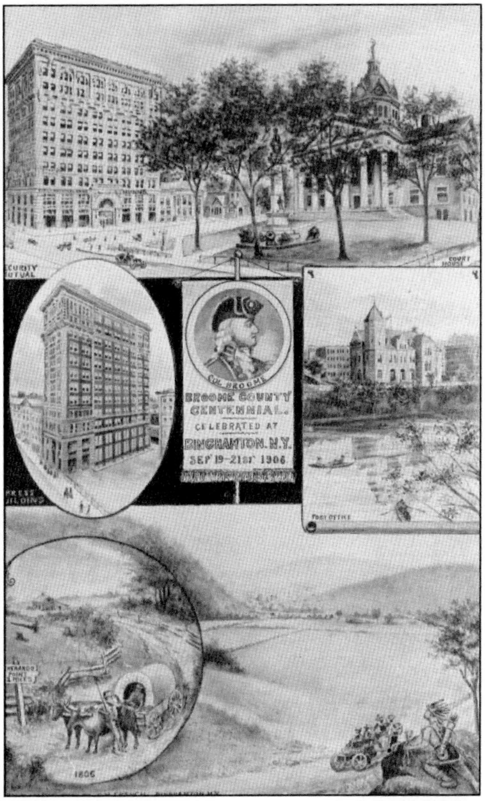

Special postcards were printed for September 19–21, 1906, the Broome County centennial celebration. The streets of Binghamton were filled with people from all over the state who came for the wide array of programs, speeches, races, and fireworks.

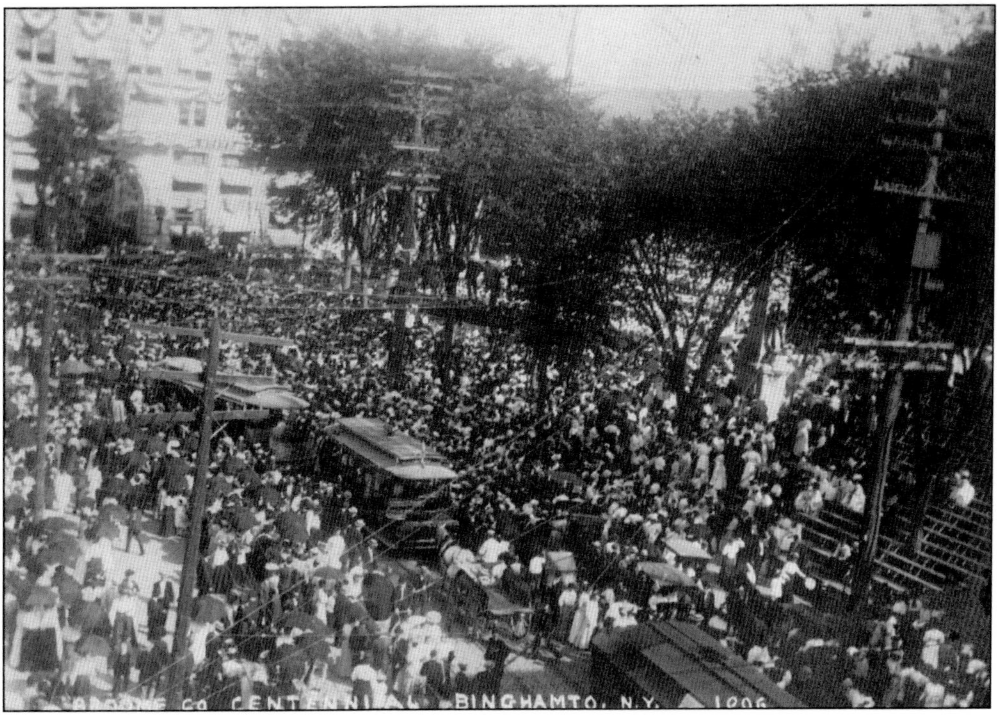

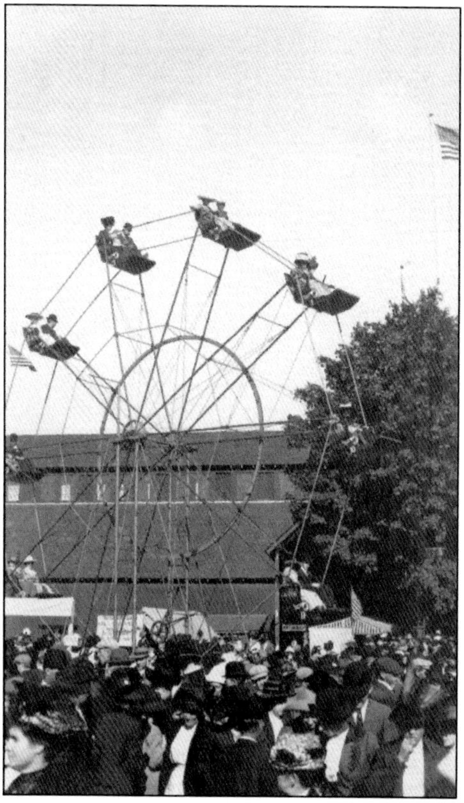

In September 1911, the crowds again stayed in Binghamton for days to participate in the County Fair. The event was held at the Stow Flats Fairgrounds, now the site of the Binghamton Plaza, near the river. This was the year the great pioneer flyer Lincoln Beachey pitted his airplane against the automobile of Barney Oldfield on the Stow Flats racetrack.

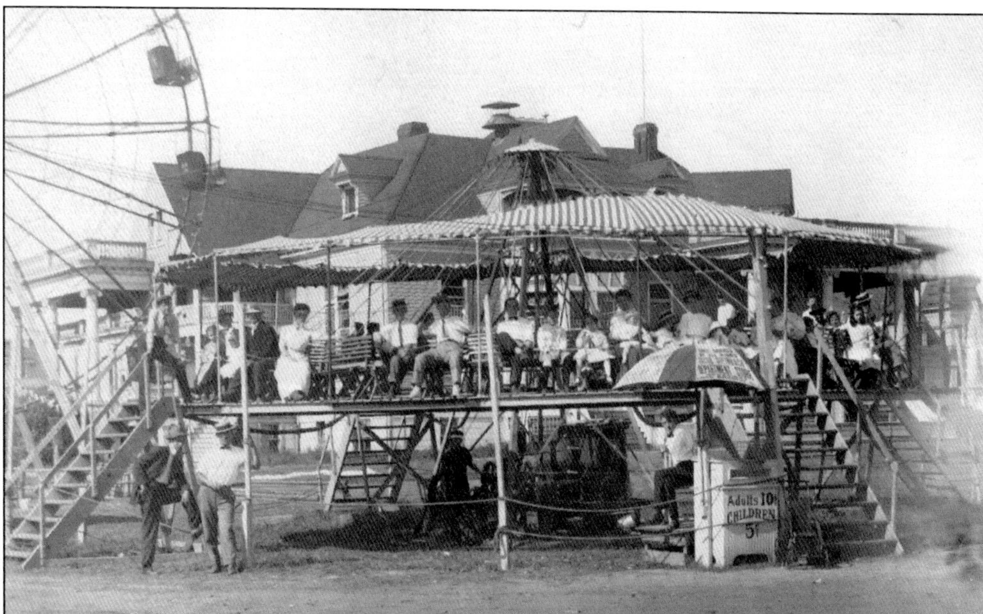

The Stow Flats Fairground was the site of many famous performances. Hundreds of people from throughout the state crowded the city of Binghamton streets, staying in hotels and boardinghouses for days to see all the sights. Carnival rides and bandstands were erected.

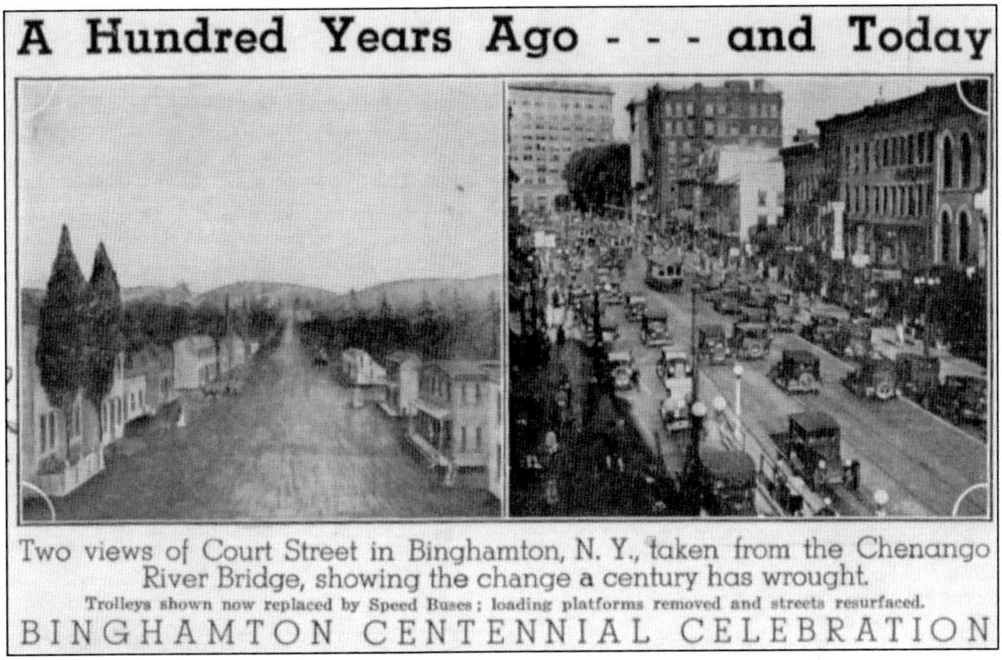

In 1934, Binghamton celebrated its own centennial with a three-day extravaganza. Drawn by George Park from his memory of the area, this postcard shows an 1810 view of the city, next to a 1934 photograph of the downtown streets. Feasts and a squadron of bi-wing bombing planes entertained the crowds. The message entices attendees to join "old home week, for pageantry, parades and Mardi Gras spectaculars."

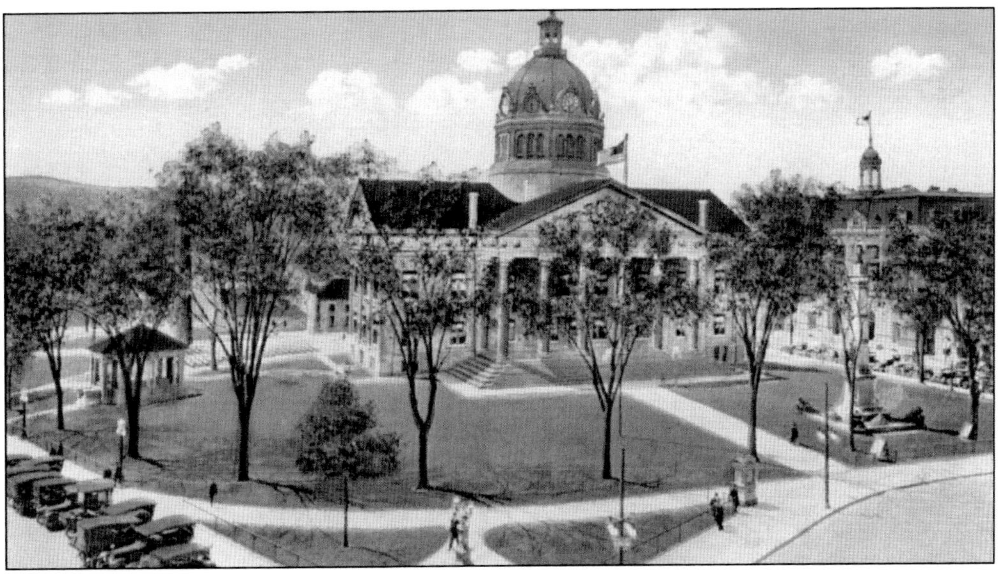

The Broome County Courthouse, located in Binghamton, is the fourth in a succession of courthouses. Built in 1897, it stands near the foundations of its predecessors. Made of Ohio sandstone, with bluestone trim and a copper dome, it is a place where "the majesty of law is asserted and vindicated." The dome and the statue of blind justice both underwent extensive restoration in the late 1990s.

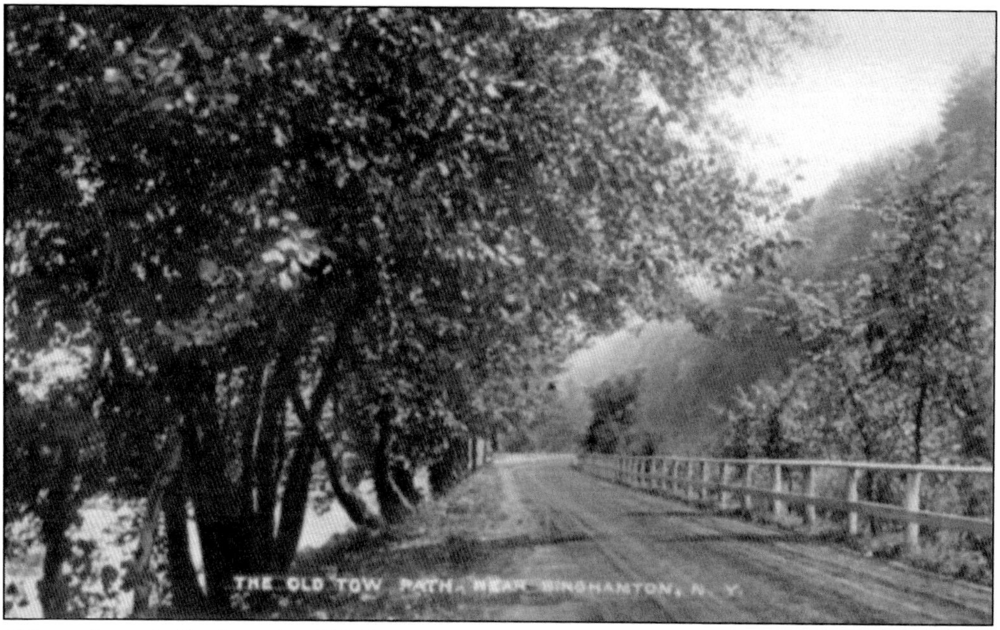

This road was built along the Old Chenango Canal towpath between 1837 and 1875. The canal attracted tough men who "held property, life, and limb cheaply." A saloon and gambling den, owned by Buckshot Adams, was located near the rear of the Sissons Store next to the canal. Gruesome stories were told of the establishment, including at least one "nefarious" murder, when the victim was weighted and dropped into the channel. Canal people, or "canalers," preferred to drink whiskey, knowing the extent of the trash dumped into the waters.

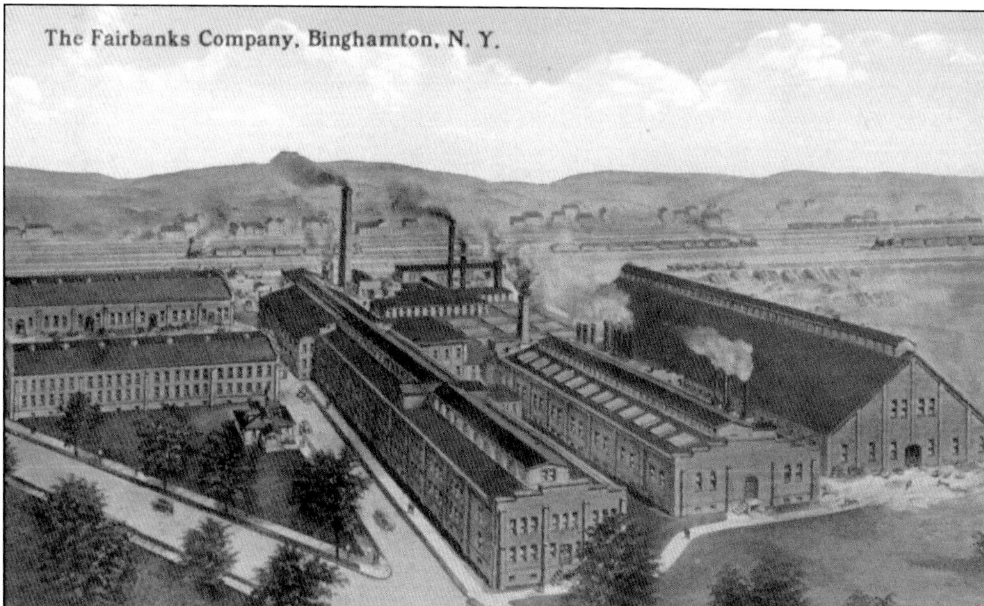

The Fairbanks Company on Glenwood Avenue in Binghamton was known worldwide for the manufacture of scales, trucks, gas engines, valves, and general merchandise ranging from pulleys to marine engines. The plant opened in 1909 in the location currently known as Foundry Plaza.

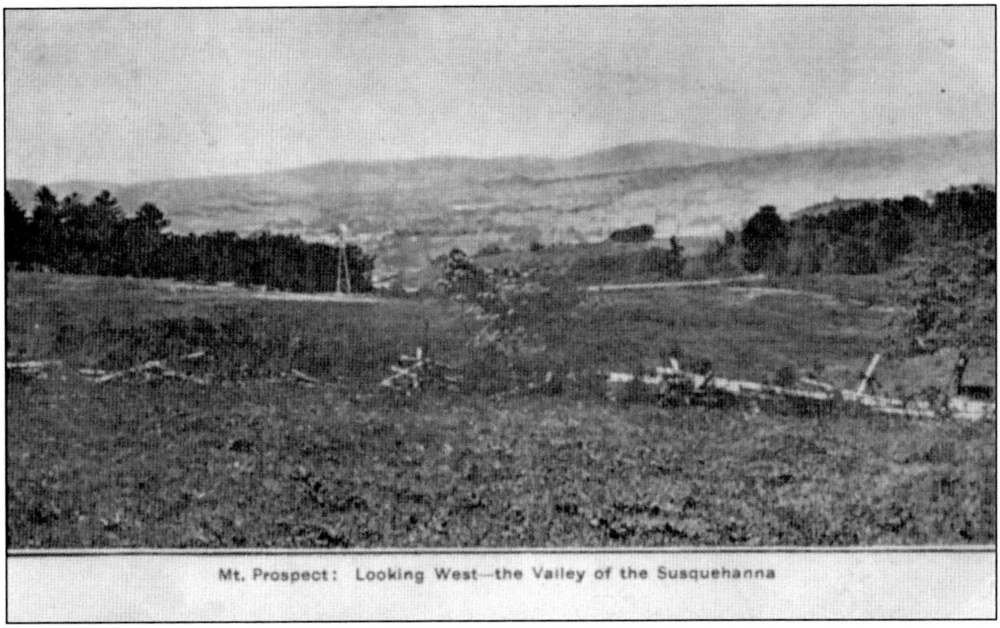

The historic slopes of Mount Prospect have sheltered several interesting enterprises. In 1849 and early in the 1850s, water therapies were said to "cure most all the evils of mankind," and the hillside harbored two of these establishments. By 1866, the West & Kress Lager Beer Brewery found a home on the mountain. This postcard was mailed as an advertisement for the Pine Tree Inn, also located on Mount Prospect in Binghamton.

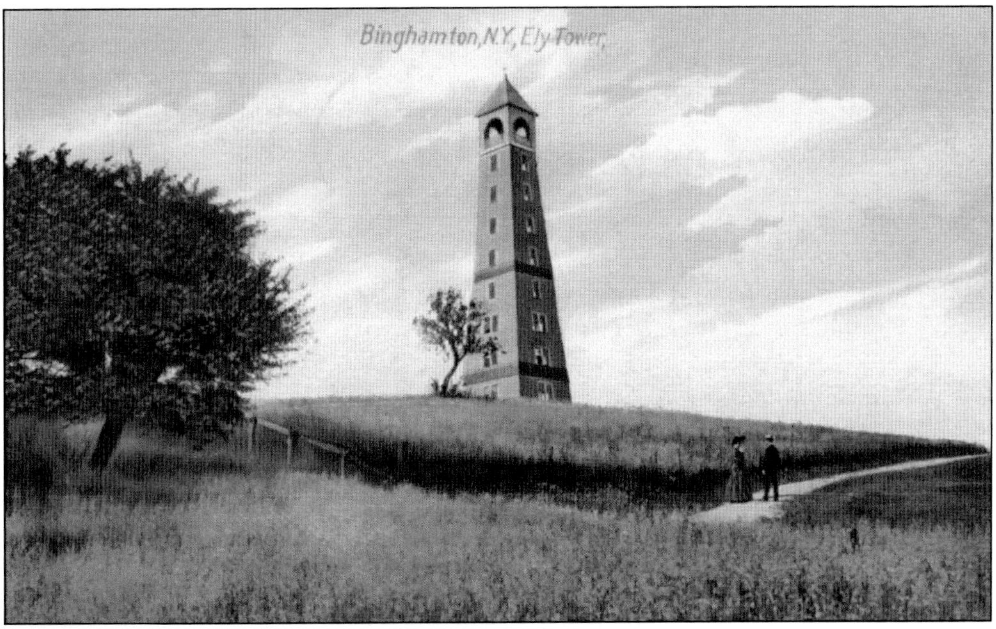

Ely Park was donated to the City of Binghamton in 1907 by S. Mills Ely. The wood used to construct this tower was recycled from a temporary temple called the Mills Meeting Hall, built in 1893 for an itinerant evangelist. Located on Mount Prospect, it was blown down in a windstorm. The tower site is now part of the Ely Park Golf Course.

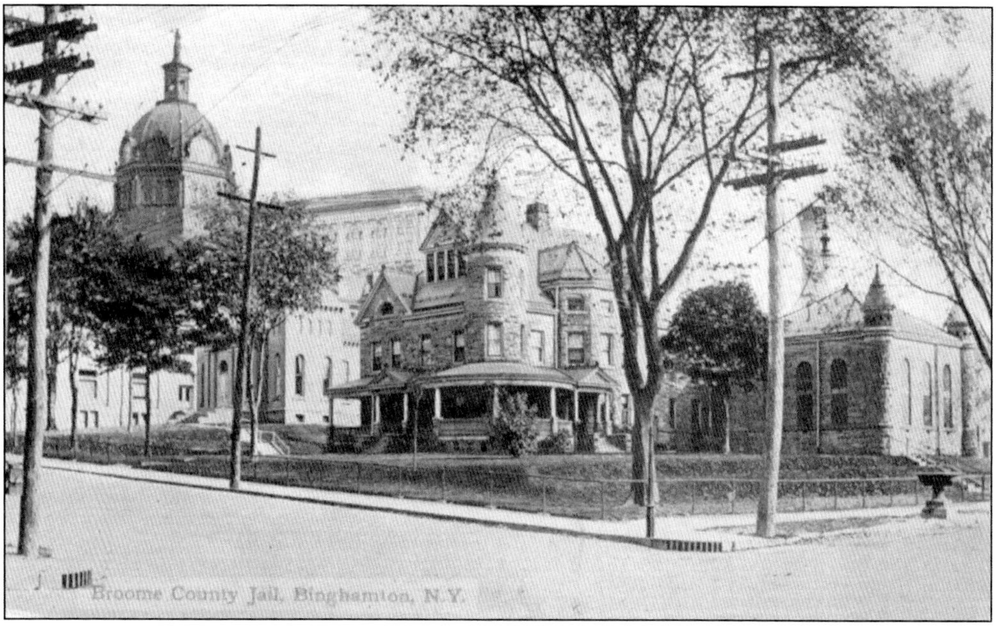

In 1896, Isaac Perry designed the second jail erected in Broome County. It not only served as a lockup for criminals, but was also home to the current sheriff. Unfortunately, it was torn down in 1939. The stone was carted away and recycled for use in building a home in Castle Creek. This postcard was mailed in 1919.

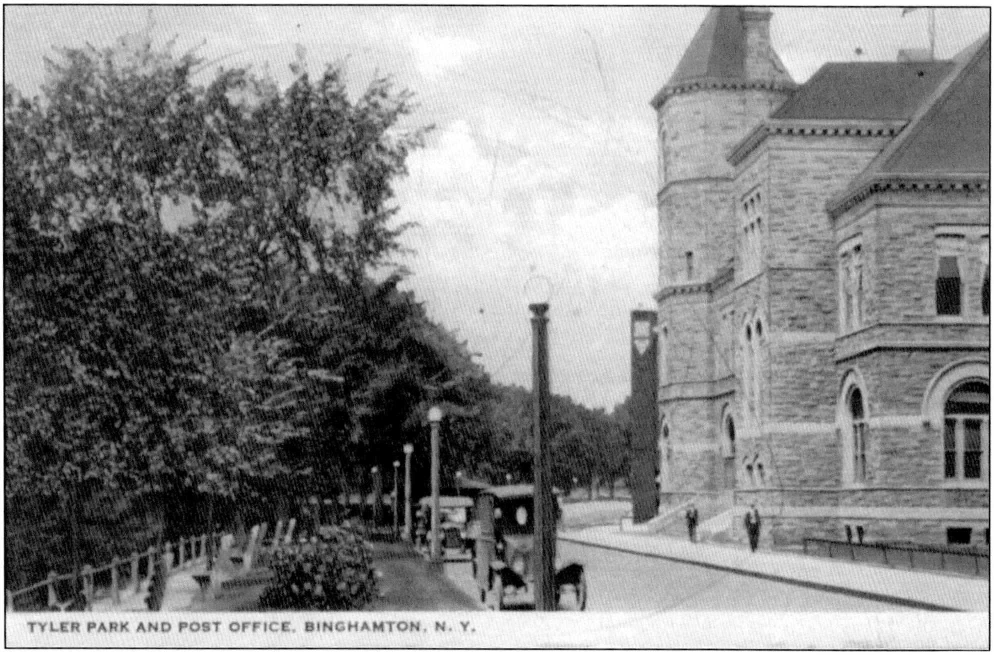

Looking as though it would last for centuries, the stone post office in Binghamton was constructed in 1891 on the corner of Wall and Henry Streets. It was severely damaged in the great fires of 1913 and was torn down in 1942. The demolition was much easier than expected, as the stone was just a façade over a wood frame building. This postcard was mailed in 1908.

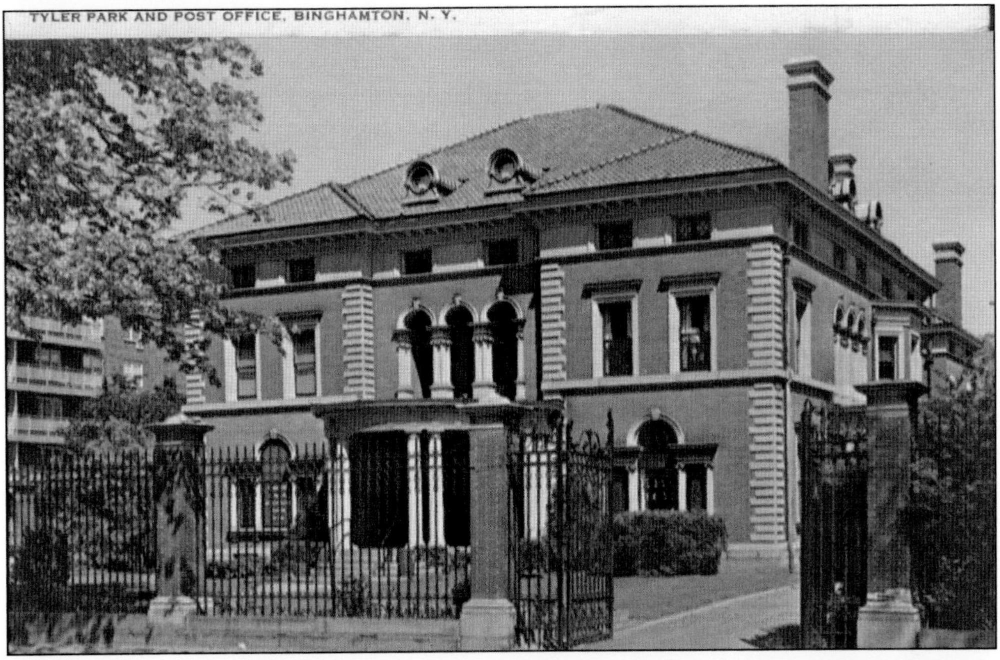

Alonzo Roberson Sr. built this stately mansion between 1906 and 1909 on Front Street in Binghamton. He used magnificent ornate woodwork throughout the home to showcase his lumber company products. The structure was donated to the community in 1954; today, it is the Roberson Museum and Science Center and home to the Broome County Historical Society.

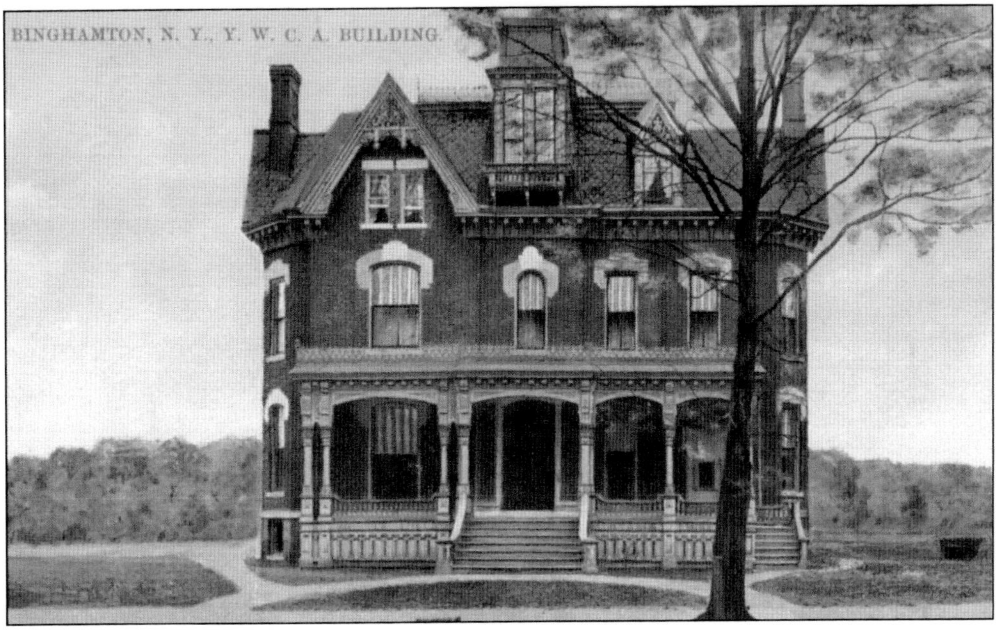

Isaac Perry was a sought-after architect in Broome County and in 1874, D.J. Sullivan requested Perry to design a house on the corner of Lewis and Washington Streets. In 1897, the home named Riverside was turned into the YWCA. The building changed hands again in 1920, becoming the Georgian Hotel.

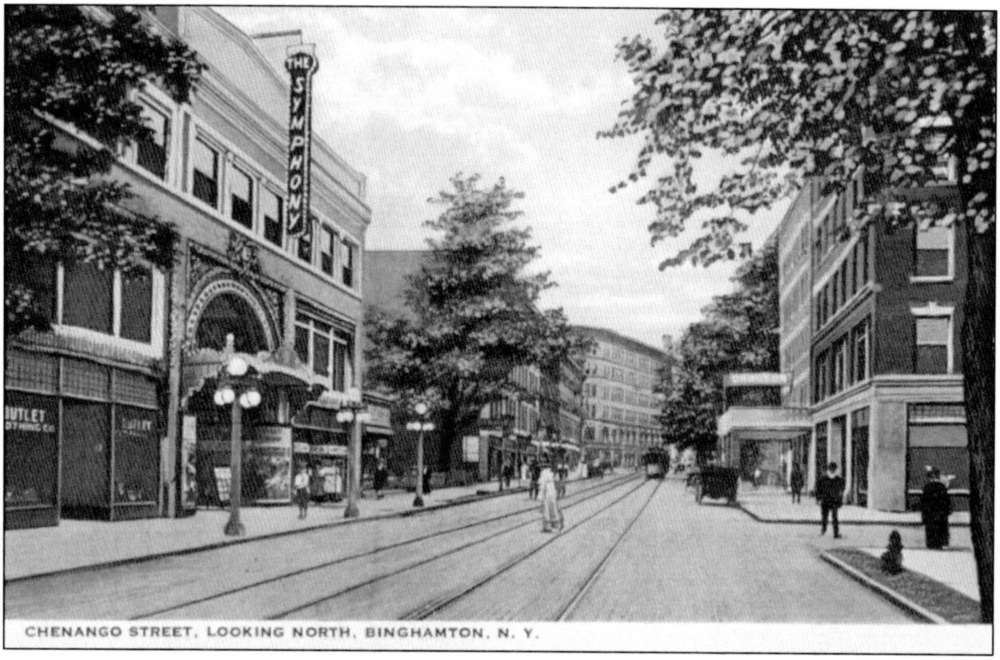

Chenango Street in 1917 was a classy locale for amusement and hostelry. The Symphony Theater showed silent films accompanied by "house music" played on a Link pipe organ. The Arlington Hotel and the Carleton Hotel were just a short way down the street.

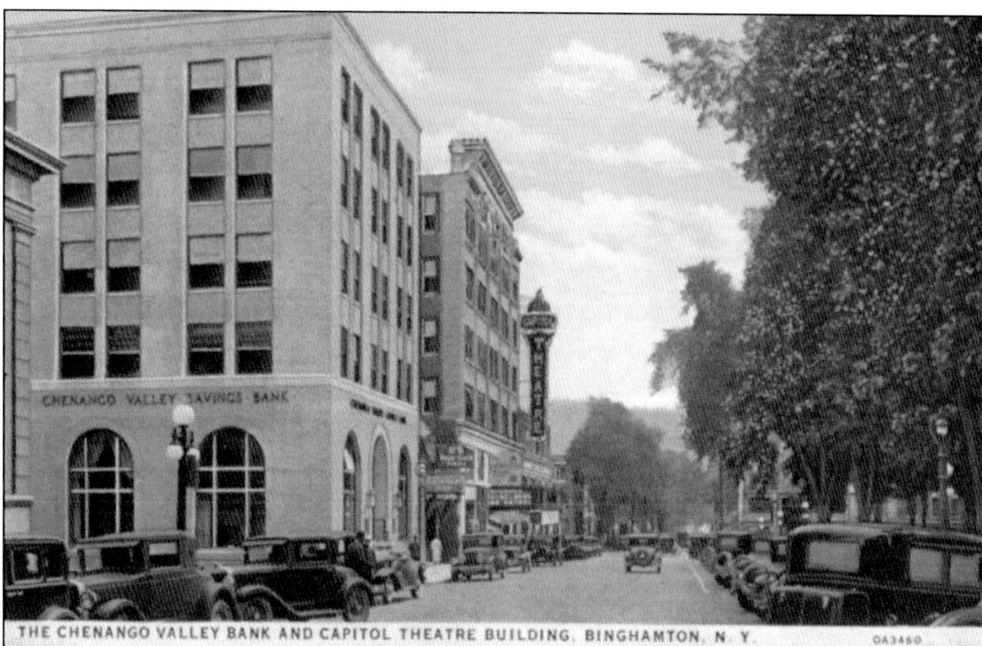

One of the largest theaters in the area was the Capitol Theatre on Exchange Street. Constructed in the 1920s, it could seat more than 1,000 people. At first it was used for vaudeville and later for motion pictures. Today, a parking lot occupies the site.

In 1892, Charles M. Stone erected the Stone Opera House. For that era, it was a complete, comfortable, and commodious structure. Many "stars of the road" played to full houses. Destroyed by fire in 1903, the opera house was rebuilt and again reigned first in the theater world. After years of bringing live performances to Broome County, it became the Riveria Theater for moving pictures, remaining in operation until the 1970s.

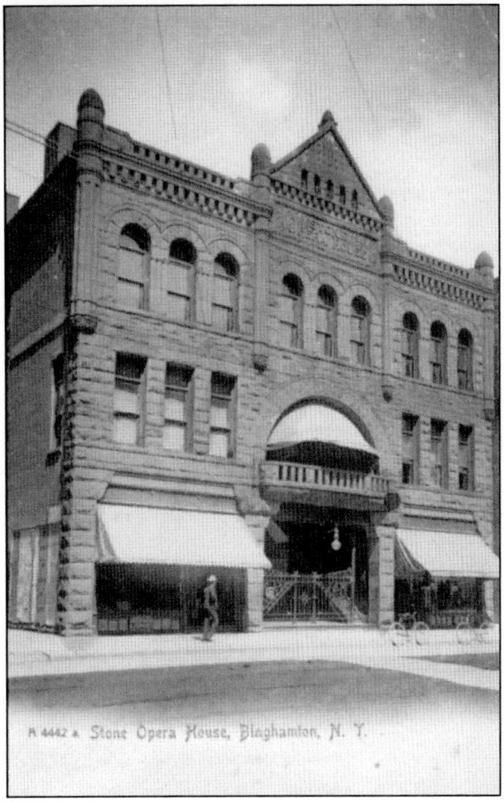

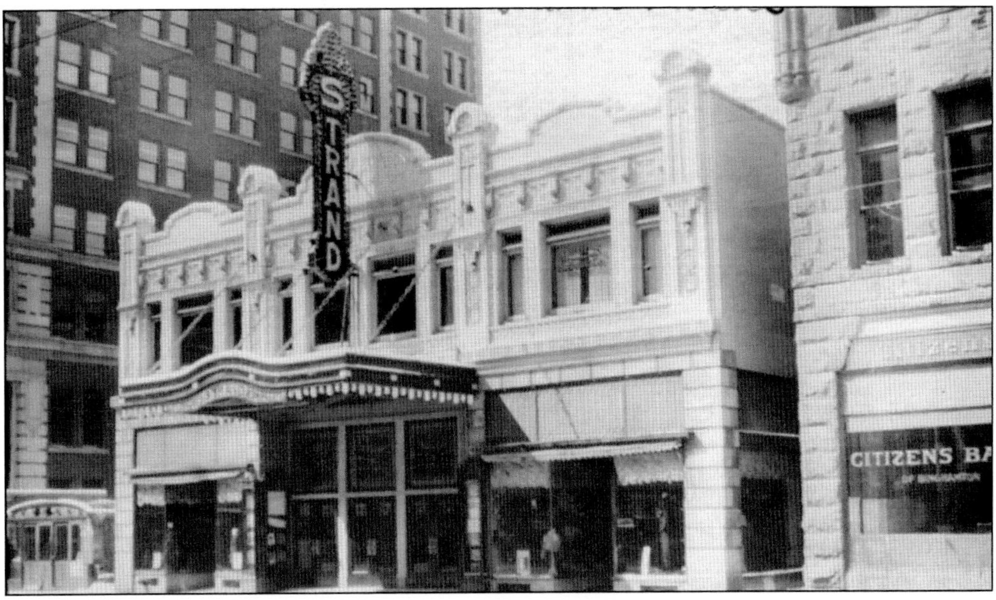

At one time, there were theaters in every neighborhood. The Strand, built in the 1920s as a motion picture house, captivated hundreds of young people at afternoon matinees until television became a lifestyle.

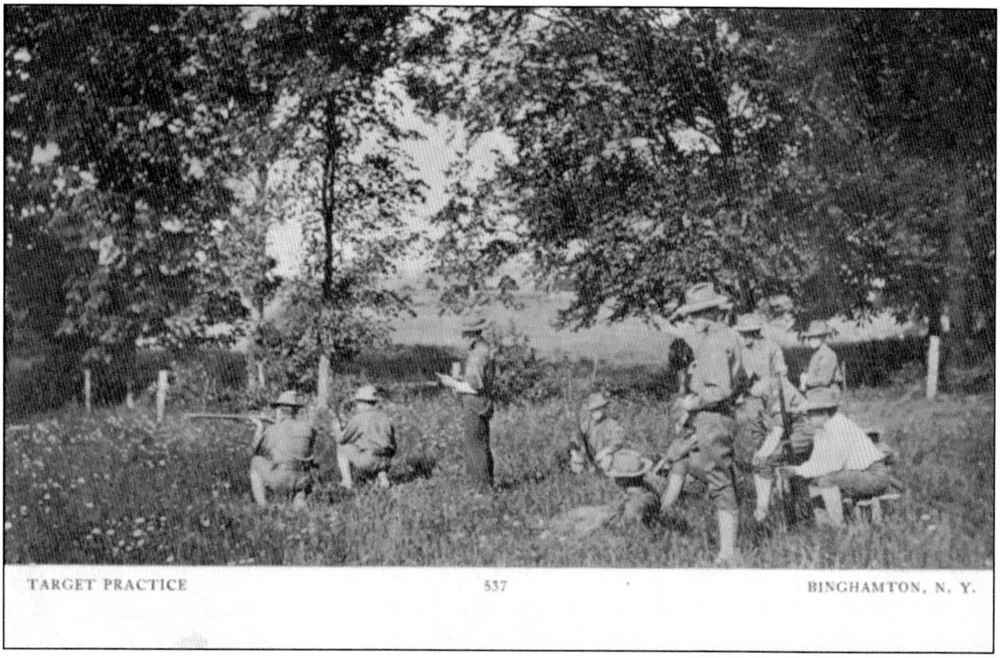

World War I, the war to end all war, was prepared for in every town and village in Broome County. These young men are practicing with firearms in Binghamton.

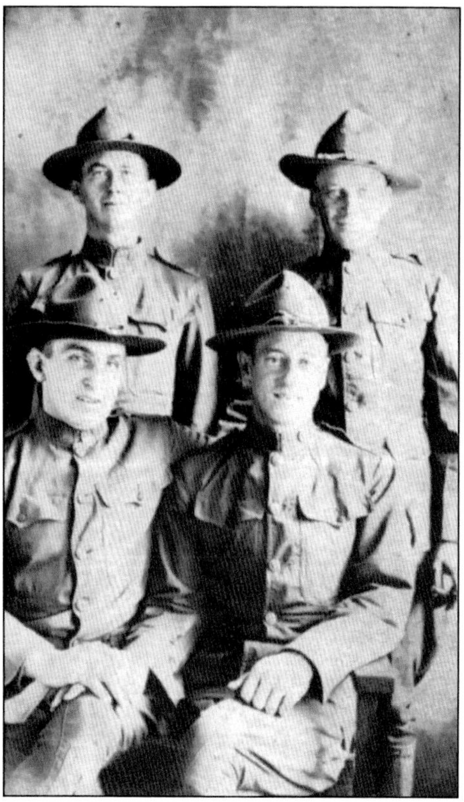

Local men show the camaraderie of war during a leave from their encampment in 1918.

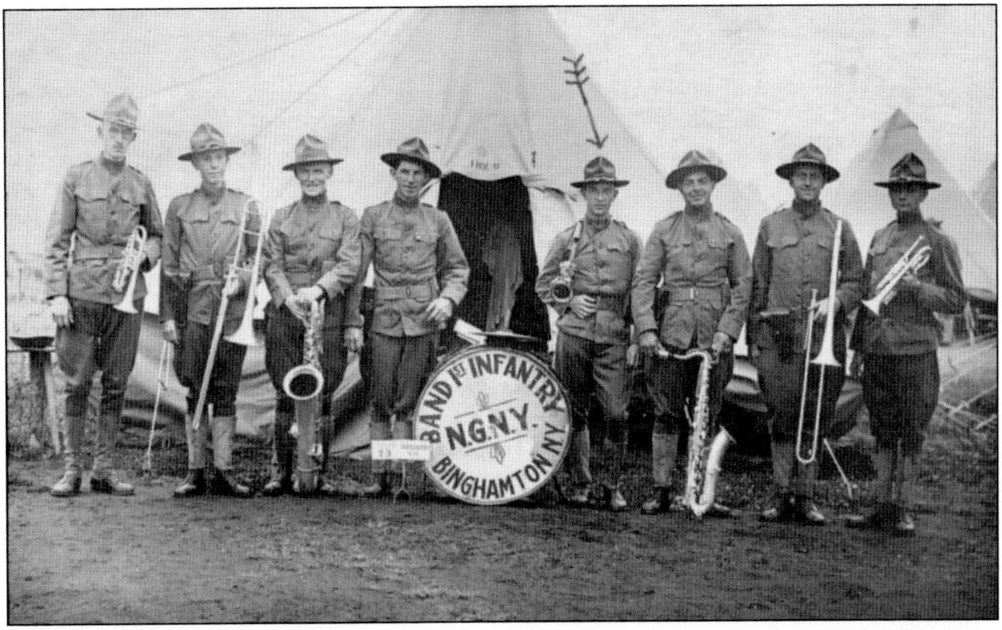

Soldiers of World War I served in many ways—with firearms and with music. The message on the back of this postcard relates, "we are all still together here in Squad #9, and I am anxious for a letter." It is signed "Jack."

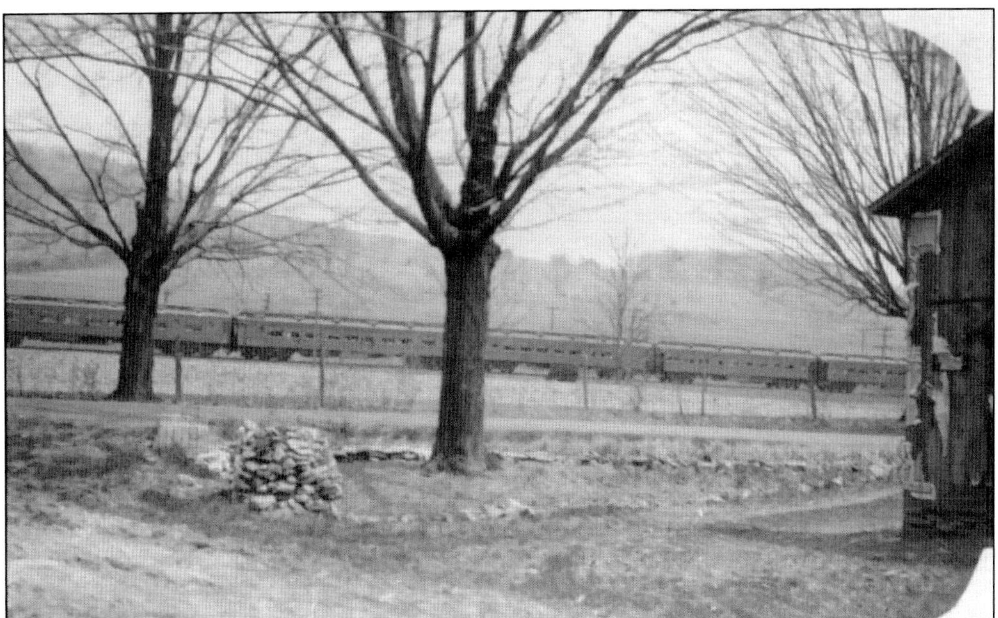

Shown is the first troop train of World War I to pull out of Binghamton, its image preserved forever on the rails of steel and fate. The historic event was recorded by an astute photographer watching the recruits leave for Camp Wadsworth.

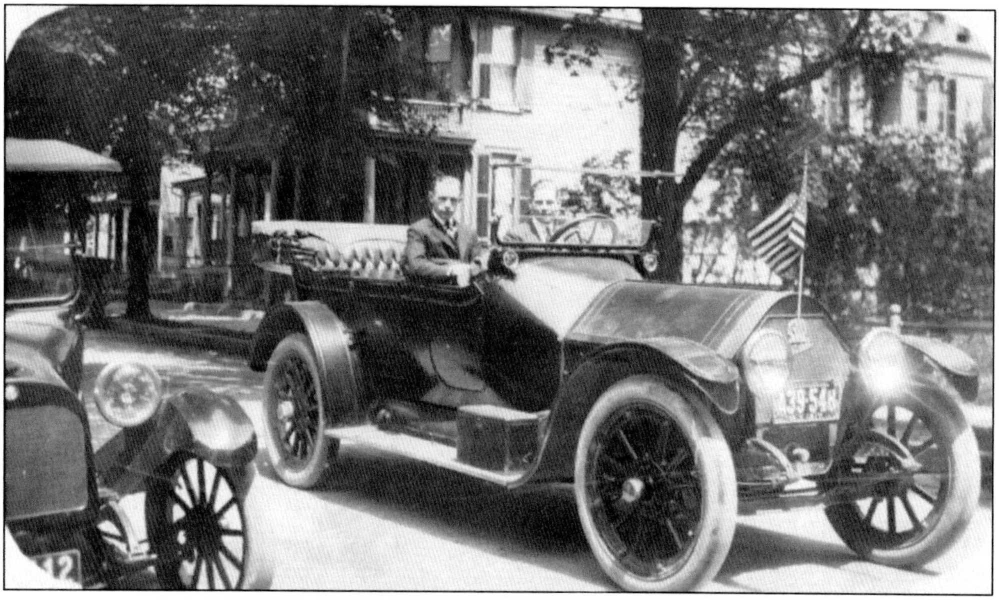

Shortly after this moment in time was captured on film in 1917, these carefree young men from Broome County were "on the firing line in France." This is a good example of a real photo postcard, a one-of-a-kind glimpse into history.

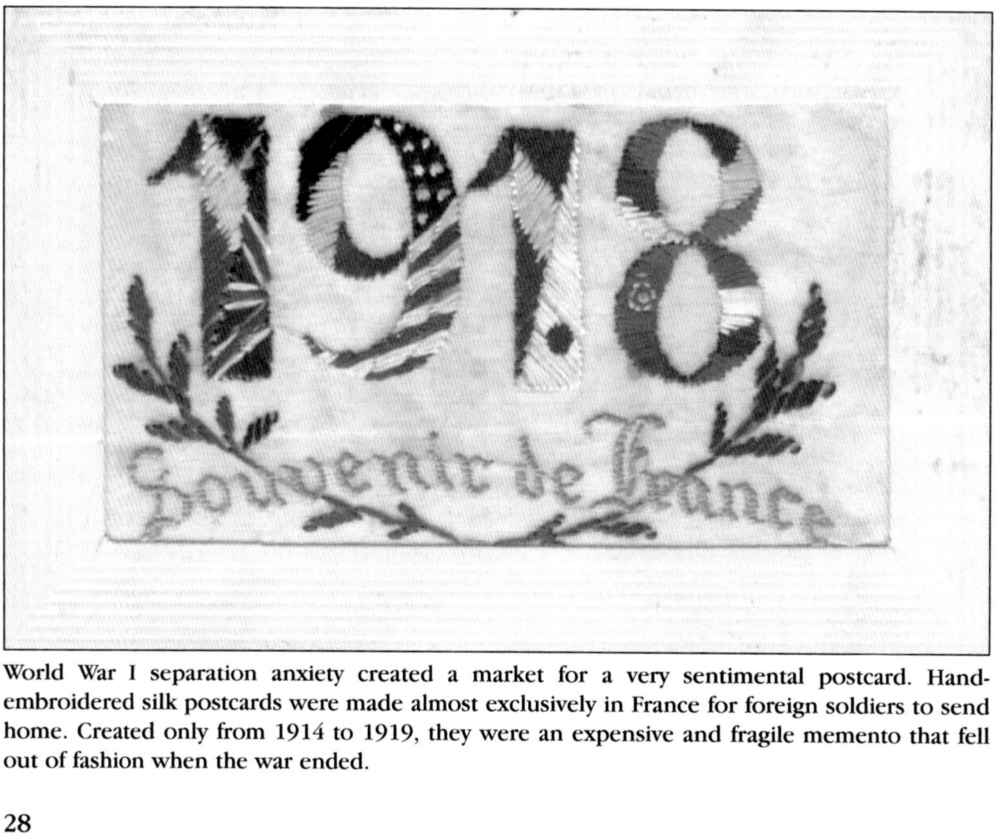

World War I separation anxiety created a market for a very sentimental postcard. Hand-embroidered silk postcards were made almost exclusively in France for foreign soldiers to send home. Created only from 1914 to 1919, they were an expensive and fragile memento that fell out of fashion when the war ended.

The Endicott Johnson Corporation made exceptional efforts to show support of men from their factories who were in service during World War I. This patriotic display represented the number of people in service, with the colors of the stars differentiating between the living and the dead. This postcard was mailed in 1918.

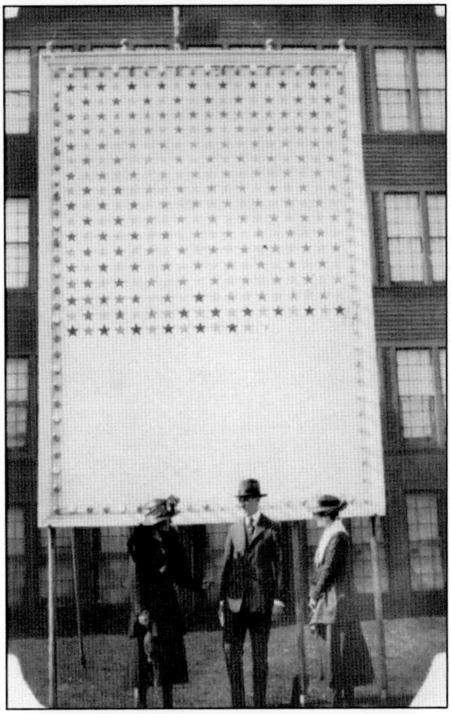

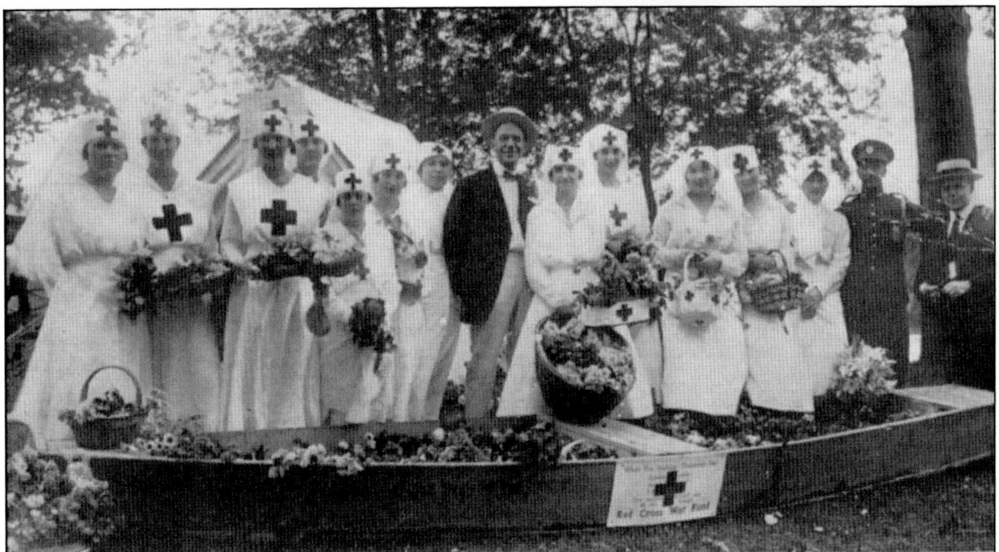

RED CROSS DAY AT IDEAL PARK, ENDICOTT, N. Y. Managed by Endicott-Johnson Workers.

The local chapter of the American Red Cross was founded in 1910. Living up to its unofficial title as "Mother of the World," the organization by 1917 had enlisted 11,000 Broome County volunteers to serve in the war effort. Canteens were staffed, money was raised, and relief supplies were sent to the front lines. During the great Spanish flu epidemic of 1918, the group nursed more than 12,000 area residents needing assistance. This postcard shows a view of Red Cross Day at Ideal Park, Endicott.

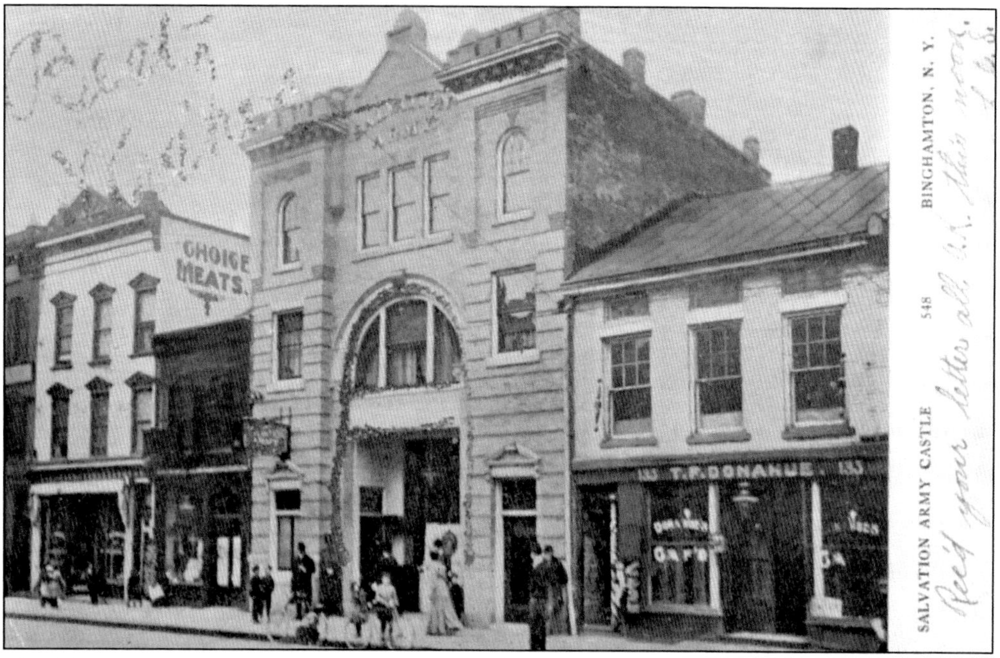

The Salvation Army came into existence in 1861 when William Booth, a Methodist minister, began independent evangelistic work. As an international charity of service, the Salvation Army came to the United States in 1880 and by 1904 had established a citadel at 131 Washington Street in Binghamton. Although remodeled inside and out, the building still stands, a reminder of the "gallant work performed by members in their warfare against evil." The organization is recognized for outstanding efforts during World War I and World War II, and at other times of public need. The postcard below was for service people in 1919 to let relatives at home know their warrior had arrived safely at a classified location. The postcard above was mailed in 1907.

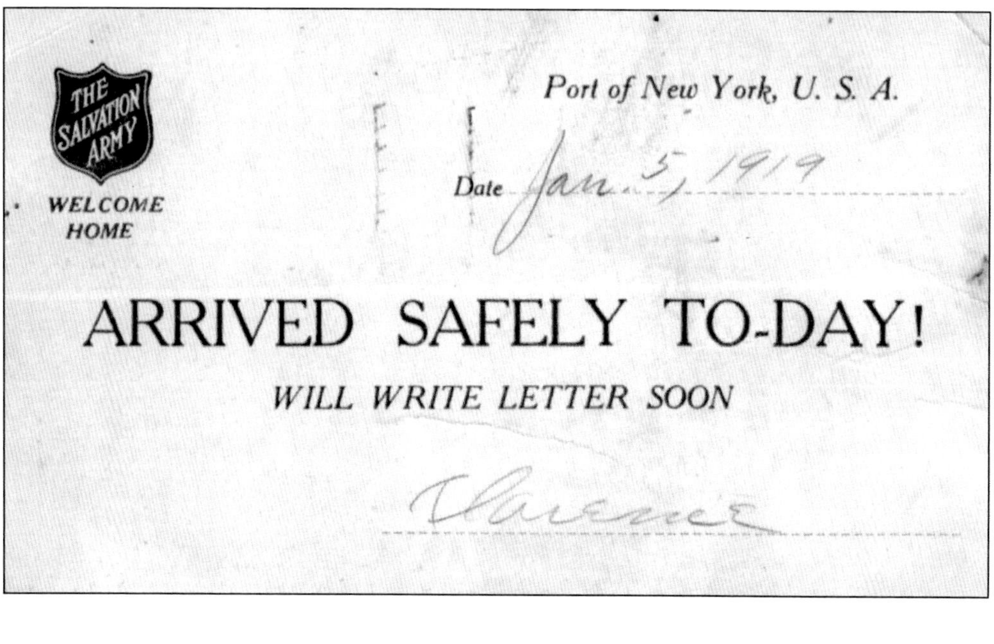

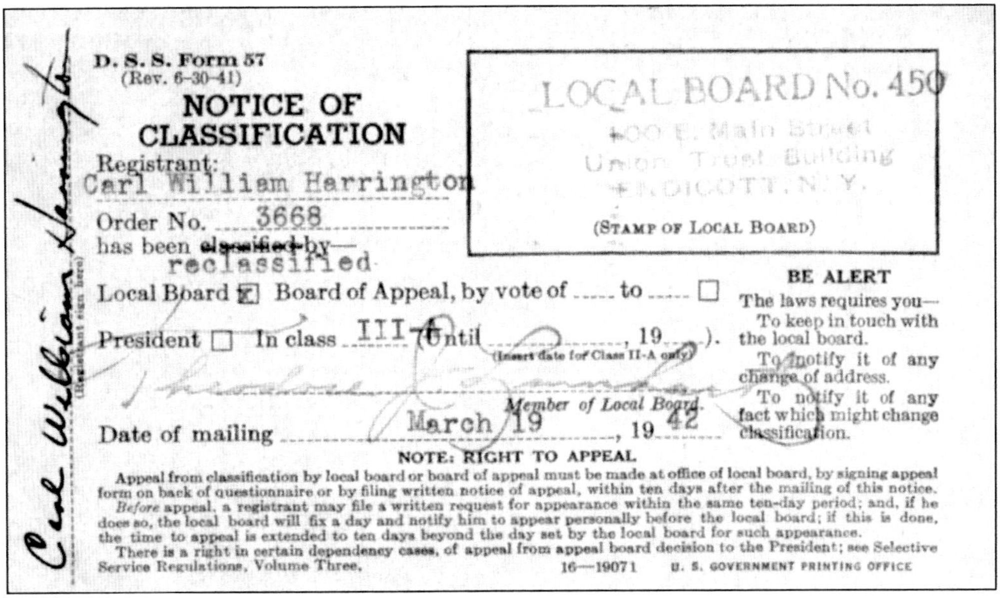
D. S. S. Form 57
(Rev. 6-30-41)

NOTICE OF CLASSIFICATION

Registrant:
Carl William Harrington

Order No. 3668
has been ~~classified by~~— reclassified
Local Board [x] Board of Appeal, by vote of ...... to ...... [ ]
President [ ] In class III-A until ...., 19....).
(Insert date for Class II-A only)

Member of Local Board.

Date of mailing March 19, 1942

LOCAL BOARD No. 450
400 E. Main Street
Union Trust Building
ENDICOTT, N.Y.
(STAMP OF LOCAL BOARD)

BE ALERT
The laws requires you—
To keep in touch with the local board.
To notify it of any change of address.
To notify it of any fact which might change classification.

NOTE: RIGHT TO APPEAL
Appeal from classification by local board or board of appeal must be made at office of local board, by signing appeal form on back of questionnaire or by filing written notice of appeal, within ten days after the mailing of this notice. *Before* appeal, a registrant may file a written request for appearance within the same ten-day period; and, if he does so, the local board will fix a day and notify him to appear personally before the local board; if this is done, the time to appeal is extended to ten days beyond the day set by the local board for such appearance.
There is a right in certain dependency cases, of appeal from appeal board decision to the President; see Selective Service Regulations, Volume Three.

16—19071 U. S. GOVERNMENT PRINTING OFFICE

(Registrant sign here) Carl William Harrington

Postcards were used to call men to serve in World War II. This 1942 postcard is from a local draft board. Carl William Harrington served in the U.S. Navy and returned home to work for International Business Machines.

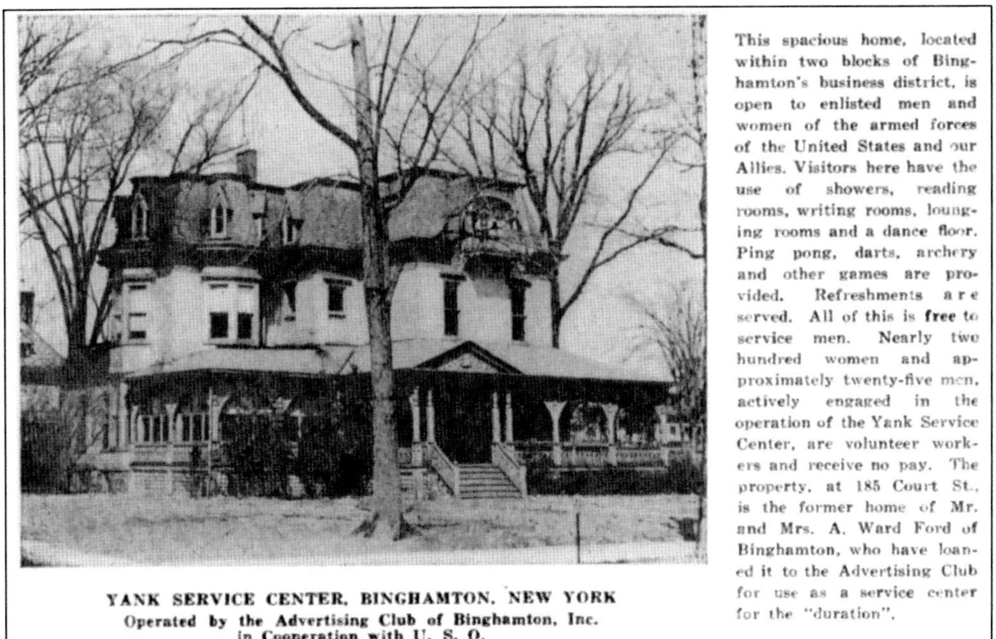
YANK SERVICE CENTER, BINGHAMTON, NEW YORK
Operated by the Advertising Club of Binghamton, Inc.
in Cooperation with U. S. O.

This spacious home, located within two blocks of Binghamton's business district, is open to enlisted men and women of the armed forces of the United States and our Allies. Visitors here have the use of showers, reading rooms, writing rooms, lounging rooms and a dance floor. Ping pong, darts, archery and other games are provided. Refreshments are served. All of this is free to service men. Nearly two hundred women and approximately twenty-five men, actively engaged in the operation of the Yank Service Center, are volunteer workers and receive no pay. The property, at 185 Court St., is the former home of Mr. and Mrs. A. Ward Ford of Binghamton, who have loaned it to the Advertising Club for use as a service center for the "duration".

The Ausburn-Birdsall House was built *c.* 1863 on Court Street in Binghamton, just west of the Monday Afternoon Club. During World War II, A. Ward Ford owned the mansion and loaned it for use as a United Service Organizations (USO) Club. It was demolished in 1946.

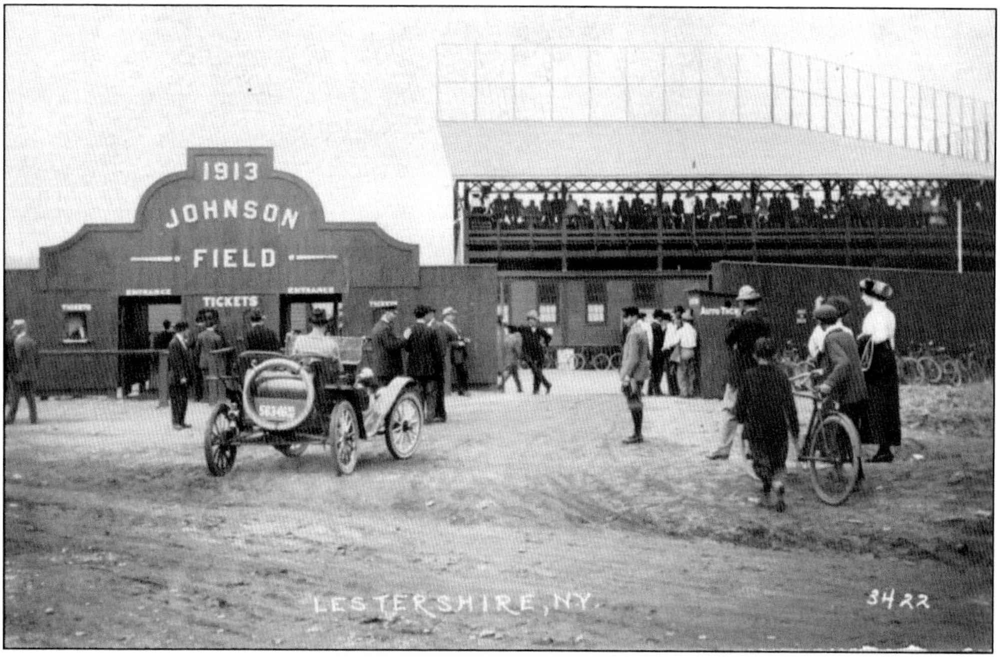

George F. Johnson and family were enthusiastic sports fans. Johnson purchased a minor league baseball franchise and built a stadium in Lestershire *c.* 1913. Johnson Field was home to the New York Yankee farm team, the Triplets. Each year, the Johnsons paid expenses for an exhibition game between the home team and the Yankee major league players. Joe DiMaggio, Lou Gerhig, Babe Ruth, and dozens of other great names in baseball gladly traveled to Broome County. On the day this postcard picture was taken, the John Philip Sousa Band was inspiring fans with patriotic music. The historic stadium was demolished in the mid-1960s to build the Route 17 expressway through Johnson City. The vehicle was built in either 1912 or 1913 and is a Hupmobile.

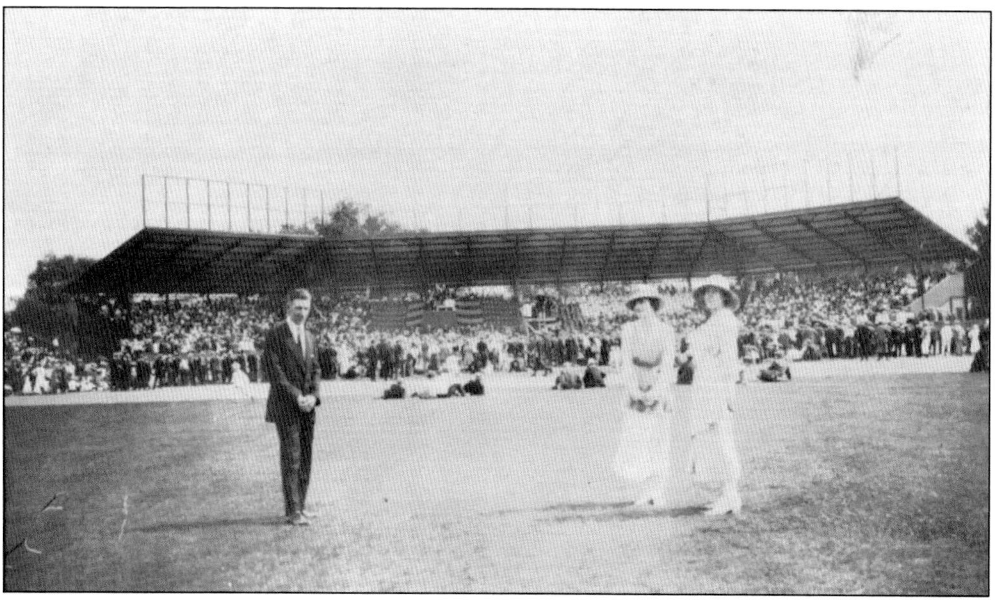

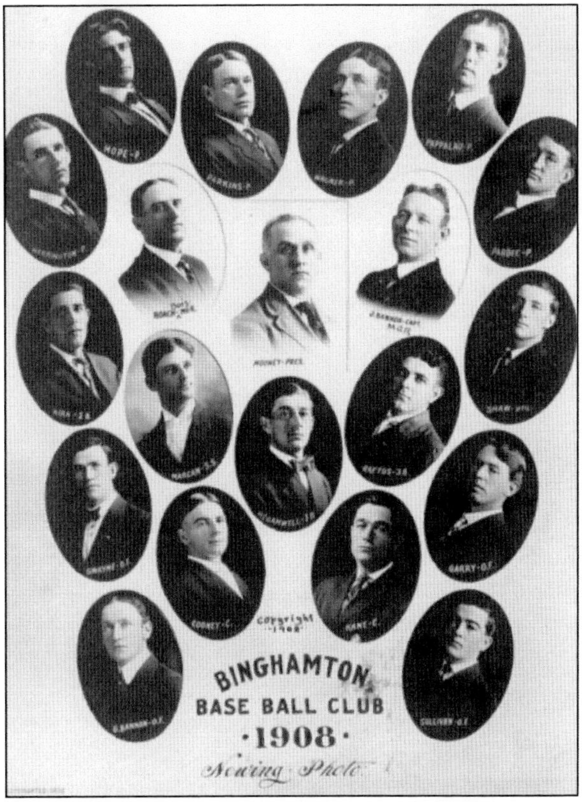

Binghamton and vicinity has always been interested in baseball, as evidenced by this 1908 real photo collage of players. In 1992, the great American pastime of baseball returned to the Triple Cities. The Binghamton Municipal Stadium was built and is home to the Binghamton Mets, a Triple A team for the major league New York Mets. The postcard below is a new aerial photograph taken from a helicopter by Ed Aswad.

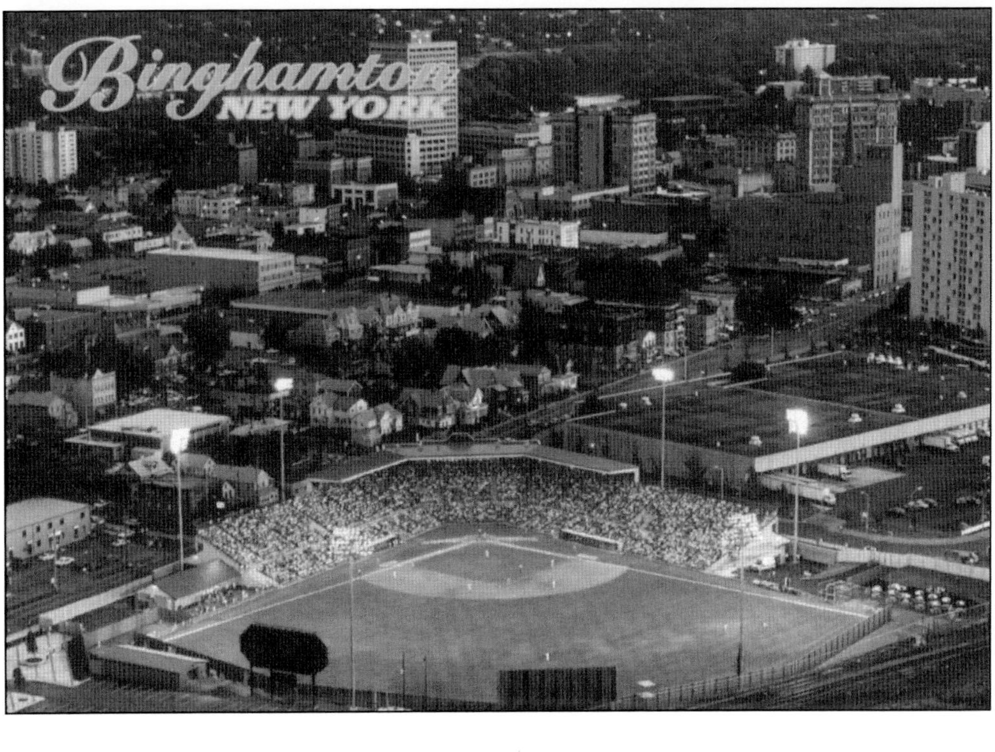

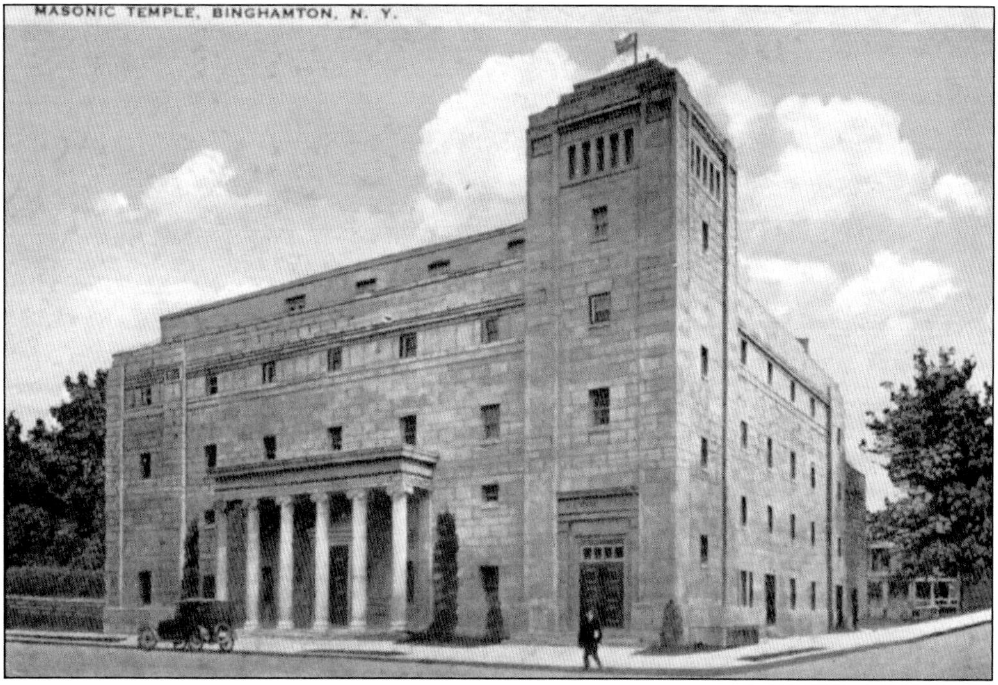

The Masonic Temple was constructed on the corner of Main and Murray Streets in 1923. Made with an impressive auditorium and stage, it contained three locally made Beman pipe organs. For a time, it was home to the Tri-Cities Opera. In the 1950s, it hosted touring Broadway presentations. Although it is still standing, it has fallen into disrepair; it is for sale and has an uncertain future.

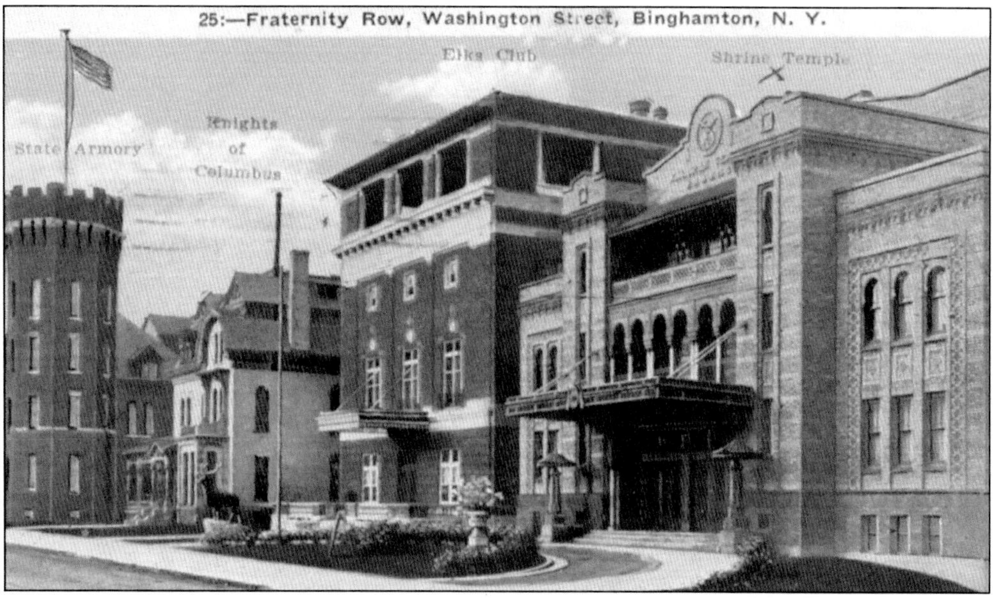

In 1918, the Kalurah Temple was built on the corner of Washington Street and Ferry Street (now East Clinton Street). The ornate interior fixtures and ornamentation that resembled traditional Moslem motifs have disappeared. The temple was sold in 1954 and is currently a church.

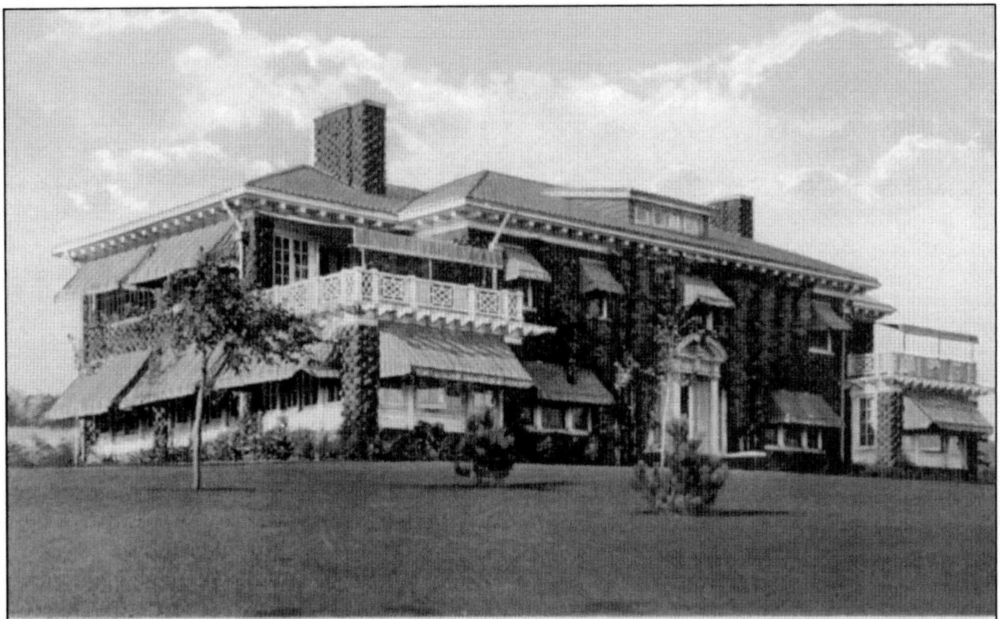

KALURAH COUNTRY CLUB, BINGHAMTON, N. Y. 107057

The Masonic fraternity enjoyed prosperity in the 1920s. By 1925, the fraternity decided to purchase the estate of Eliot Spaulding in the town of Union for $100,000. It became the Kalurah Country Club and was elaborately furnished for another $42,000. Because of the Great Depression, the facility liabilities made it impossible to continue ownership. It was foreclosed upon in 1934, and the furnishings were sold for $1,400. The building and golf course have been the International Business Machines (IBM) Homestead for many years, but is again being offered for sale. The photograph at right shows three Masons—two from Pennsylvania and one from Broome County—attending a Masonic convention in Atlantic City in 1927. The Masons are the oldest fraternity in the world.

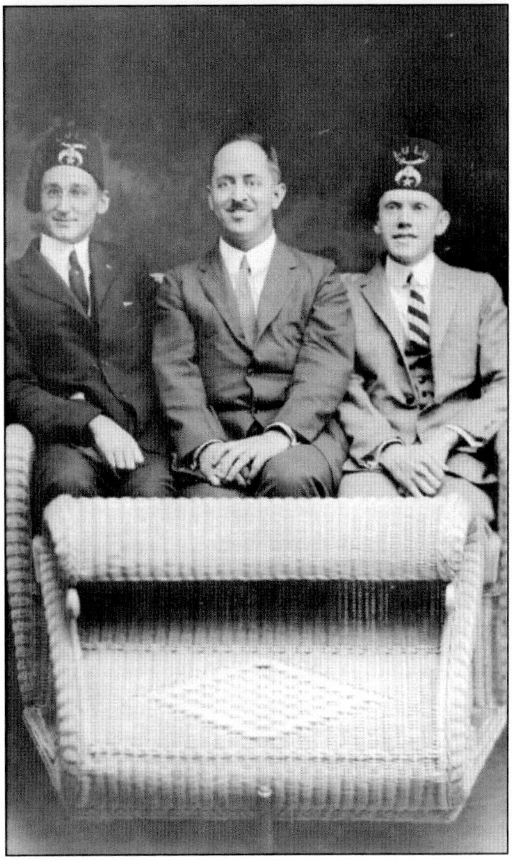

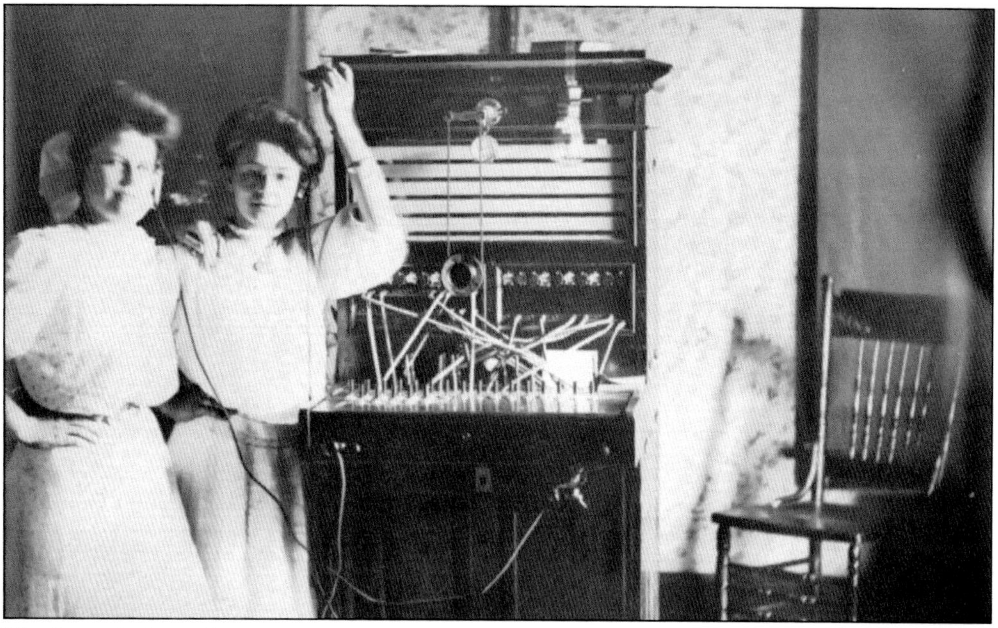

The first telephone line in Broome County was owned by local entrepreneur and comb factory owner Joseph P. Noyes. He was recognized as a telephone pioneer but was unable to acquire a long-distance line until about 1883. Operators often worked at home on switchboards similar to the one being used by these women.

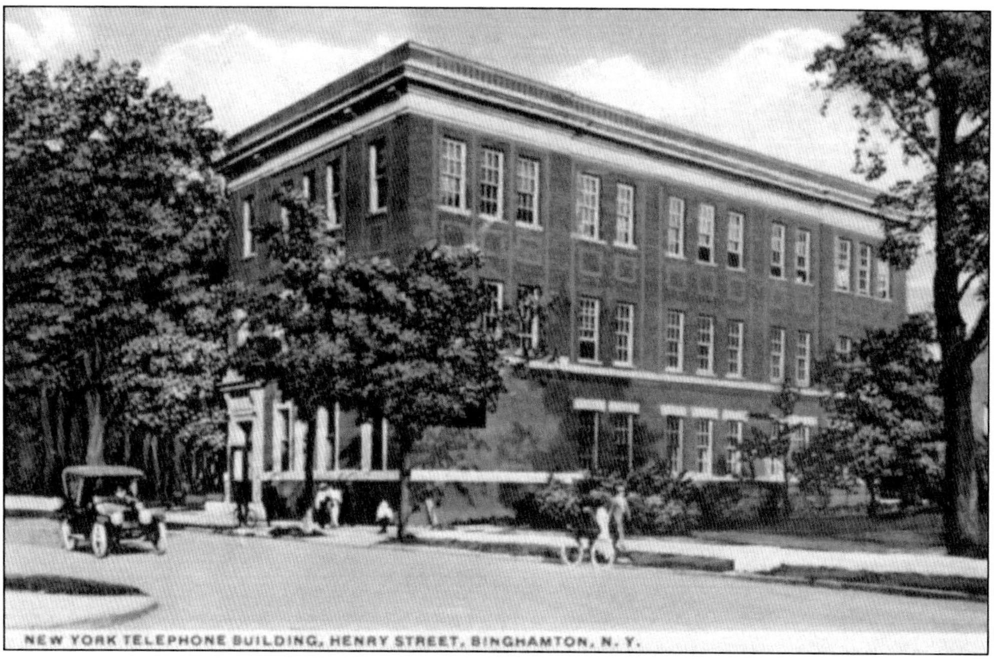

Alexander Graham Bell invented the telephone in 1876. Broome County was quick to grasp the concept and benefit of the device, especially for the business community. By 1880, the original telephone system for Broome County had been established. In 1915, the New York Telephone Company opened for business on Henry Street in Binghamton.

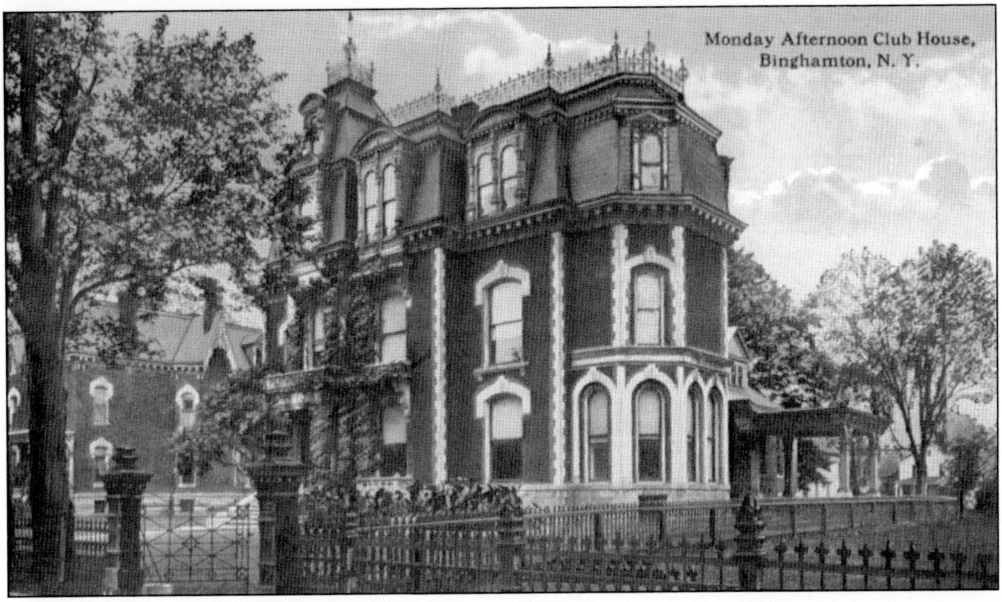

In 1890, the Monday Afternoon Club was established by women dedicated to the mental improvement of their limited membership. In 1905, the club acquired the Sherman D. Phelps Mansion. Designed by Isaac Perry *c.* 1870 in a Victorian style, the building is skillfully crafted, with an opulent interior of rare wood and marble. Beautifully preserved, it is a vital part of the community. Recent plans called for the mansard roof, which was removed years ago, to be restored. This postcard was mailed in 1917.

PICTURESQUE BINGHAMTON--Preserve This--More Coming

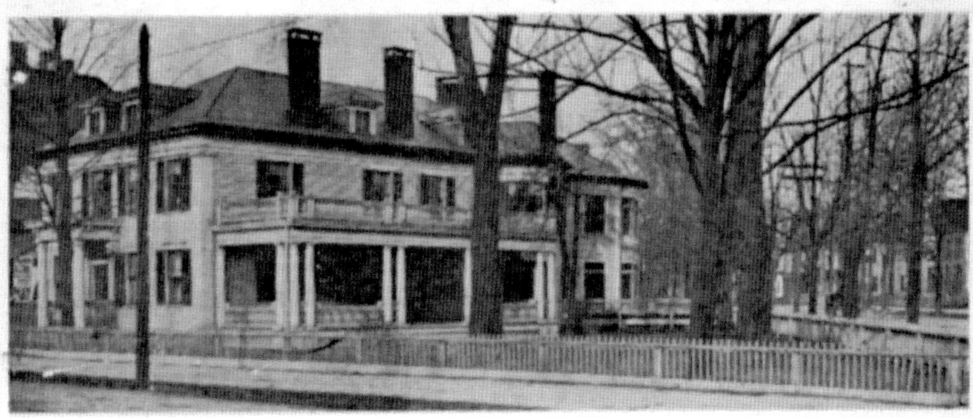

BINGHAMTON CLUB

The following statement shows the net circulation of THE BINGHAMTON PRESS for the week ending October 29, 1904, all exchanges, free copies and spoiled papers not included: Monday, 21,378; Tuesday, 21,384; Wednesday, 21,452; Thursday, 21,348; Friday, 21,601; Saturday, 22,730; total 129,893.

NET DAILY AVERAGE CIRCULATION 21,649

The Binghamton Club was organized by 39 of the area's most influential businessmen in 1886. The building pictured was on the corner of Chenango and Henry Streets. In 1924, the club built a magnificent brick Georgian Colonial clubhouse on Front Street. The new accommodations included lounges for smoking, cards, reading, and billiards, as well as a restaurant. At that time, the club was for men only. This postcard was mailed in 1904.

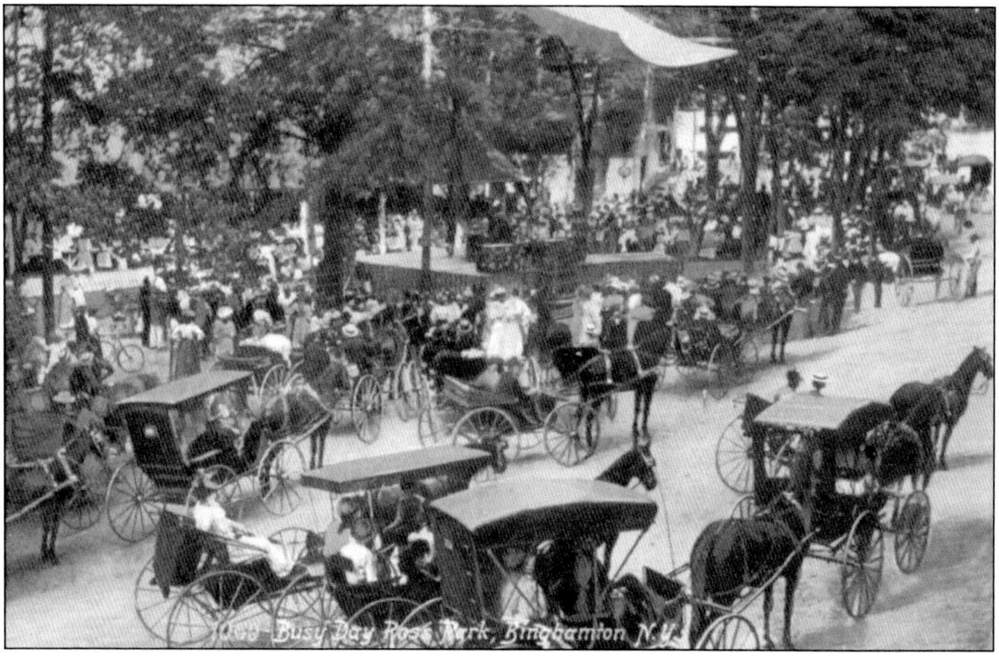

Most of the south side of Binghamton was once known as Rossville in honor of Erastus Ross, who gave the city a 90-acre park in 1875. The extraordinary glen landscape, thrill rides, and band concerts drew crowds on trolley and carriage. Ross Park is the home of an antique carousel donated by George F. Johnson in the 1920s. The park also contains the fifth oldest zoo in the nation. The postcard was mailed in 1909.

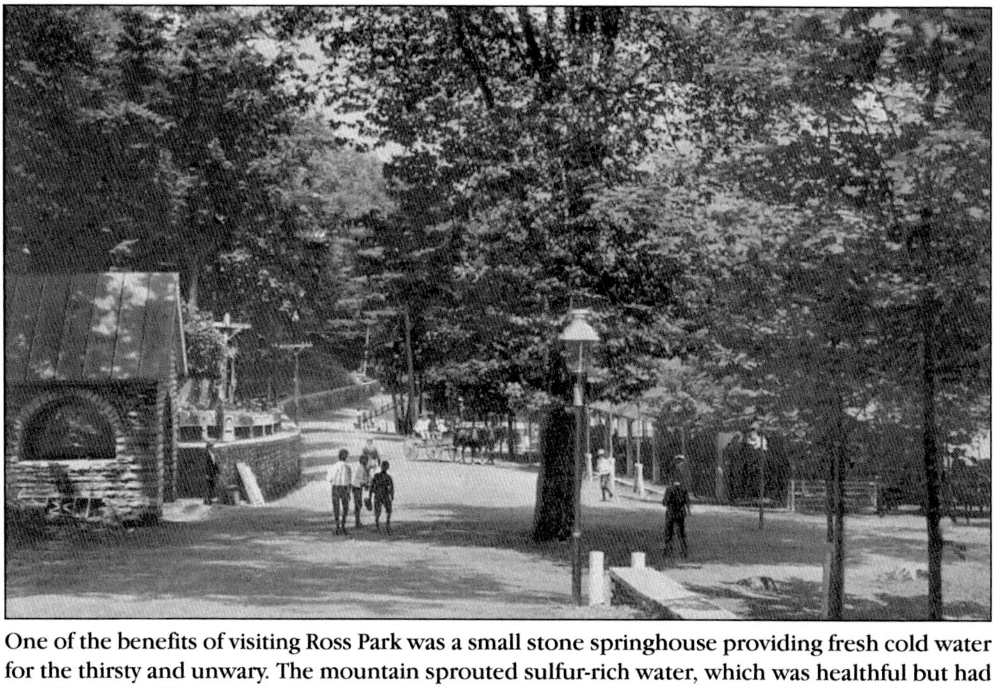

One of the benefits of visiting Ross Park was a small stone springhouse providing fresh cold water for the thirsty and unwary. The mountain sprouted sulfur-rich water, which was healthful but had an odor much like rotten eggs.

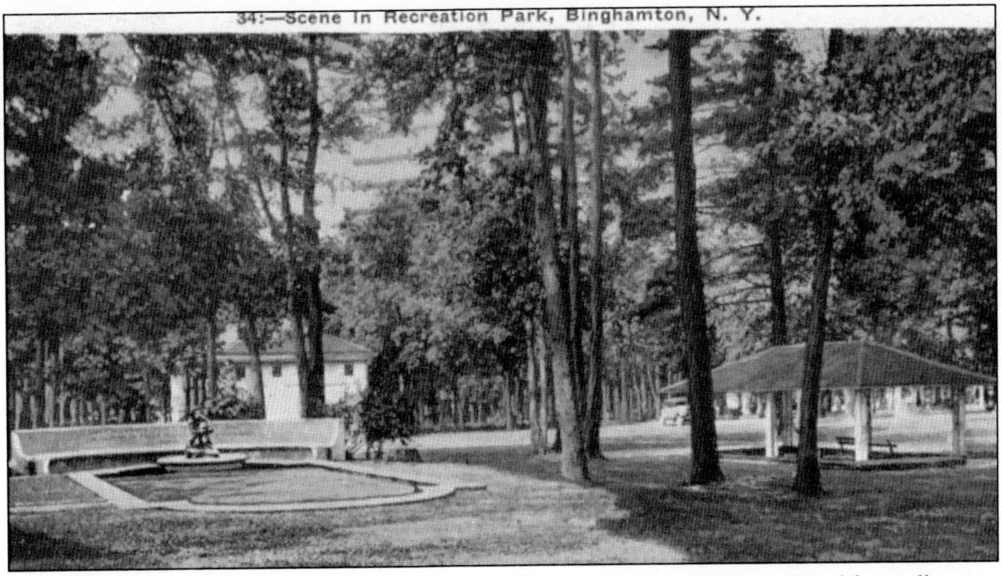

The Binghamton Railway Company had an excellent marketing division. Travel by trolley was encouraged by offering excursion rates to entertainment facilities owned by the company. Bennett Park, known during the 1890s as Bennetts Grove and later as O'Neil Park, served this purpose well. It contained a springhouse, a dance pavilion, ball fields, and picnic areas. Eventually purchased by George F. Johnson, who donated it to Binghamton, it is now Recreation Park. This postcard was mailed in 1939.

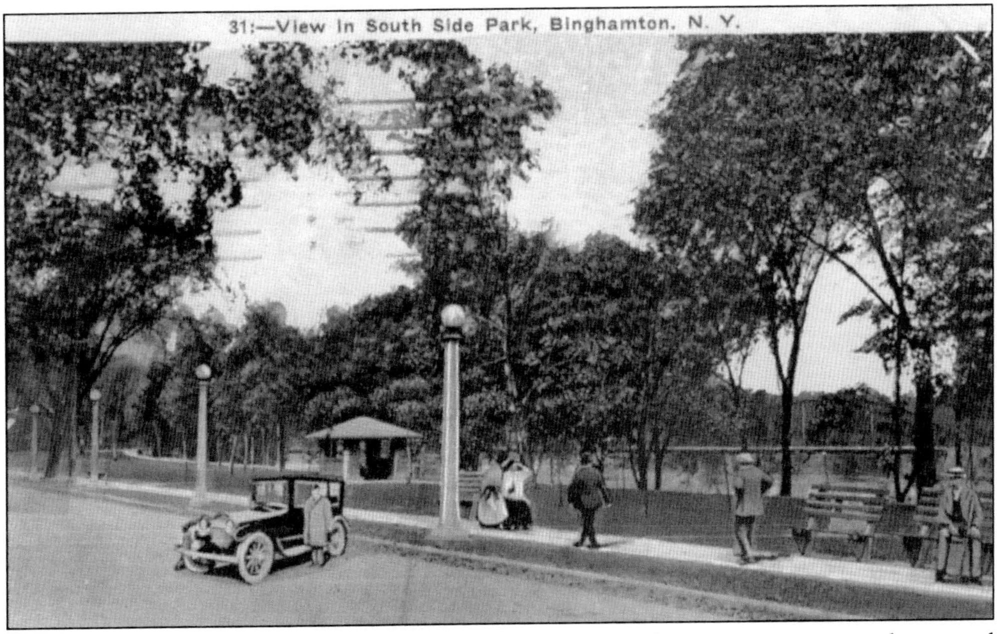

The ruins of the unused Chenango Canal extension provided a space to preserve the natural beauty of the riverbanks by developing a public park. The idea of a South Side Park began in 1900; by 1916, possession of the land was secured. It remains today as a lovely expanse along Conklin Avenue, a passive recreation area, interspersed with benches and war memorials. The postcard was mailed in 1939.

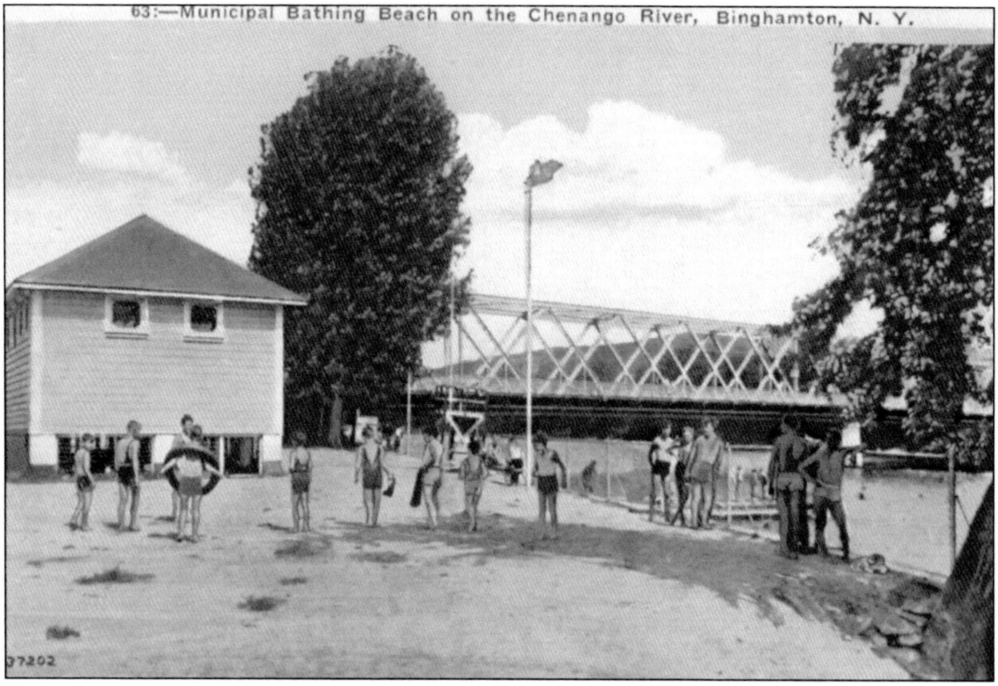

These public bathing facilities, the boathouse, and beach along the Chenango River near the De Forest Street Bridge were all washed away in the great flood of 1935. The bridge, too, has disappeared and has been replaced by the Bevier Street Bridge.

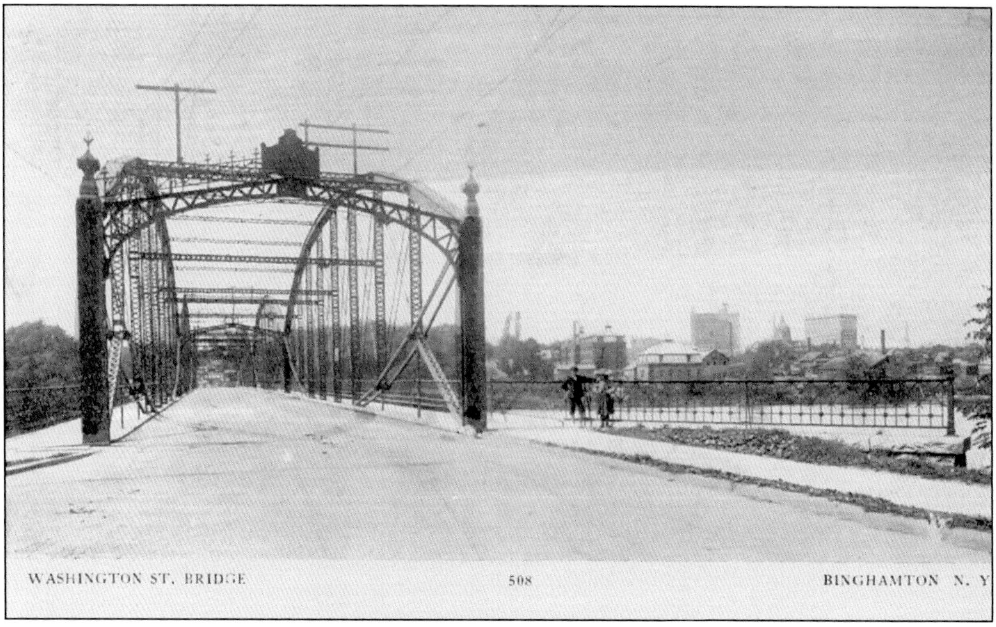

In 1825, a traditional covered wood structure was built across the Susquehanna River. It was called the "White Bridge," and a toll was charged. By 1886, it was replaced with what is today one of the last triple parabolic arch bridges left in New York. The South Washington Street Bridge is now a noted historic site used only for foot traffic.

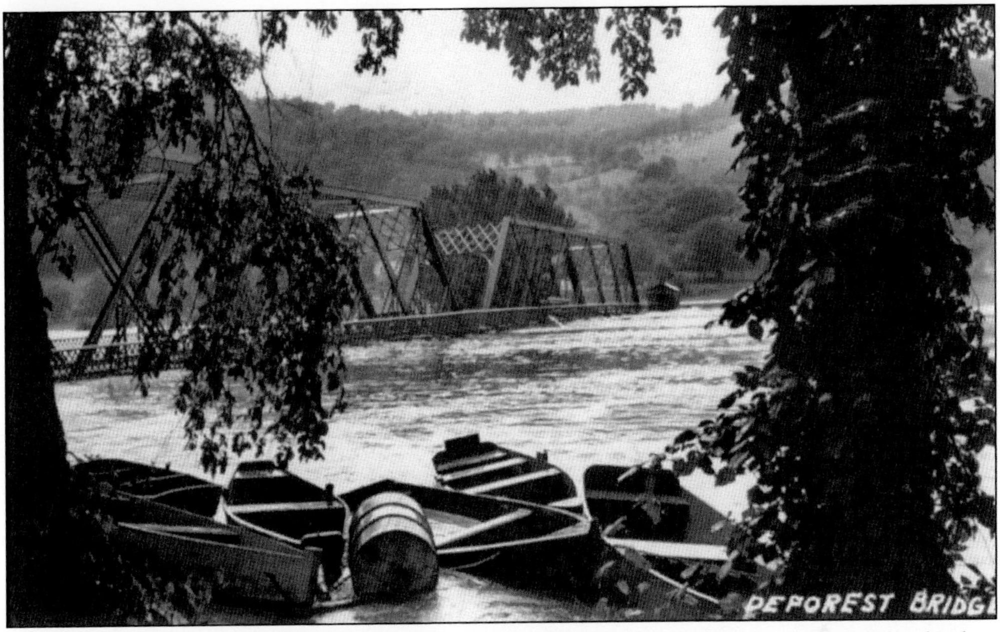

In 1793, a ferry operated at the end of De Forest Street. It was replaced in 1897 with a bridge. This postcard shows the structure being inundated by floodwaters in 1936. The street and bridge were named for Captain De Forest, a Revolutionary War soldier personally acquainted with George Washington, Alexander Hamilton, and Benedict Arnold. His house at Three De Forest Street, was a modest log structure, long since lost in time.

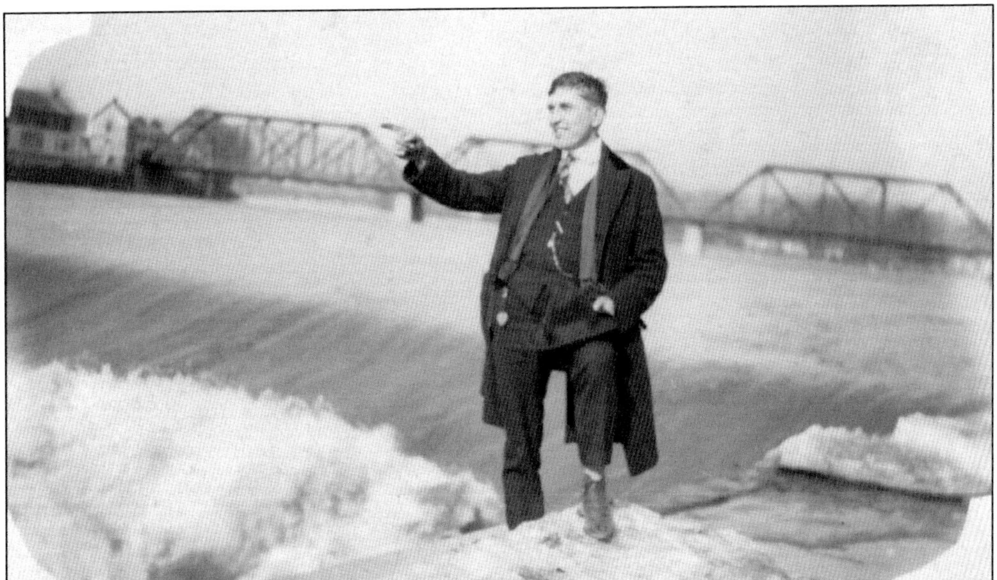

The Rock Bottom Dam was constructed in 1871 as part of the scheme for extending the Chenango Canal from Binghamton to Owego. The dam was necessary to convert the Susquehanna River into a great feeder. It is 400 feet in length and more than 7 feet high. It was constructed on a regular curve, with the convex side breasting the current to give it superior strength. This real photo postcard was taken in 1920.

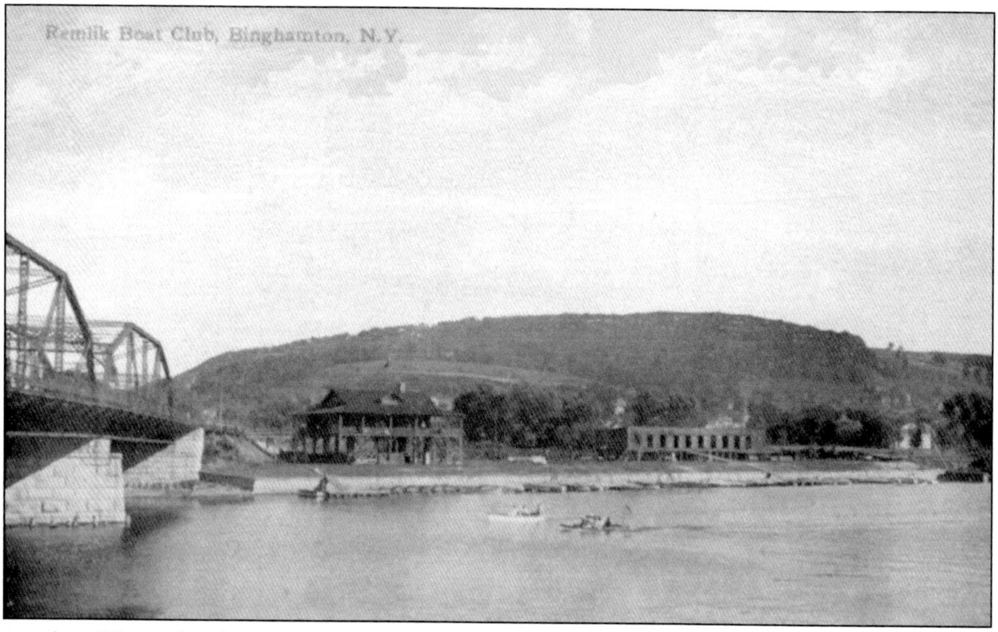

Another Kilmer family enterprise was the boat club along the Susquehanna River near the Tompkins Street Bridge. The name of the facility was Remlik, or Kilmer spelled backwards. The club no longer exists.

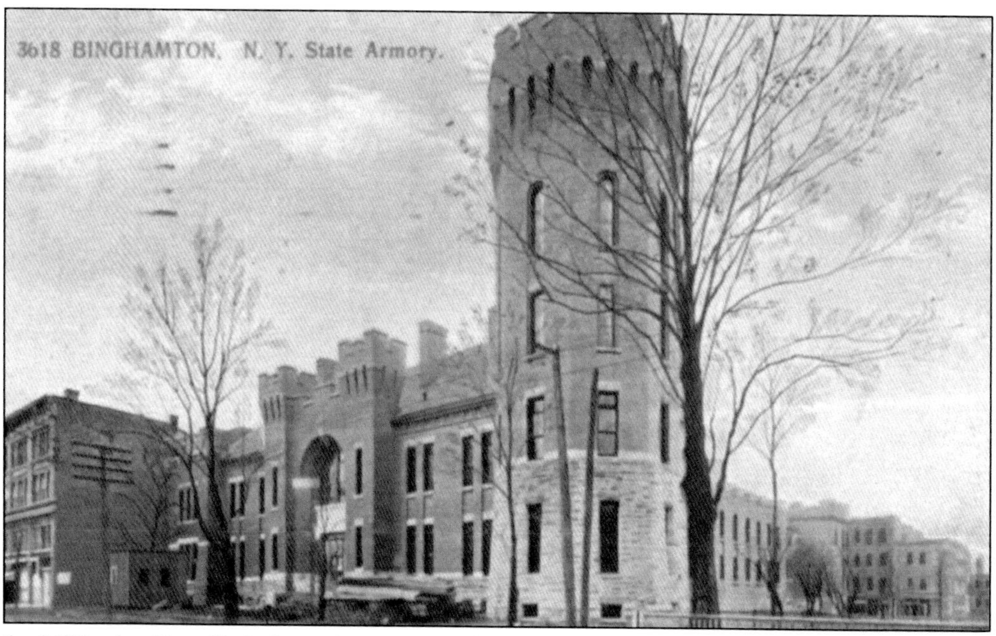

In 1905, the New York State Armory was built on Washington Street in Binghamton, the second armory in the city. The New York State Institute of Applied Sciences used the facility for classrooms for many years; the school became Broome Community College. This armory burned to the ground in 1951, despite the valiant efforts of firefighters, one of whom lost his life in the inferno. This postcard is from 1908.

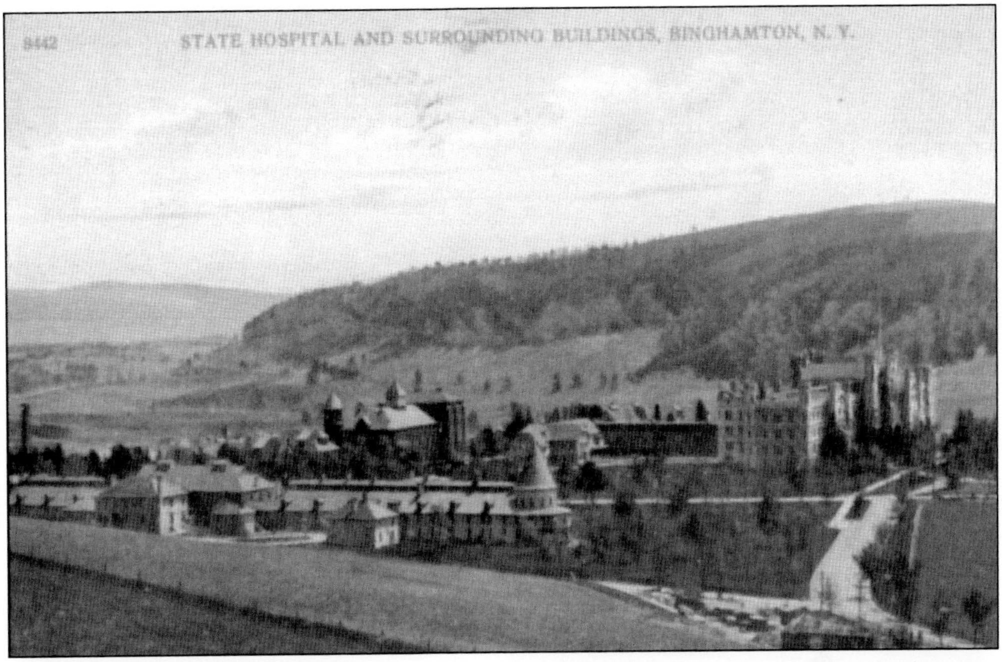

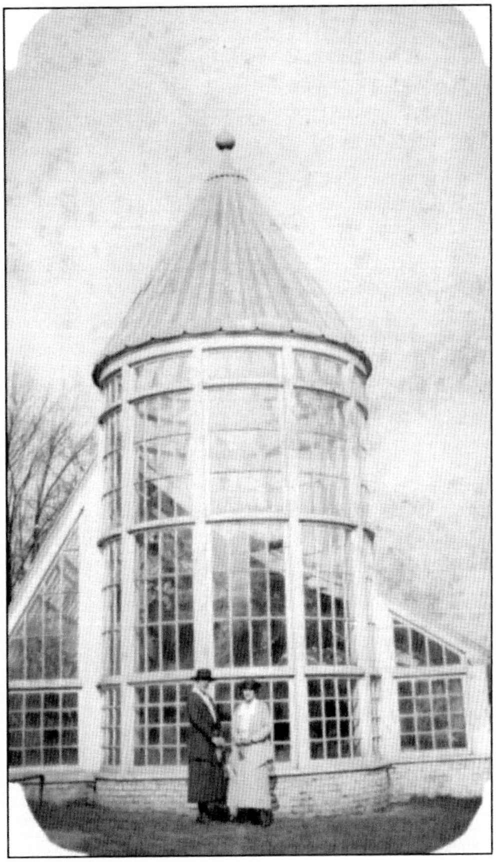

Broome County led the nation by recognizing alcoholism as a physical dependency and treating it as a disease. The first New York State Inebriate Asylum was erected in 1858 on a 252-acre site just outside the city of Binghamton, with a commanding view of the river valley. A great quantity of Syracuse limestone composed the front and decorative details of the castellated Gothic-style building. The rear walls and the interior were all of local stone and brick. The building was designed by architect Isaac Perry and is now recognized as a national historic landmark. The grounds contained all the elements necessary for therapy and survival, including a greenhouse with a tower (at right). People from the valley regularly visited the parklike lawns for fairs and picnics. Just a few years after opening, the facility became a psychiatric center. In 1999, it was abandoned and put up for sale. The landscape view of the asylum (above) was mailed in 1910.

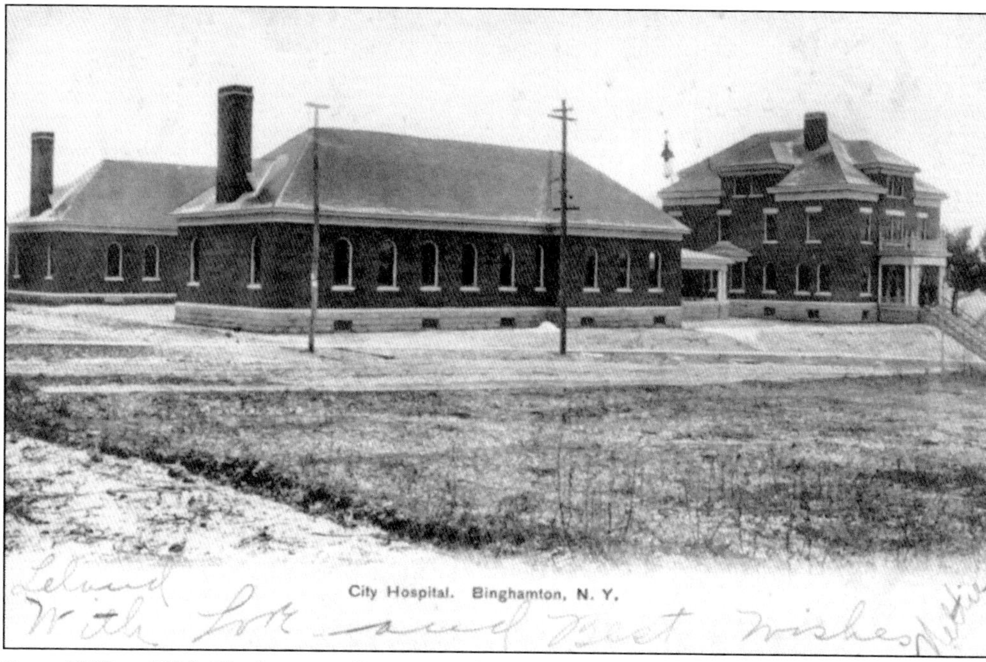

From 1888 to 1895, Binghamton City Hospital operated from a house on Court Street. In 1896, it opened facilities on Mitchell Avenue. A nurse was selected as superintendent of the hospital and directress of nurses at a salary of $600 per year.

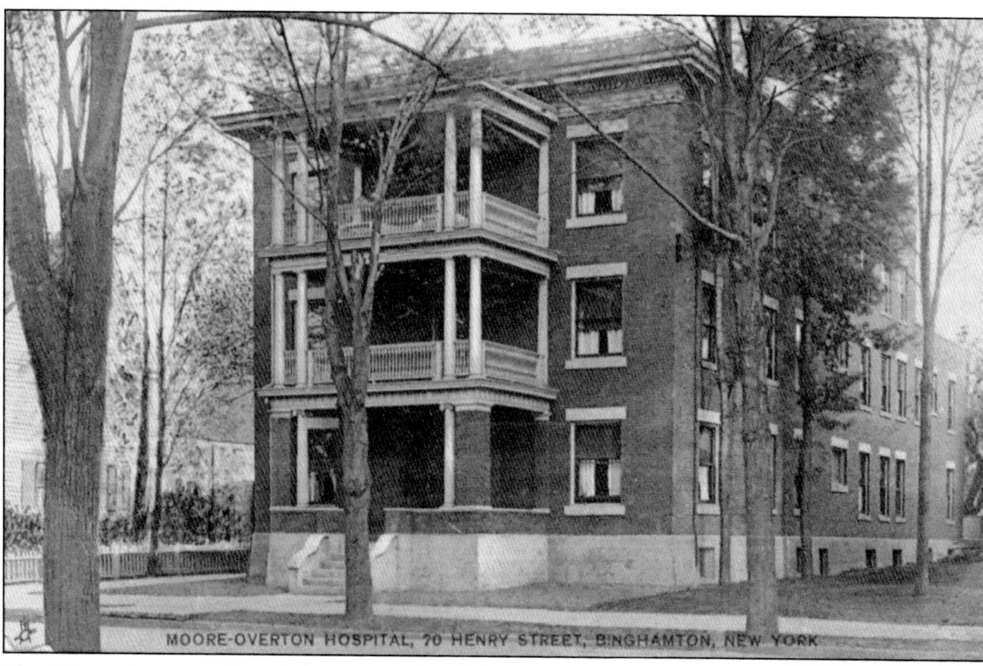

The Moore-Overton Hospital opened in 1909 as a private institution on Henry Street in Binghamton, with a capacity for 16 patients. In 1920, it added a nurses' home. In 1922, an addition was built so that 22 people could receive care. The postmark on this card is 1912. The hospital is no longer in existence.

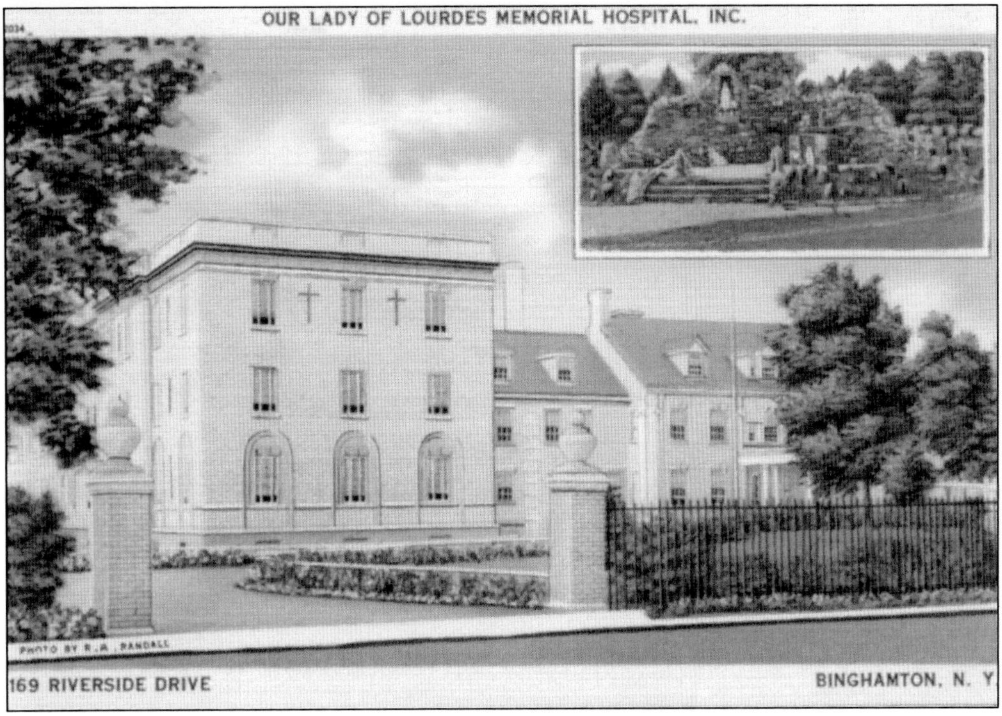

Lourdes Hospital was established in 1925 in the Corbett Mansion on Riverside Drive in Binghamton. Operated by the Sisters of Charity, it was a pioneer in Catholic health care. From its beginnings as a 25-bed unit, Lourdes has grown to become one of the largest nonprofit health care providers in the nation.

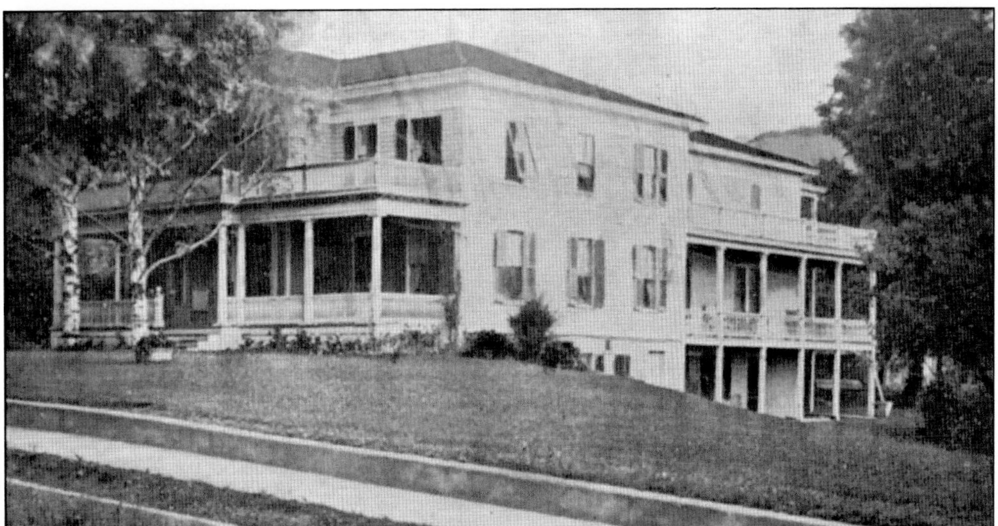

Broome County has always been proud of its ability to care for the indigent and needy, as exemplified by the creation of the Home for Aged Women in 1891. A house in Binghamton was donated for the purpose, and it served 14 women over the advanced age of 60. The women were asked to donate a one-time fee of $300 and thereafter had life residence.

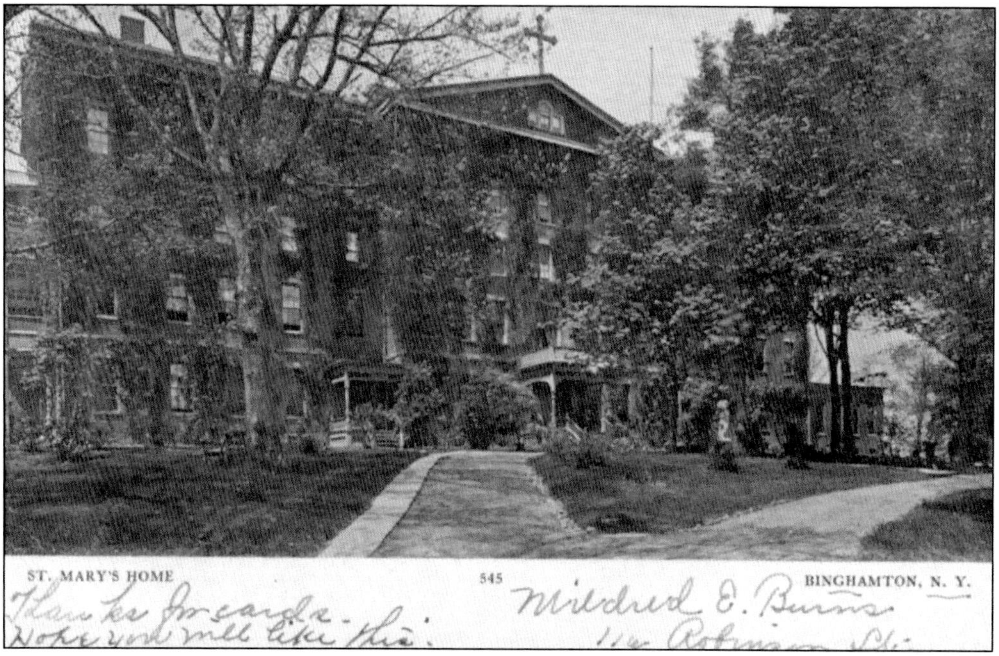

The building that was the Susquehanna Valley Seminary in 1855 and later Dean College came to be St. Mary's Home for Orphans Asylum in 1881. Located on Chestnut Street in Binghamton, the building was demolished in 1963 and is now the site of Seaton Catholic High School. This postcard was mailed in 1906.

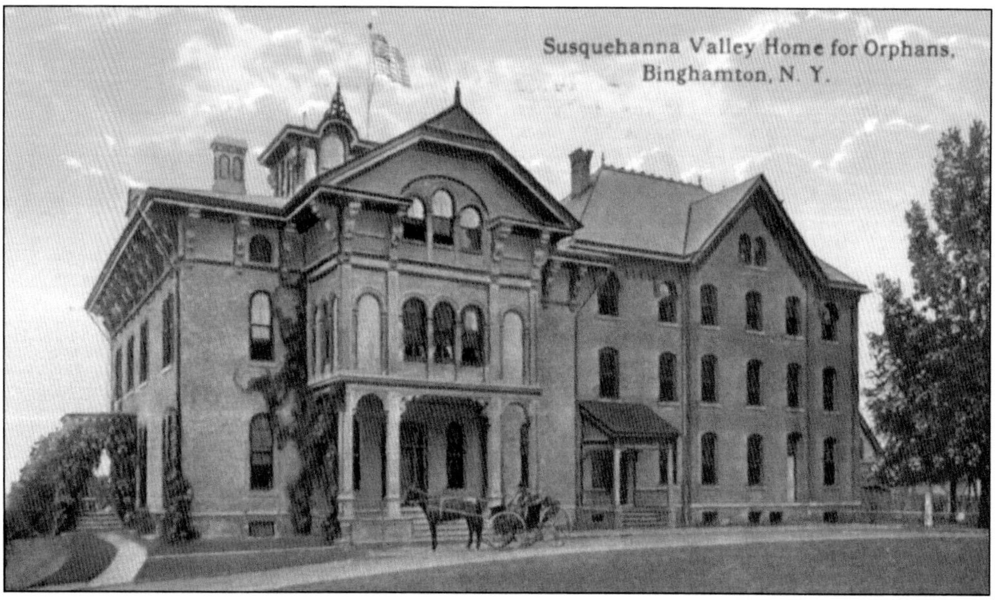

River Mound, a mansion built in the style of an Italian villa, was located on 45 acres near the river on the south side of Binghamton. By 1871, it was the Susquehanna Valley Home for Needy Children. The institution intended to solve "hereditary pauperism, and give the little waifs of fortune cast upon its care, the refining influences of a Christian home, and habits of industry." It was demolished in 1956.

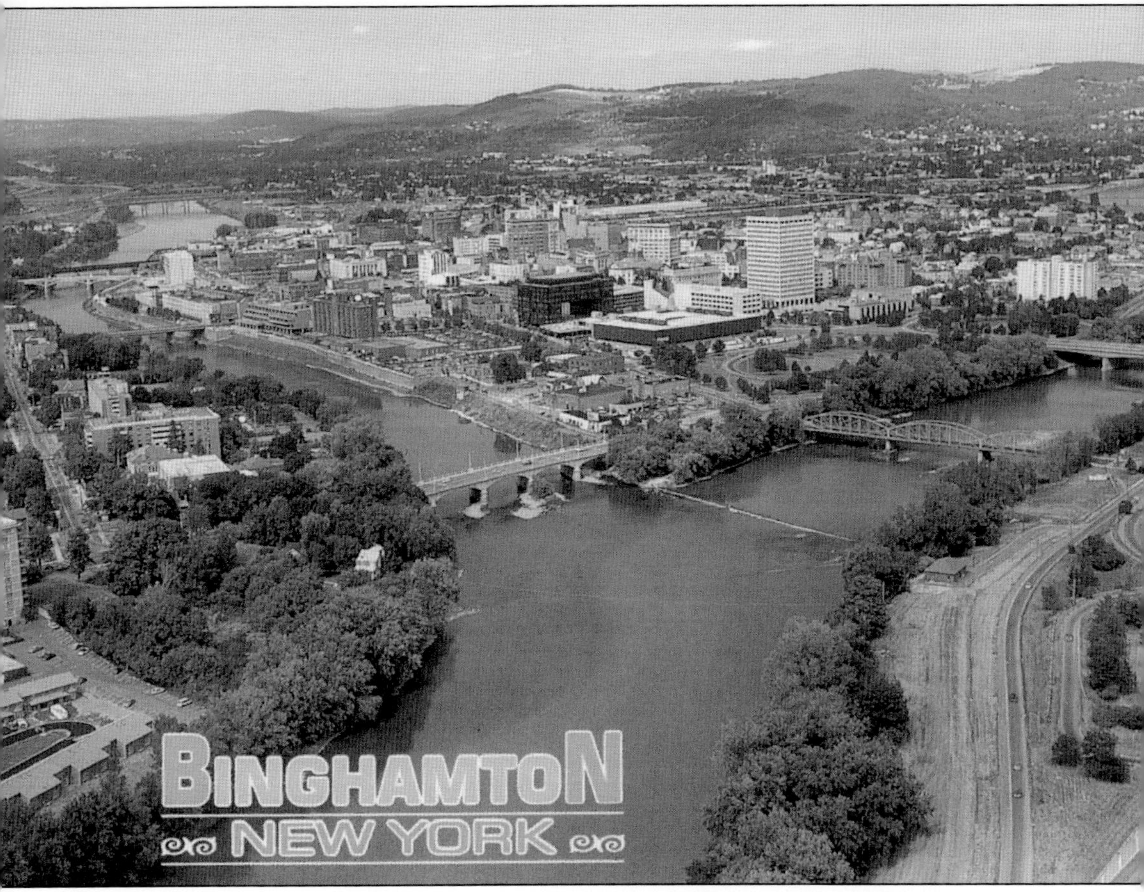

The Chenango and Susquehanna Rivers converge in the Broome County seat of Binghamton. Used for food, water, transportation, and power, the rivers have exercised an influence that has been integral with local development. Before it was known that a waterway could die, the depths were also used for other purposes. In the 1790s, flat-bottomed boats, arks, and log canoes carried settlers into the deeply forested valleys. By 1813, the New York State Legislature declared the rivers state "hi-ways." In 1859, an article published in the local newspaper said, "dead horse hooked by fisherman, again." In the 1920s, slot machines, stills, and other illegal apparatus were dumped in the rivers by law enforcement agencies. All along the riverbanks, sewers and household waste emptied into the coursing waters. Today's era of environmental awareness has resulted in renewed appreciation and cleansing, and once again the rivers bring signs of life and hope to the Valley of Opportunity. This view is a new postcard by photographer Ed Aswad.

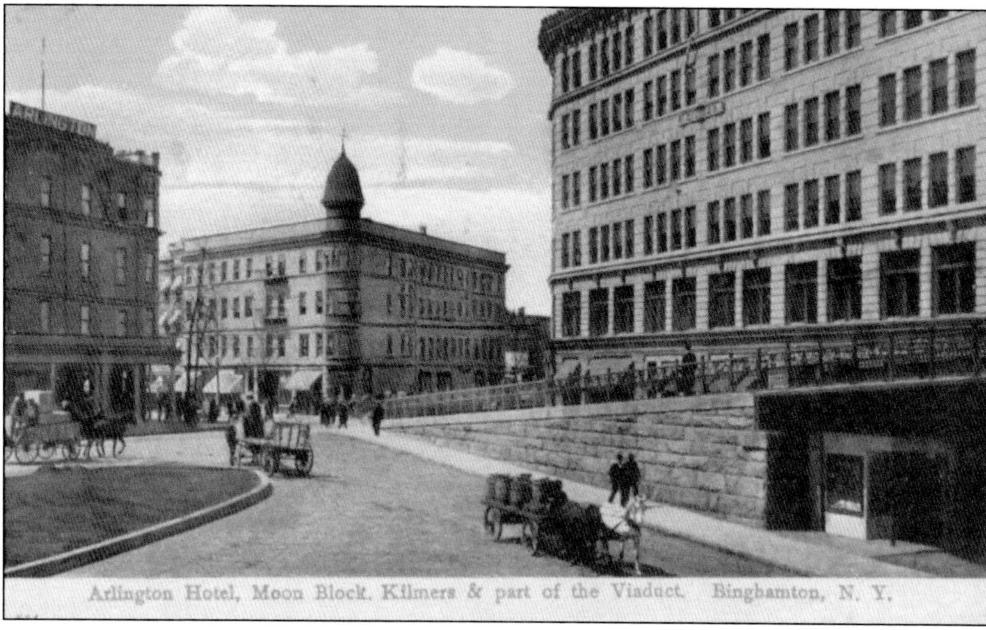

Dr. Kilmer & Company was established in 1878 and produced a patent medicine so popular that it was sold around the world. Swamp Root was claimed to cure almost any human ailment. The healthy dose of alcohol added to the roots and herbs in each bottle probably did induce a temporary good feeling. The Kilmer family had a large influence on Broome County, liberally spending the millions earned with Swamp Root. Distinctive mansions were constructed on Riverside Drive, including a world-class racing stable, Sun Briar Court. Some of the finest thoroughbred horses in the country were raised on this estate, including the great Kentucky Derby winner of 1917, Exterminator. The stables and track where the "horse was king" have disappeared into the Lourdes Hospital Complex. The Kilmer building where the concoction was bottled remains an impressive but empty edifice at the corner of Chenango and Henry Streets. The postcard above was mailed in 1908. The one below was sent in 1905.

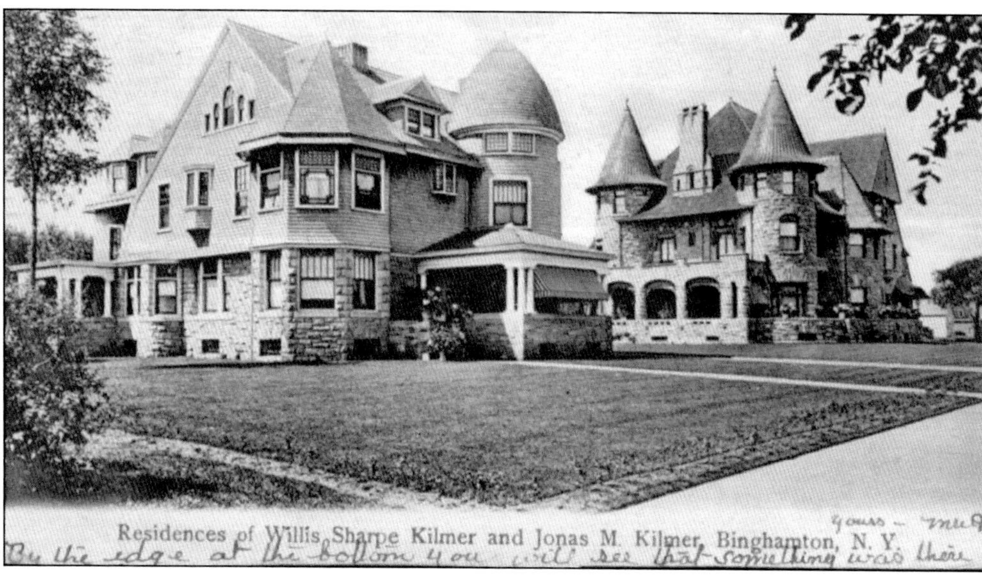

In 1904, millions of Swamp Root dollars were used to establish the Binghamton Press. Willis Sharp Kilmer, angered by the notoriety he was receiving in the existing newspaper, opened his own publication. The Press Building was the area's first skyscraper and has housed local history for years. In 1924, the New York State Ku Klux Klan ran operations from offices at the site. During World War II, the Kilmer family donated the entire top floor for use by the Red Cross.

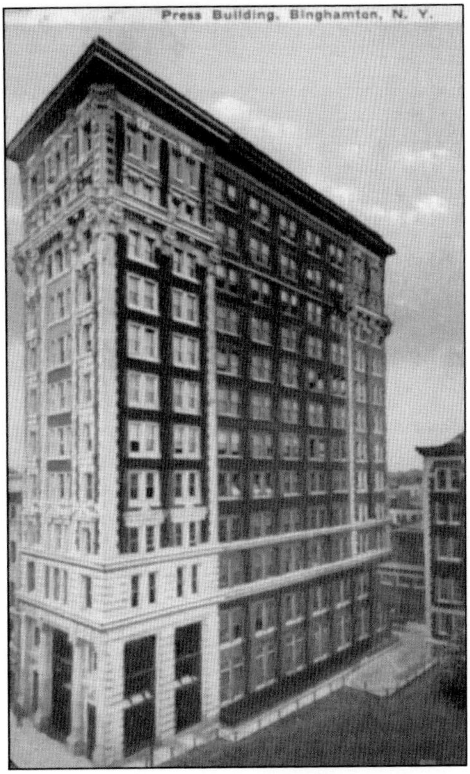

Dr. S. Andral Kilmer changed the hamlet name of Osborne Hollow to Sanitaria Springs and built a mountain sanitarium. Located in the town of Colesville, the facility took advantage of the "healing waters" of sulfur and advertised a completely "successful non surgical de-cancerizing system of treatment." Using "plasters" that drew out the cancer, supposedly "marvelous recoveries were effected every day." This postcard was mailed in 1907.

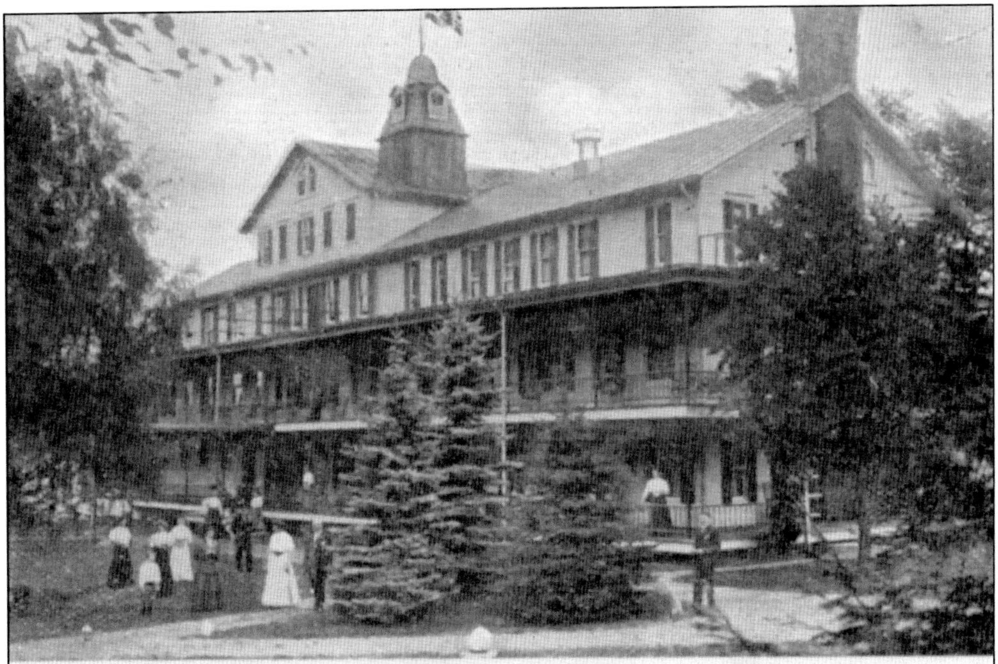

Dr. S. Andral Kilmer's Sanitarium-in-the-Mountains, Sanitaria Springs, N. Y.

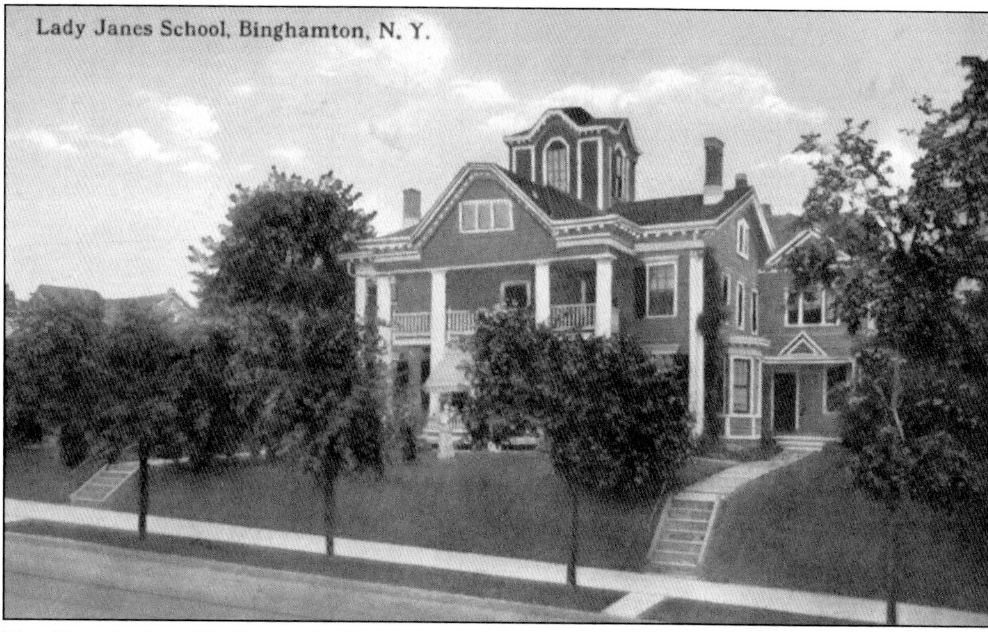

The Brandywine Hotel was built in 1810 on the corner of Court and Liberty Streets in Binghamton. In 1882, it was the Lady Jane Gray School. Young ladies "of good family" from all over the state were sent here to be "finished appropriately to enter society." Run by some of the most "refined and cultured teachers found anywhere," the school operated until 1923. The building was demolished in 1926.

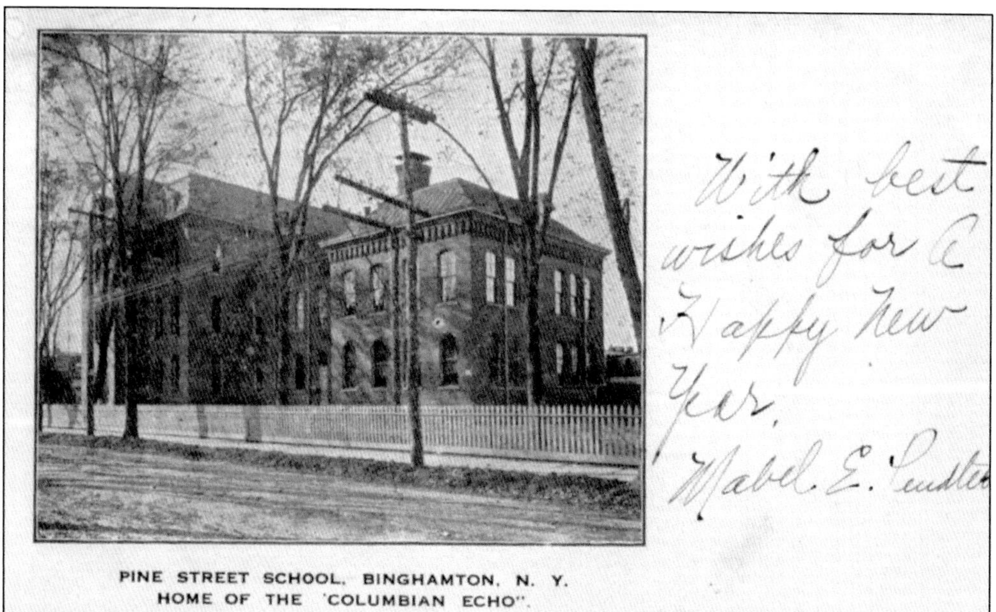

Schoolhouse No. 4 on Pine Street had a rare reputation for being fiscally sound. Through the efforts of T.J. Clark, trustee of the district in 1859, "the school was made self sustaining without the collection of a single rate bill." This postcard is from 1907, by which time many enlargements had been made and bills had been sent to taxpayers.

The Binghamton High School was erected on Main Street between 1871 and 1872 at a cost of some $100,000. In 1895, the school had 510 pupils and 16 teachers. The instructors took home a combined salary of $12,559 per year. Additional school expenses came to a grand total of $4,000. The building was torn down in 1913. Today, the present high school occupies the site.

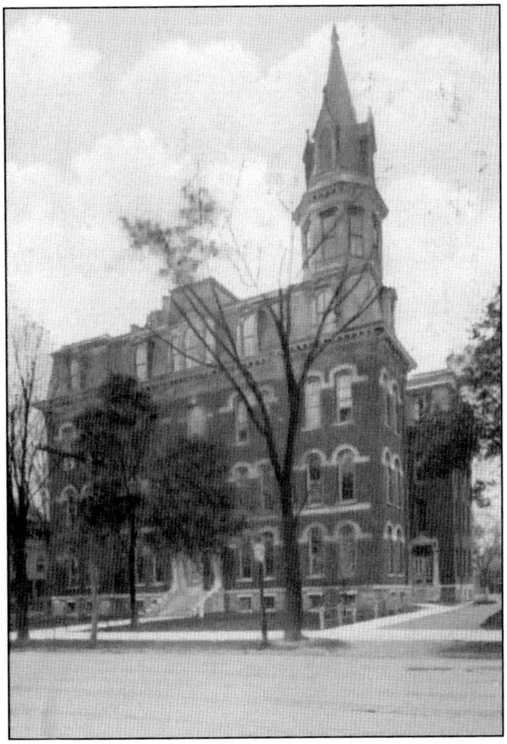

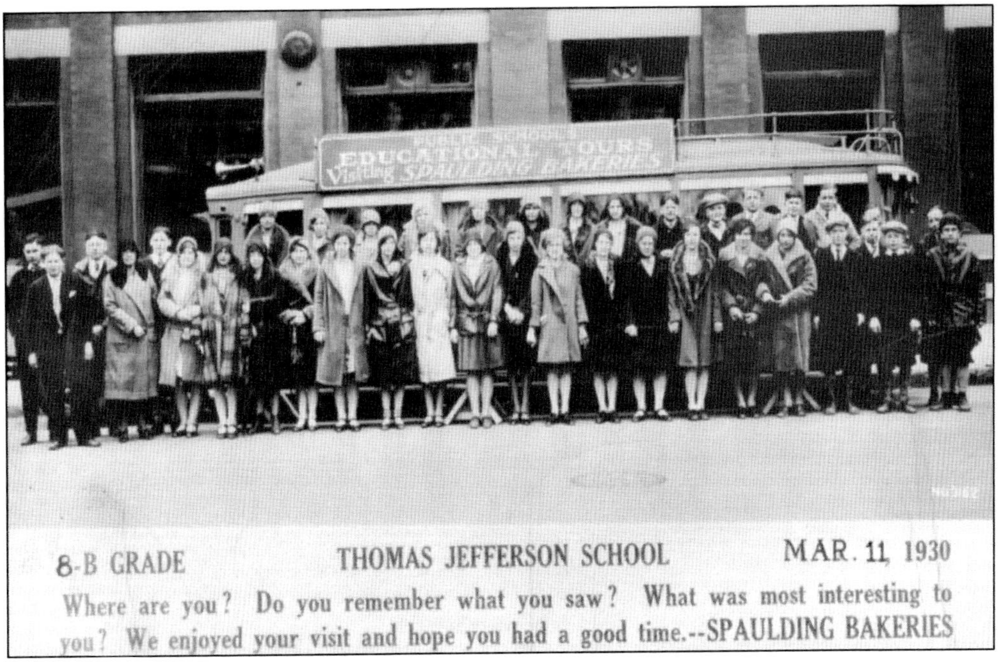

Spaulding Bakeries, originally known as the Russell Spaulding Bakeries, was located on Exchange Street in Binghamton. The company was famous for its crullers as well as its community involvement. Schoolchildren enjoyed the bakery's hospitality, which extended over its entire 50 years of existence. This postcard was sent to visitors in 1930 as a souvenir.

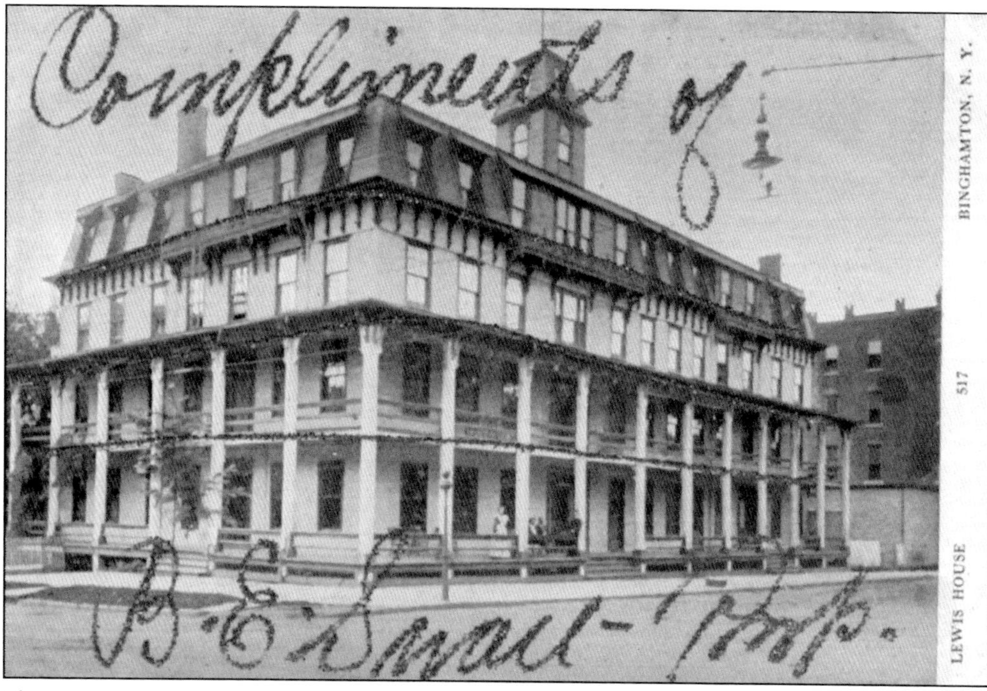

The Lewis House Hotel was built on the corner of Lewis Street and Prospect Avenue in 1849 by Hazard Lewis. A landmark popular with railroad travelers, the hotel boasted that it was the best in the city and advertised "first class accommodations for $2." Eventually, it was demolished to make way for a gas station. A generous sprinkling of glitter on the lettering was an advertising attempt to make the postcard noticeable.

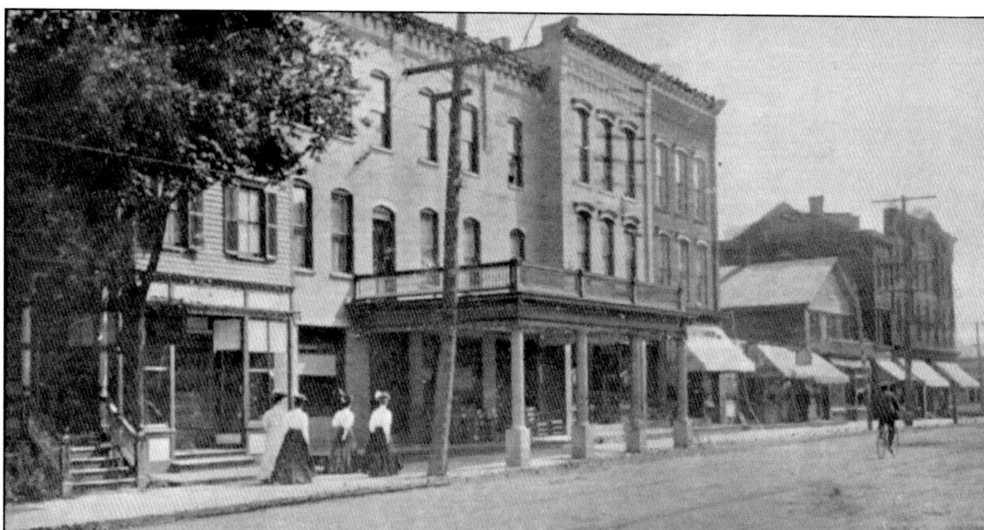

Charles Wales, born in 1836, has been remembered as a public-spirited citizen who devoted his energy to developing and improving the portion of Binghamton that lies north of the railroad. In 1884, he built the Wales Hotel, also known as the North Side Hotel, which consisted of 40 "classically efficient" rooms. His friends said that Wales was "a faithful citizen, who of course, voted Republican."

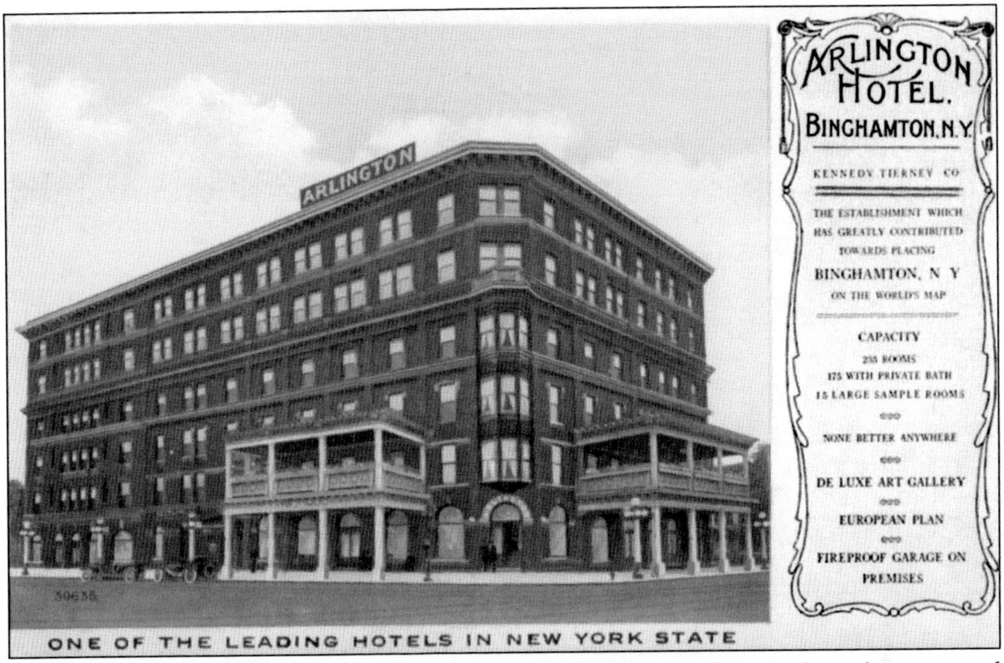

Perhaps the best-known hotel in Broome County was the Arlington Hotel, whose doors opened for business in 1888 on Chenango Street near the railway station. It advertised 300 rooms, modern in every particular, for $2 to $3. The Arlington became a luxury landmark, even boasting an art gallery that featured the work of Douglas Arthur Teed. The hotel was demolished in 1967 so that a parking lot could be built on the site. The postcard below shows the famous Arlington Spanish Ballroom.

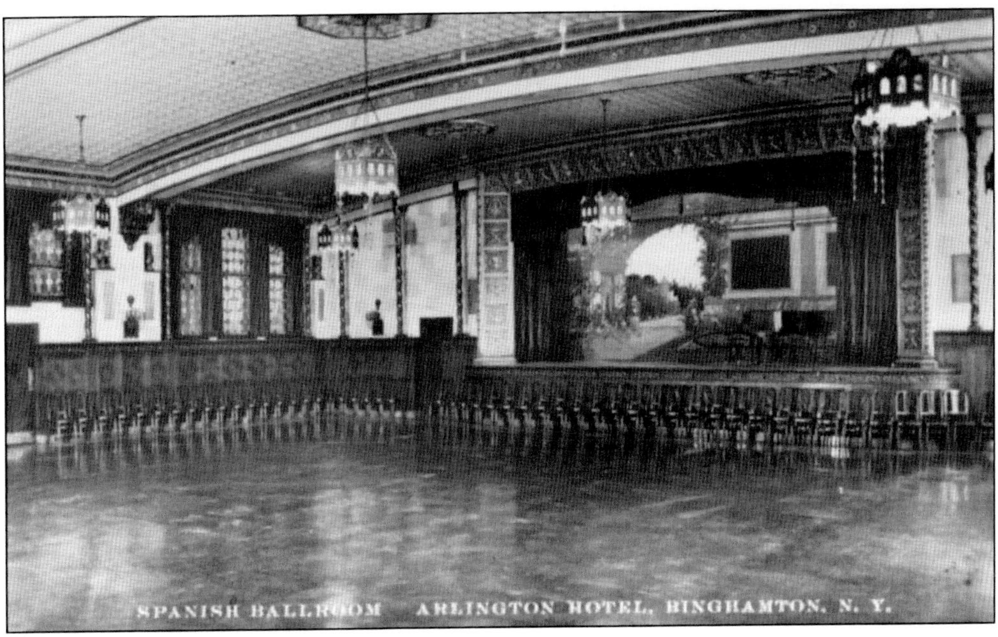

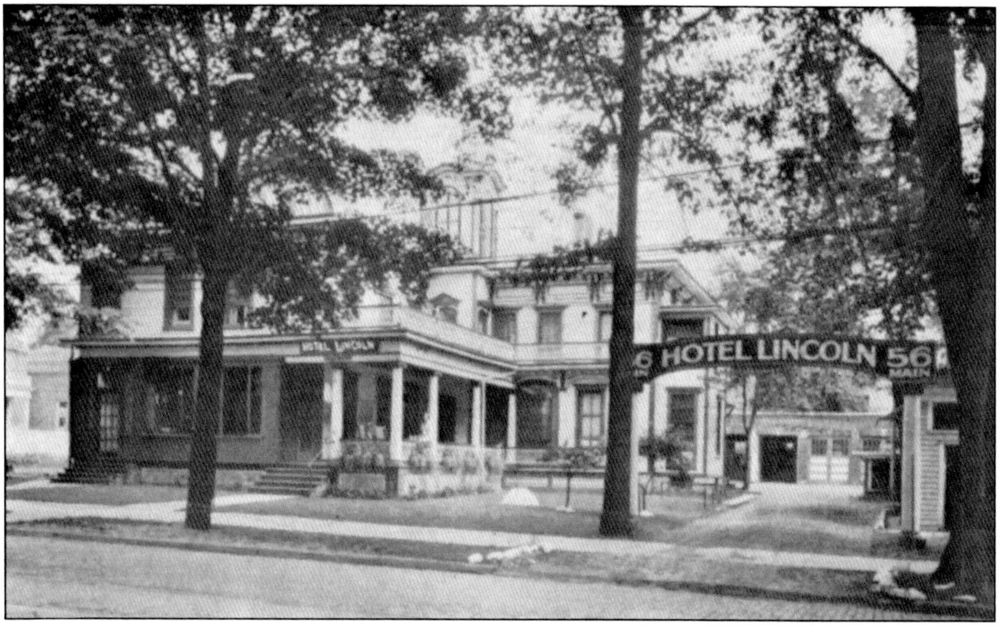

Binghamton's Popular Price

European Plan Hotel

Rates $1 - $1¼ - $1½

MODERN rooms with and without private baths. All rooms have running hot and cold water, are steam heated, clean and well kept, have electric light and splendid beds. Good moderate price restaurant attached; also garage and service station. Individual fire-proof auto stalls (lock up your car and baggage), mechanic and car washer in attendance. Barber and Tailor; sample room; spacious porches; a homelike welcome atmosphere awaits you. Prices right. Always a room. Most central and quiet; away from train noises. Any car from R. R. station passes our door. About six minutes ride.

56 MAIN STREET

Near Masonic Temple and High School

TELEPHONE 5249

JOHN L. MOORE, Owner
HUGH HEARON, Manager

Pictured in this 1926 postcard is the Lincoln Hotel at 56 Main Street in Binghamton. A lovely mansion was converted into a hotel with character. The grand old hotel was torn down and replaced with a cinder-block building and tar parking lot. The hotel's advertising postcard was distributed at many local sites, including the railroad station. The reverse side is printed with a large stop sign and words advising visitors to "ask anybody, this is a good place." As another advantage to staying at the Lincoln, the hotel proclaimed to have "the best fire proof auto stalls in the city, for only fifty cents a night."

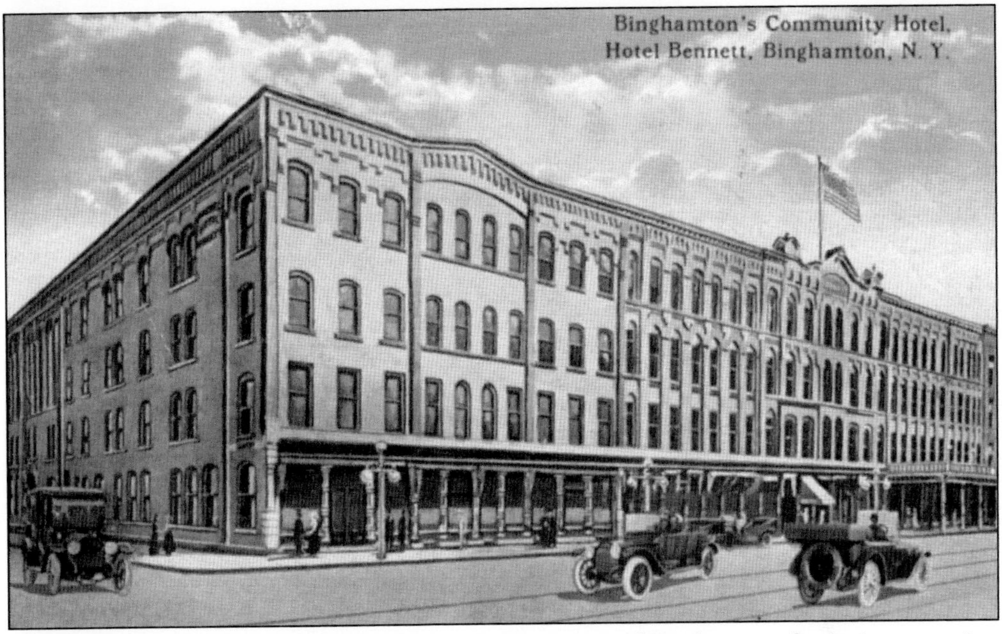

Abel Bennett was born in 1818 and served as the first mayor of Binghamton after its incorporation in 1867. As an industrious businessman, Bennett invested heavily in local real estate; in 1877, he built the Hotel Bennett. The establishment was appointed to the standards of the finest public houses in the country. Through his continued public spirit and benevolence, he earned the unusual reputation as a "wise, conservative and popular . . . politician."

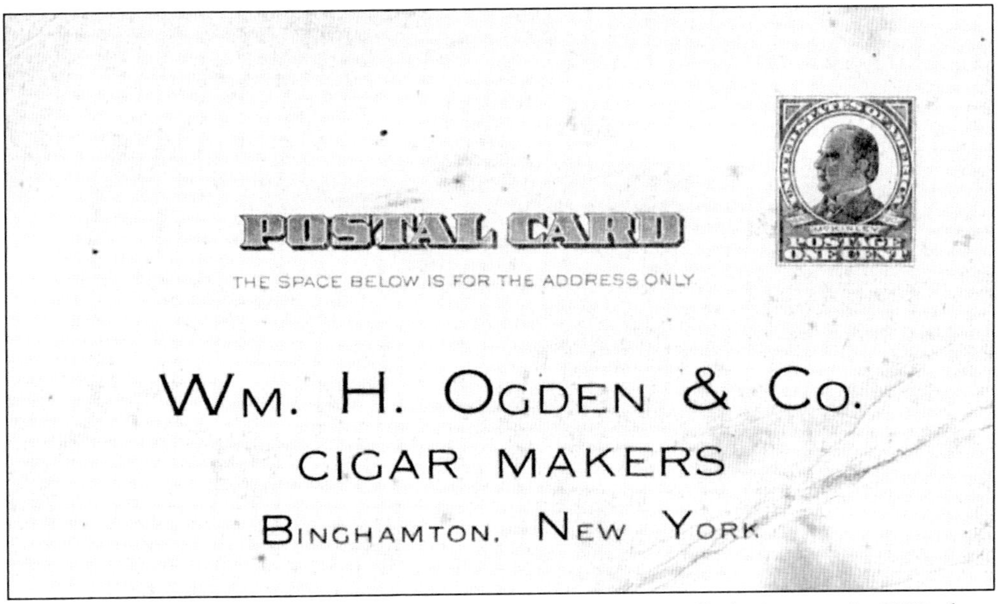

From the 1850s, successful commerce in Broome County was spelled c-i-g-a-r-s. In 1890, there were 50 local cigar factories. The industry reached its height in the 1920s, with the city being fifth in production in the United States. The promotion printed on the back of this postcard is an offer for "250 Cedulas for examination and trial . . . for 30 days." Cigar making has now disappeared from the county.

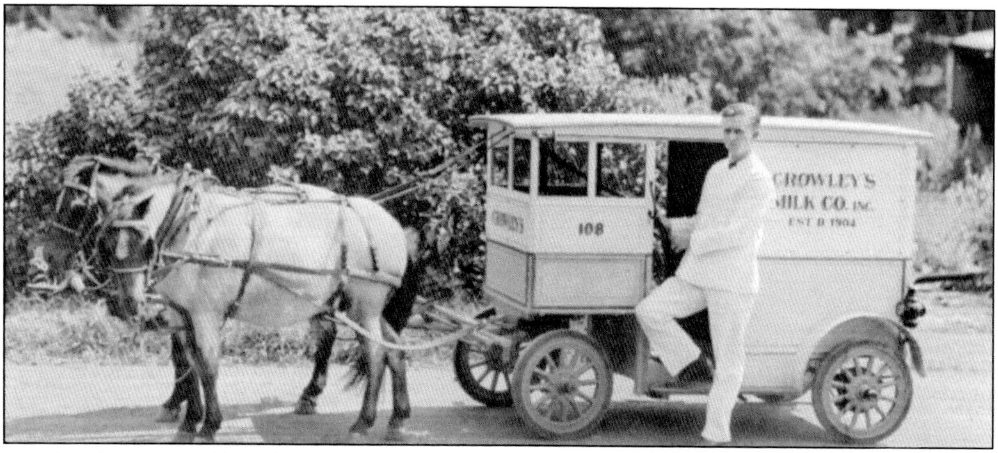

J.K. Crowley invested his life savings of $500 into purchasing a dairy business in 1904. He became the proud owner of a horse and wagon, an icehouse, a barn, and a milk route. It was one of the first distributors to use the pasteurizing process and sterilized bottles. Crowley Foods is still producing quality dairy products in a facility along the Susquehanna River in Binghamton. It is speculated that this vehicle was only used for exhibition and parade purposes.

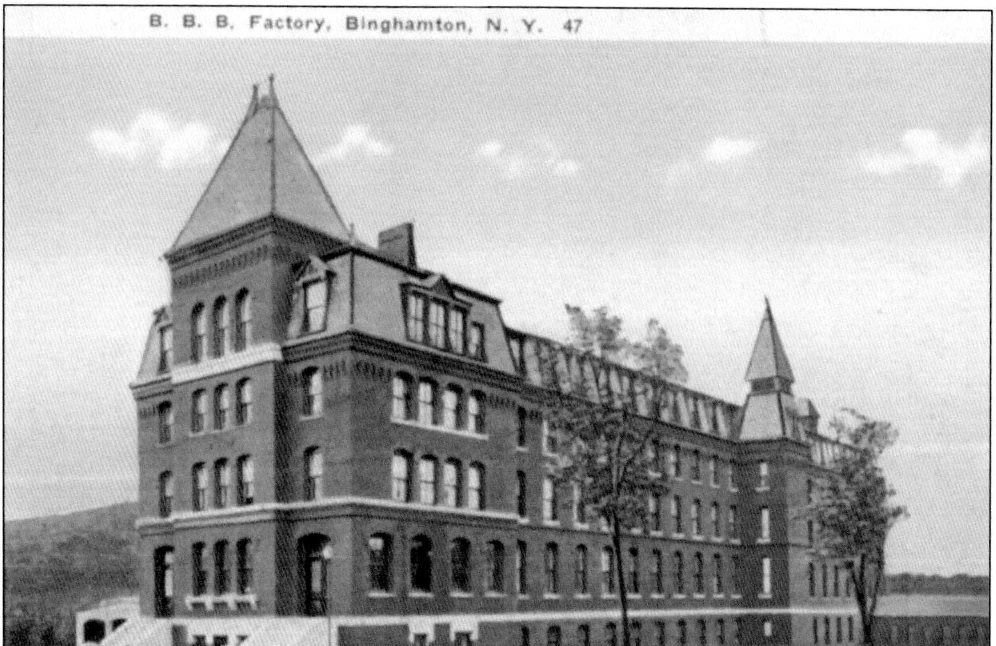

Constructed sometime before 1876, this building was the Weeds Tannery until it was purchased by the Endicott Johnson Corporation and renamed the BBB Factory. At its best, Weeds processed 1,200 hides a week and was one of the largest manufacturing concerns in Broome. Located near the Memorial Circle on Susquehanna Street in Binghamton, the building was torn down in 1966.

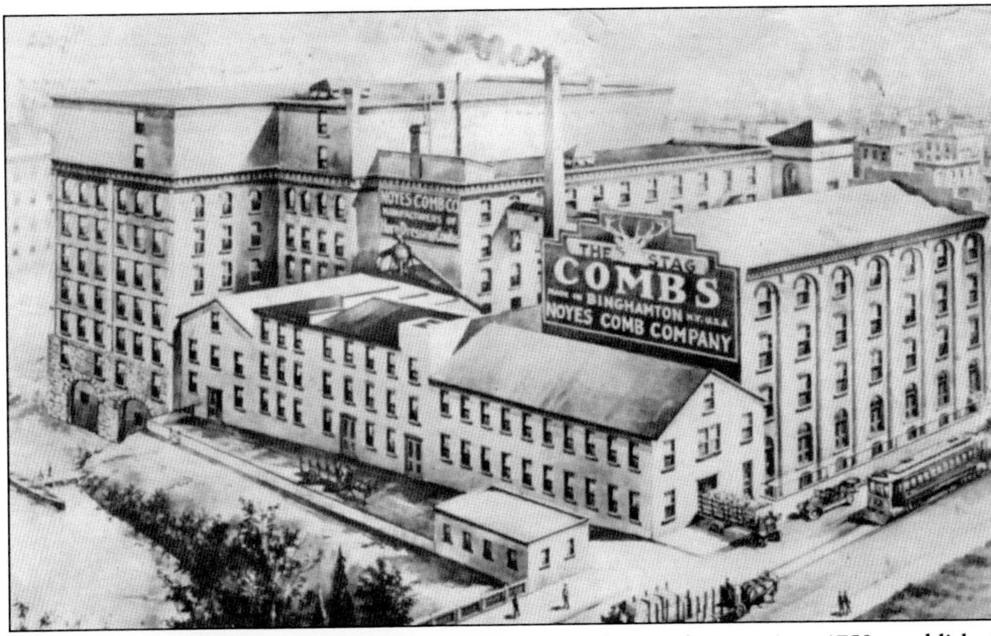

Two members of the Noyes family, comb manufacturers of Massachusetts since 1759, established a factory in Binghamton in 1865. Patents for combs, buttons, and sewing machines contributed to the success of their business locally for more than 60 years. The factory complex grew to encompass a large area along the banks of the Chenango River and included an island just offshore.

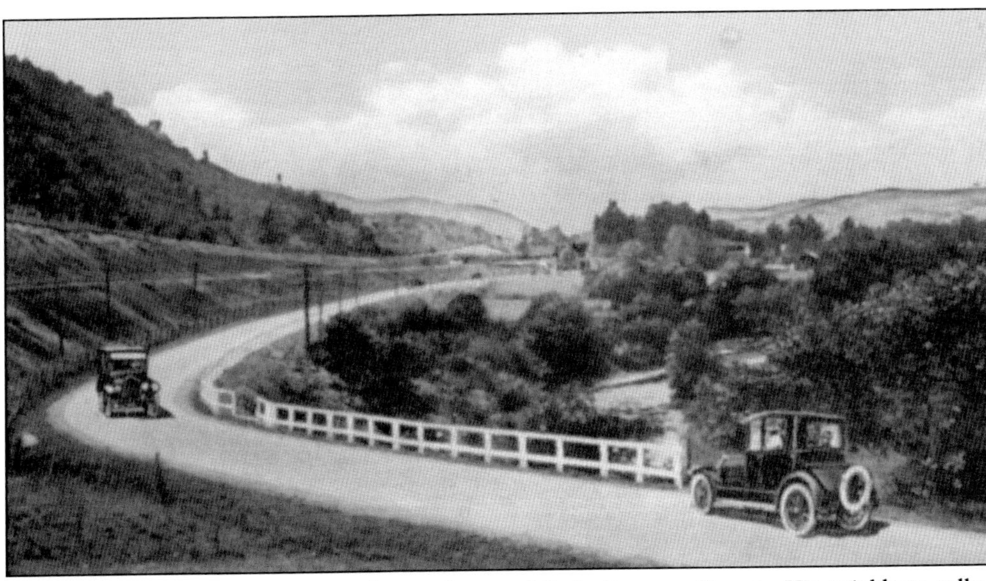

J.K. Noyes was the first person to have a Locomobile in Broome County. His neighbors called it a "freak wagon" and berated him for driving at the reckless speed of 10 miles per hour and frightening their horses. However, his vehicle was the local inspiration to own automobiles. Twenty years later, in 1922, a modern roadway, the Lackawanna Trail, was established between Scranton and Binghamton. Built on land given by the railroad system, the Lackawanna Trail it covered 62 miles.

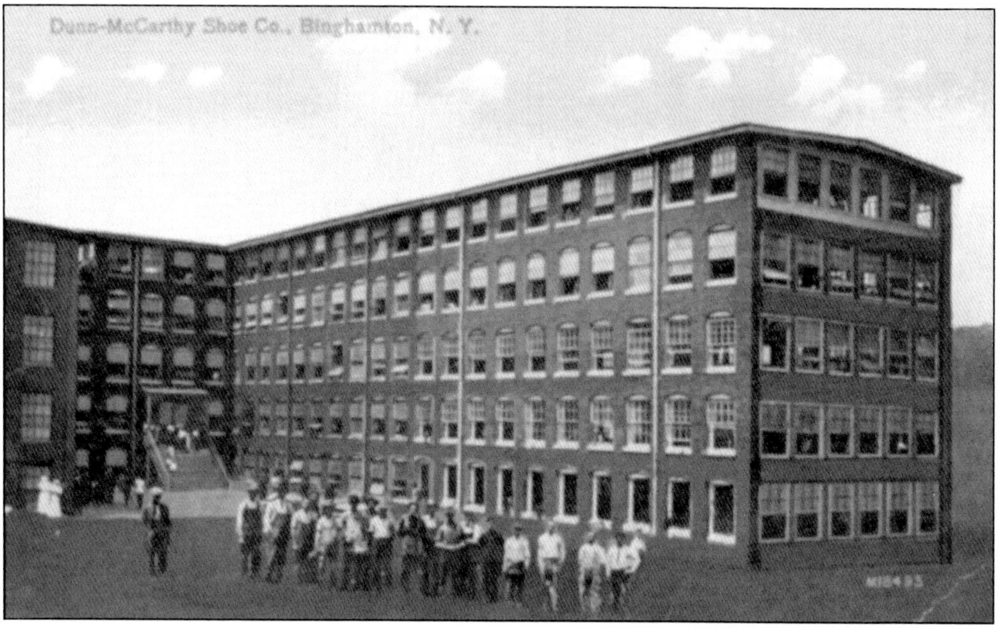

The Dunn-McCarthy Shoe Company began operations in Binghamton in 1907. By 1922, it was the largest industry in the area, employing 1,200 people. Free medical services were provided by the corporation to all employees and their families.

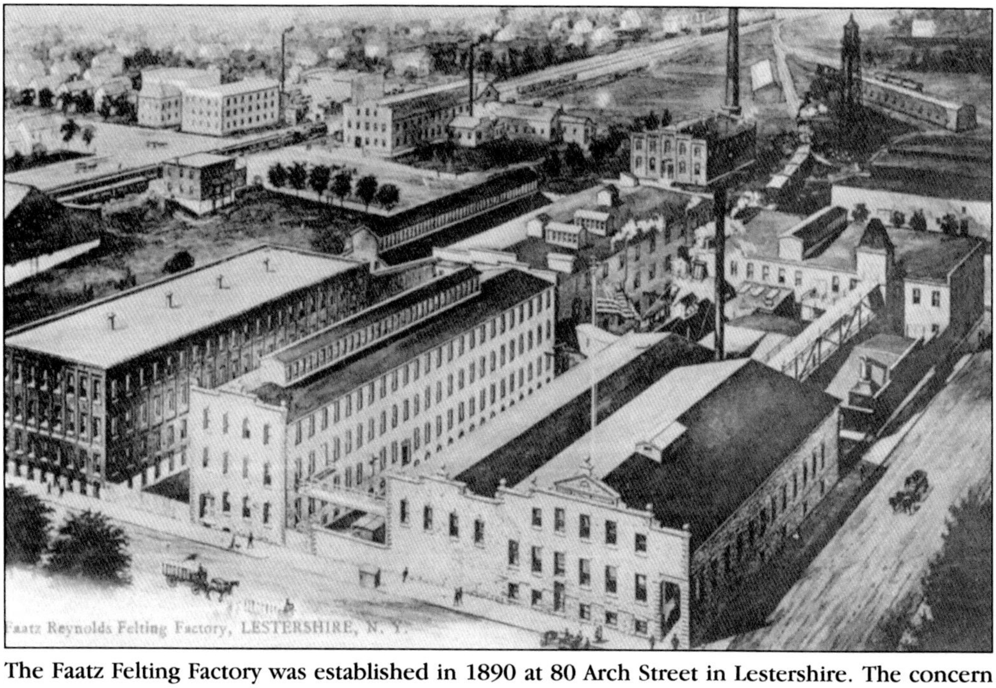

The Faatz Felting Factory was established in 1890 at 80 Arch Street in Lestershire. The concern was a combination of three felt businesses: the Diedricke Company, the Bowden Felting Company, and the Footy Reynolds Company. The concern began with the manufacturing of horse brushes and felt blankets. Felt was made by beating wet wool to pack the fibers together. The more often it was beaten, the harder the felt would get.

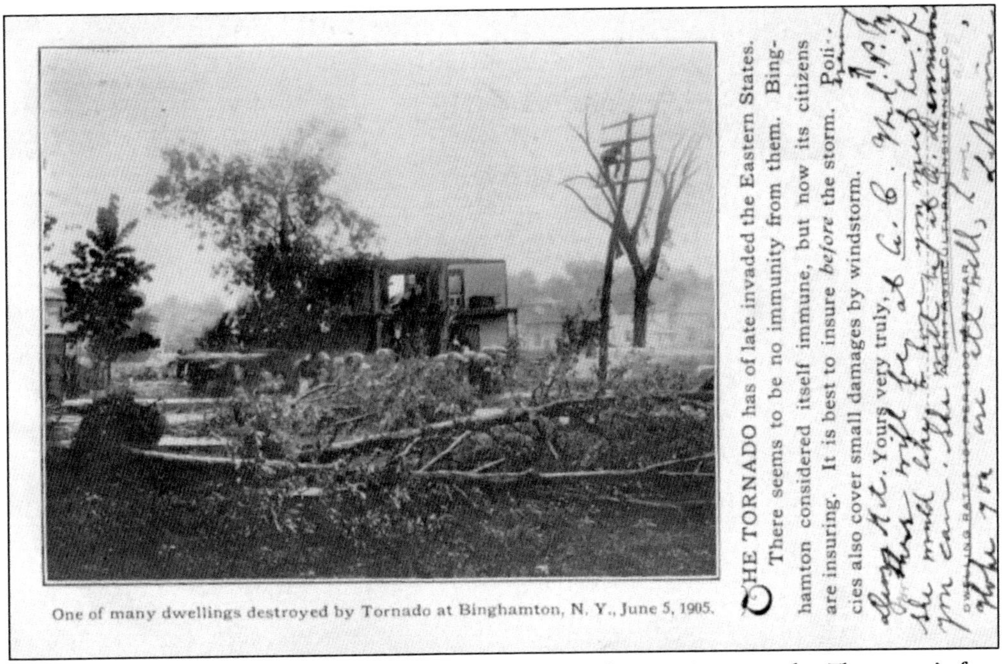

In 1905, the south side of Binghamton was the target of a massive tornado. The storm's fury destroyed many homes and businesses. It prompted a resourceful insurance company to capitalize on the disaster by sending photographs of the devastation on postcards to potential clients. Storm insurance was advertised at 10¢ per $100 per year.

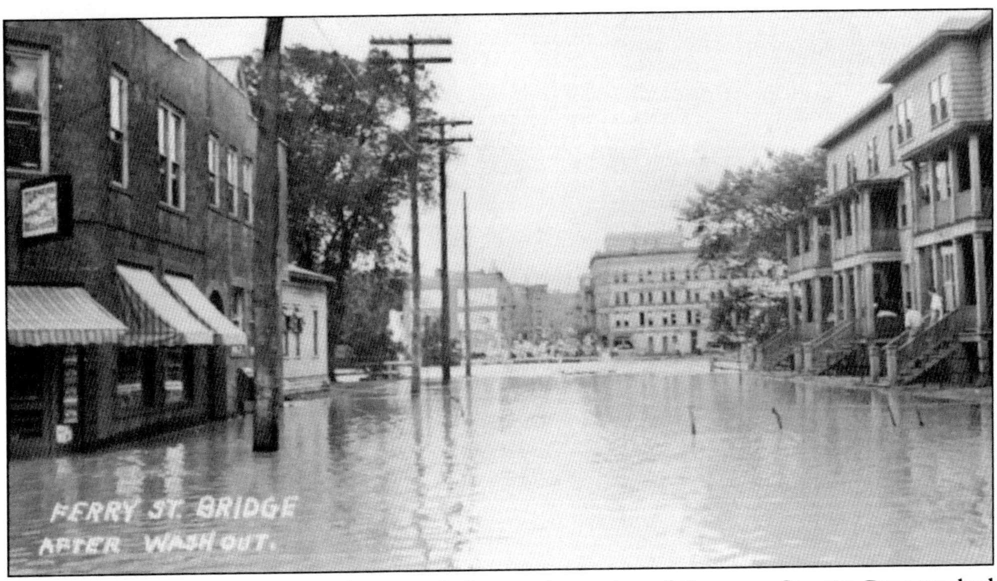

The Great Flood of July 1935 devastated the southern tier of Broome County. Broome had suffered drought conditions for many weeks when the sky darkened and water became the Devil's domain. Torrents drained over the baked hard land, dams collapsed, and bridges washed away. Thousands of homes and businesses were 5 feet deep in water, and still it rained, sweeping death and loss into the wet debris. The crisis stimulated flood control programs all along the valley.

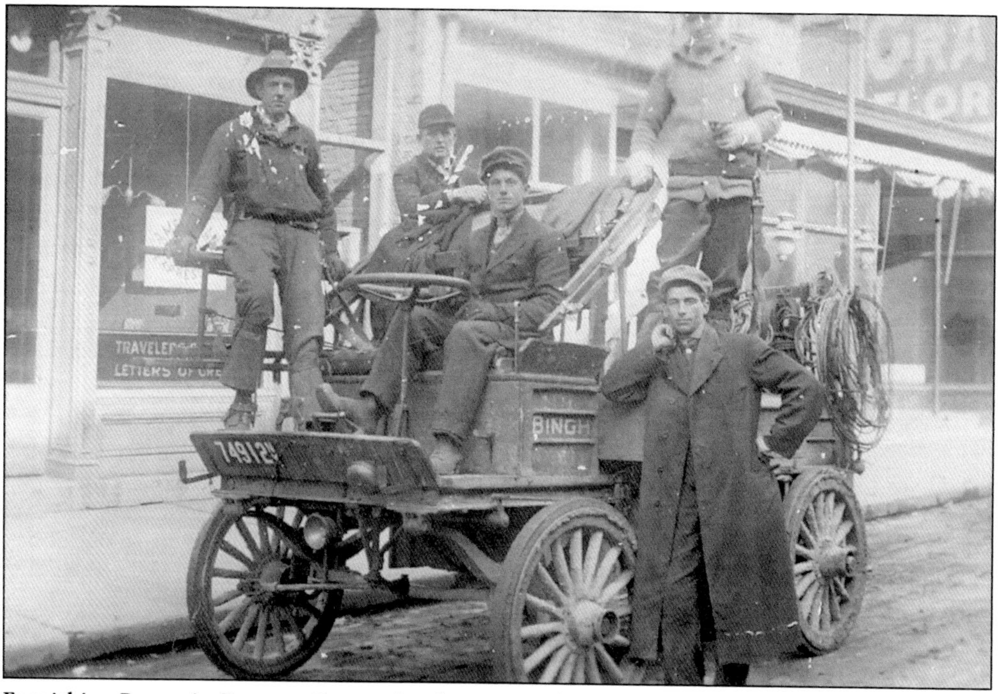

Furnishing Power in Broome County has been a profession for experts since the early days of waterwheels and wires. The men in the postcard above brought their expertise to locations in Binghamton and surrounding areas in a modern motoring device. The men below are engineers and firemen at the Deposit Light Plant, established in 1891.

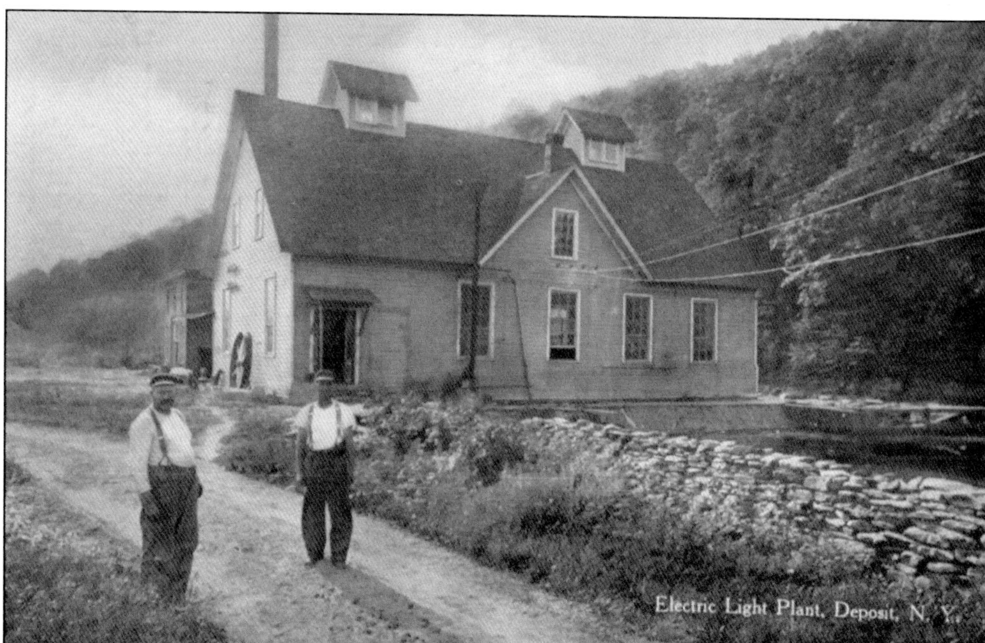

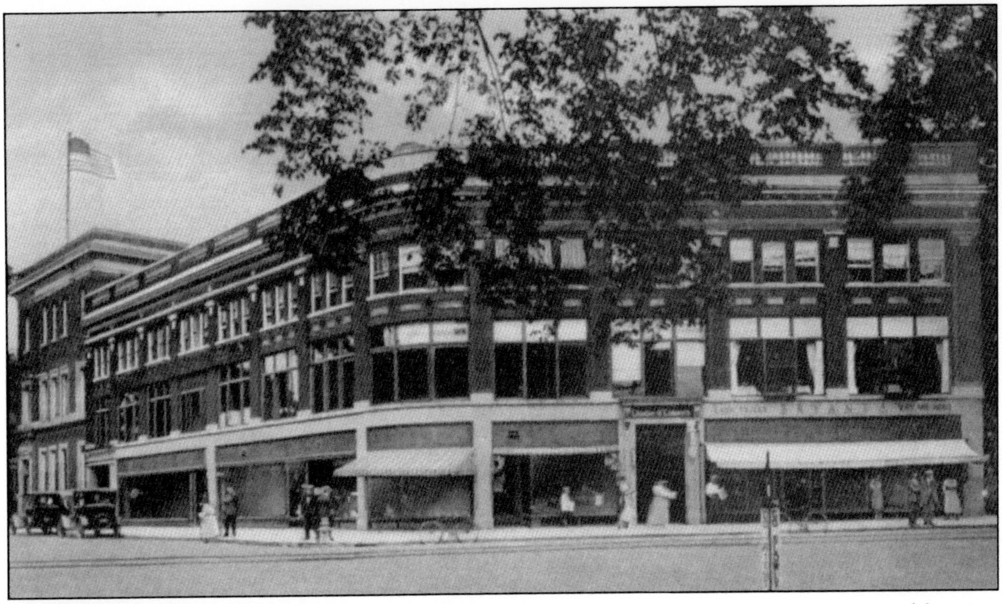

Established in 1823, the *Broome County Republican Press* remained in continuous publication for 100 years. Taken over by William H. Hill and named the *Morning Sun,* the newspaper needed a large facility in 1920. The company chose the corner of Chenango and Henry Streets and incorporated into its structure a Victorian mansion on the site, built in the 1850s by Waring Weed. In the 1960s, the paper merged with the *Evening Press.* This postcard is from 1922.

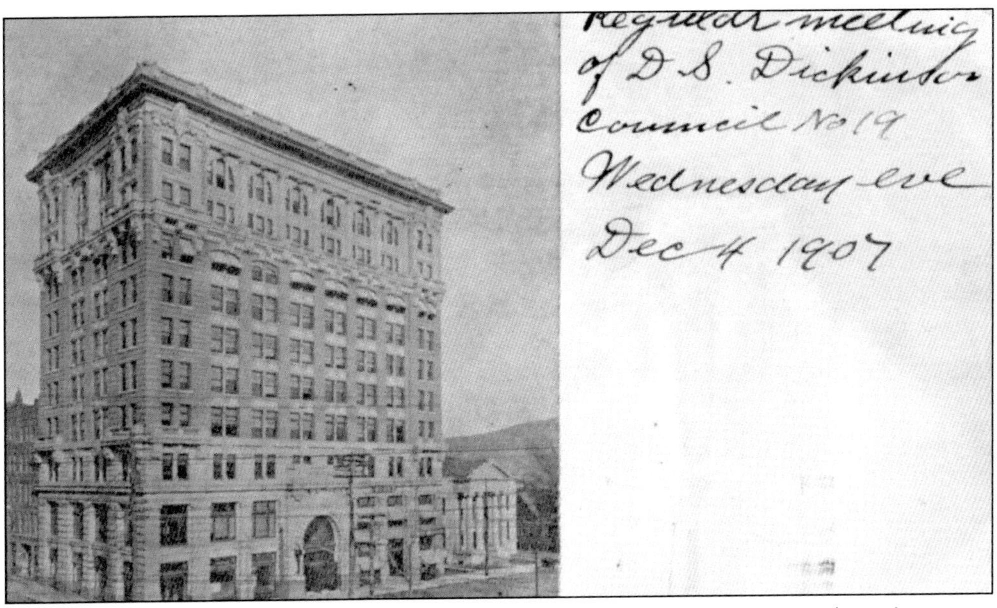

The Security Mutual Insurance Company built a ten-story home office in 1904 on the corner of Court and Exchange Streets. A technical curiosity of modern invention were the hydraulic elevators, which caused much excitement in the community. Still standing, the building features a stone arched entry that leads to another era of craftsmanship: a lobby with twin staircases of glistening marble. The postcard from 1907 announces a meeting for members of the Daniel S. Dickinson Council No. 19.

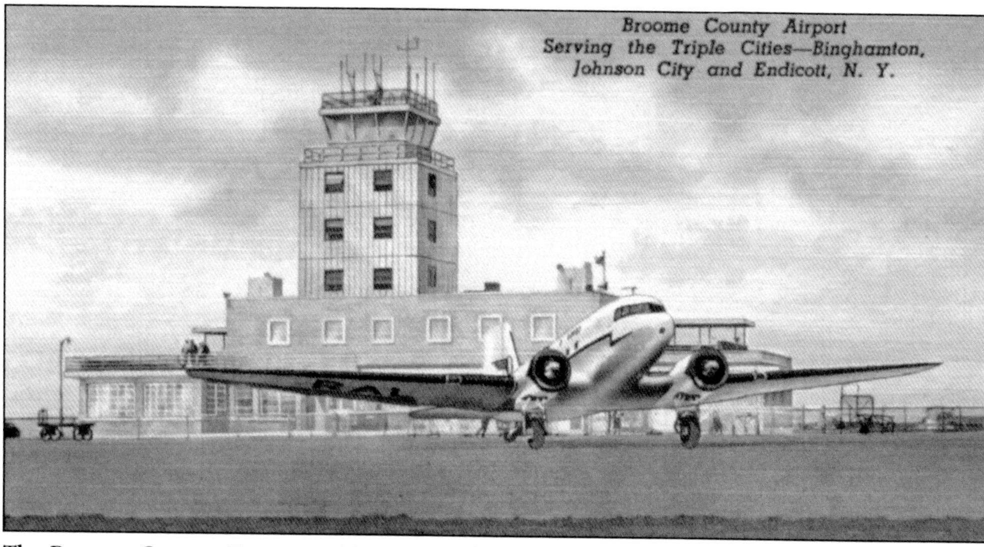

The Broome County Airport on Mount Ettrick in the town of Maine was officially dedicated in 1951. The Hogg family settled on the site in the 1830s and named it for a relative, the Scottish poet James Hogg, who was known as the "Ettrick shepherd." Mount Ettrick seemed more suitable a name than "Hogg Hill," as the mountain was often referred to by locals. In 2000, extensive renovation of the airport was completed.

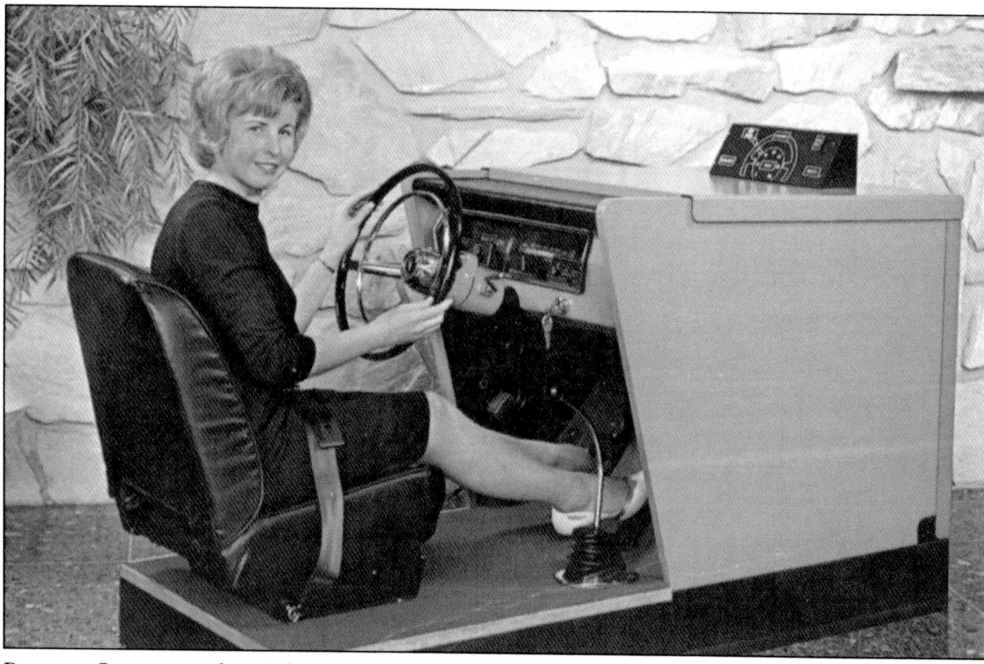

Broome County resident Edwin Link, a nationally known inventor and entrepreneur, patented the first ground-based pilot-training device in 1929. For decades, his corporation Link Aviation was a major influence in the field of simulation technology. During World War II, Link's Blue Box trainer revolutionized the training of pilots. The invention is credited with saving thousands of lives by preparing pilots and crews for the reality of flight. Link's talents extended to inventions of musical organs and submersibles.

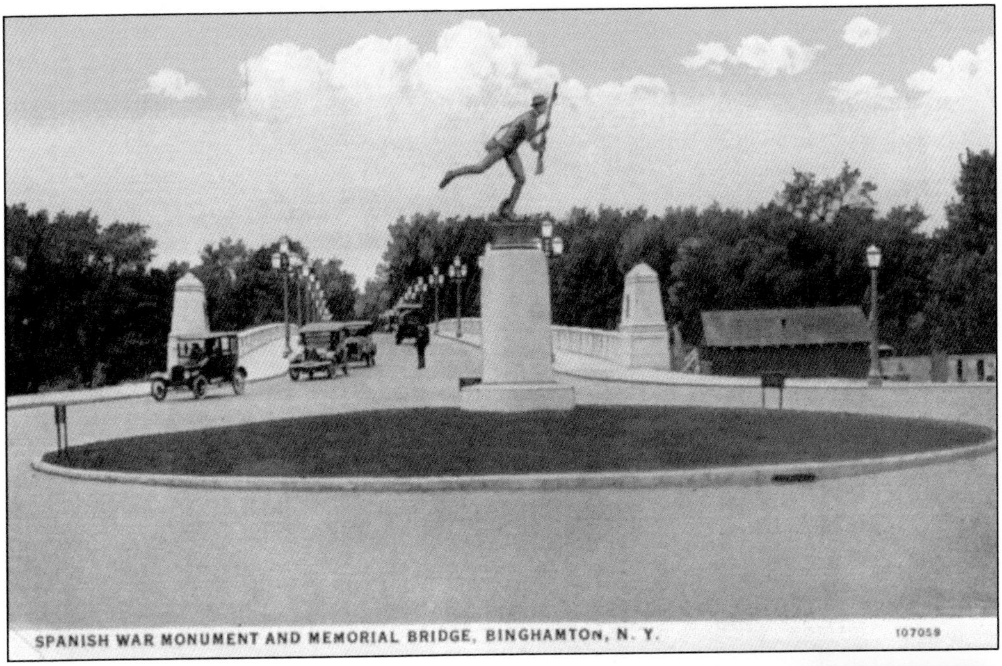

The Skirmisher, a Spanish-American War memorial designed by Robert Atkin, N.A., in 1924, still stands near the South Washington Street Bridge in Memorial Circle. Local children of the 1930s and 1940s were encouraged to remember veterans with this simple rhyme: "Throw a kiss [to the skirmisher], in memory of the men we still miss."

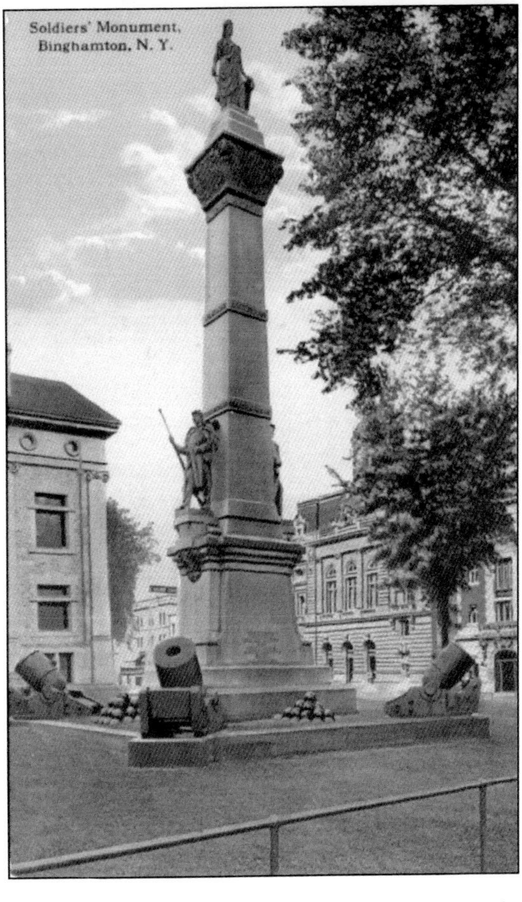

The Soldiers' Monument was erected on the lawn of the Broome County Courthouse in 1885. It was the first war memorial in Binghamton and was locally designed and manufactured by Barnes & Company of Chenango Street. In 1888, it was dedicated to the "defenders of our union [in] memory of those who have gone to that country from which no traveler returns."

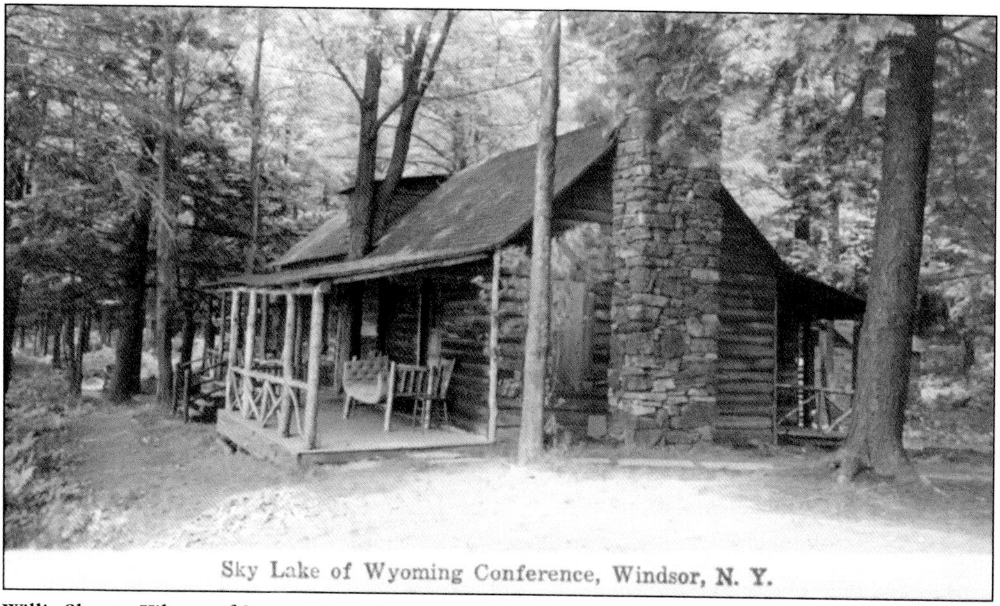

Willis Sharpe Kilmer of Swamp Root fame owned the top of Tuscarora Mountain in Windsor, New York. The estate was purchased by the Methodist Conference in 1947 to be used as a religious retreat. Now known as Sky Lake, it includes a lake, cabins, trails, and a modern lodge and is a singularly spiritual location for contemplation and fellowship.

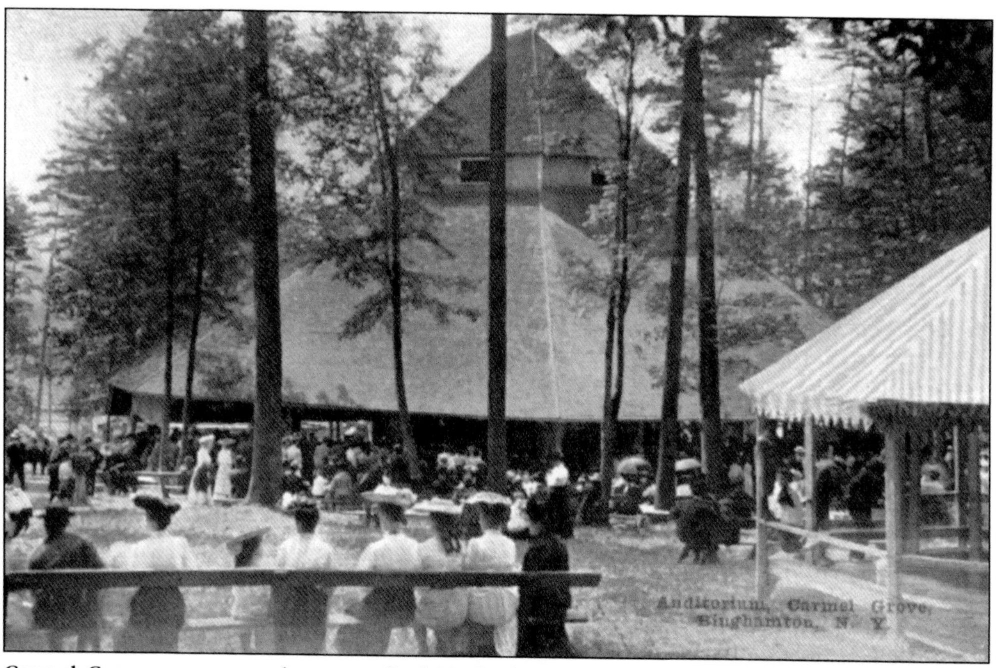

Carmel Grove was a popular evangelical Methodist campground from 1892 to 1914. Located at the far edges of civilization, in an area that is now Endwell, it was known as the "City in the Woods." The grove's 12.5 hillside acres were covered with tents and cabins, as well as a modern hotel. It was not unusual for 5,000 people to attend, shattering the peaceful wilderness with volleys of praise and preaching.

Three

The Broome Environs: Villages and Towns

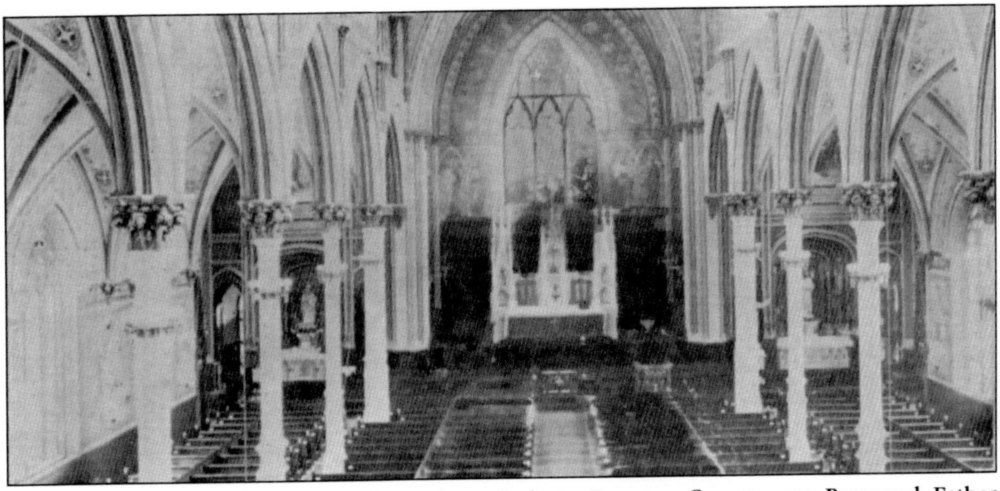

One of the most interesting of the early arrivals in Broome County was Reverend Father Hourigan, born in 1815 in Ireland. He was appointed a missionary priest in 1847 and became known as the "Keeper of the Peace." He patrolled the towpath on a handcar, going up and down the Erie line looking to suppress trouble. He was a pacifist who carried peace in the form of a cudgel. When there were brawls, the police force, whose numbers were few, sent word to the Irishman, and he came with his blackthorn. If the "good word" failed to convince the disorderly of the error of their ways, he would administer the blackthorn heartily and judiciously. Respected by all who knew him, he did what was necessary to bring God and civilization to Broome County. He was responsible for the founding of St. Patrick's church and St. Mary's Orphanage. Isaac Perry was the architect for St. Patrick church, built between 1867 and 1872. Still a well-loved house of worship, it is a fine example of early skill and craftsmanship, which lacks only the originally designed steeple.

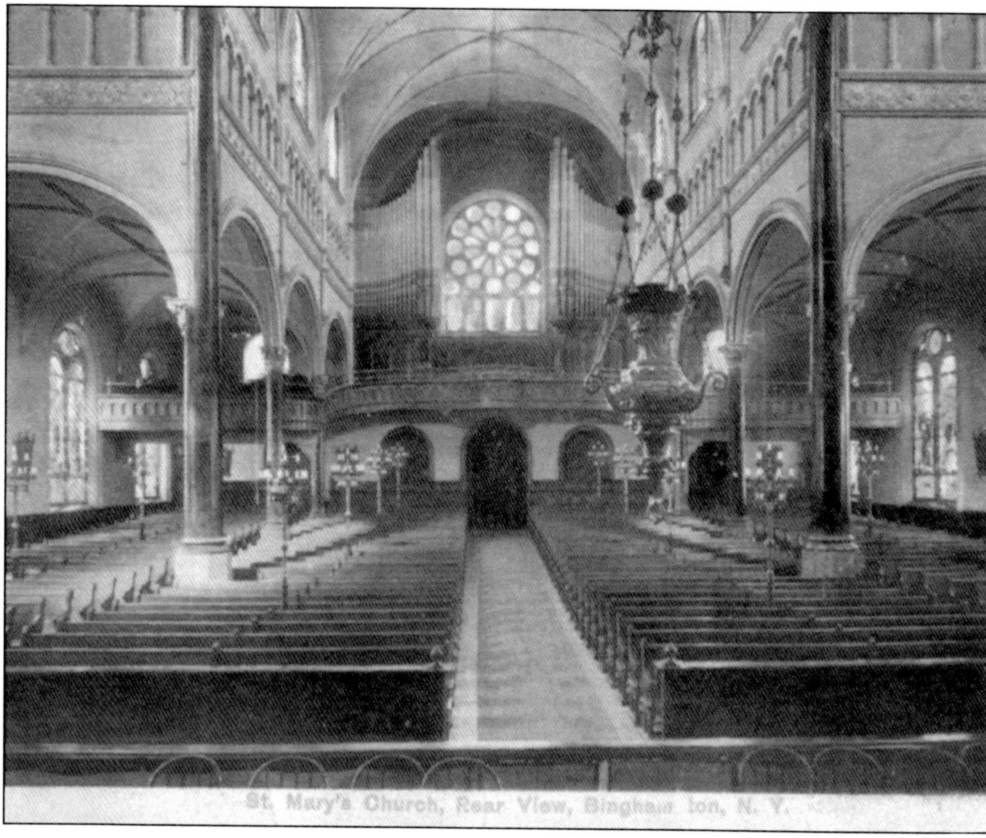

In 1920, the Beman Organ Company advertised that the oldest electric pipe organ in New York State was located in St. Mary's Catholic Church in Binghamton. Beman installed the instrument in 1894 and kept it in fine condition, bragging that it had never missed a service in 26 years. This card, posted in 1907, shows the interior of St. Mary's.

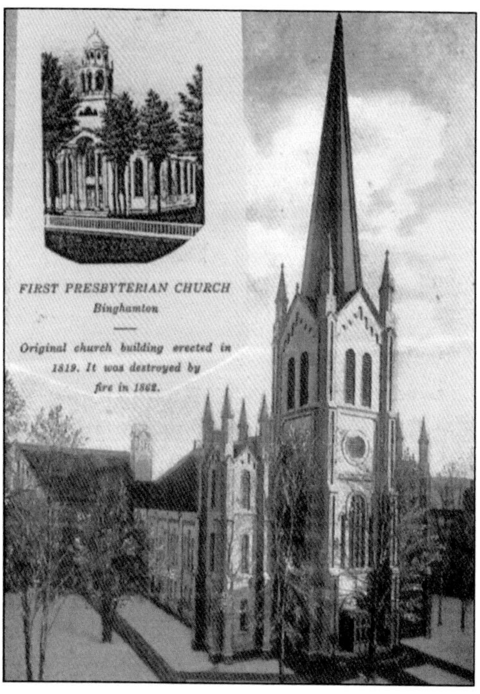

Even the Civil War could not stop the construction of a new brick First Presbyterian Church in Binghamton. The original frame church, built in 1819, was destroyed by fire in 1862. The insert on the postcard shows the old church. The new building, constructed in 1863, is still considered one of the most beautiful and stately churches in the country and a city landmark.

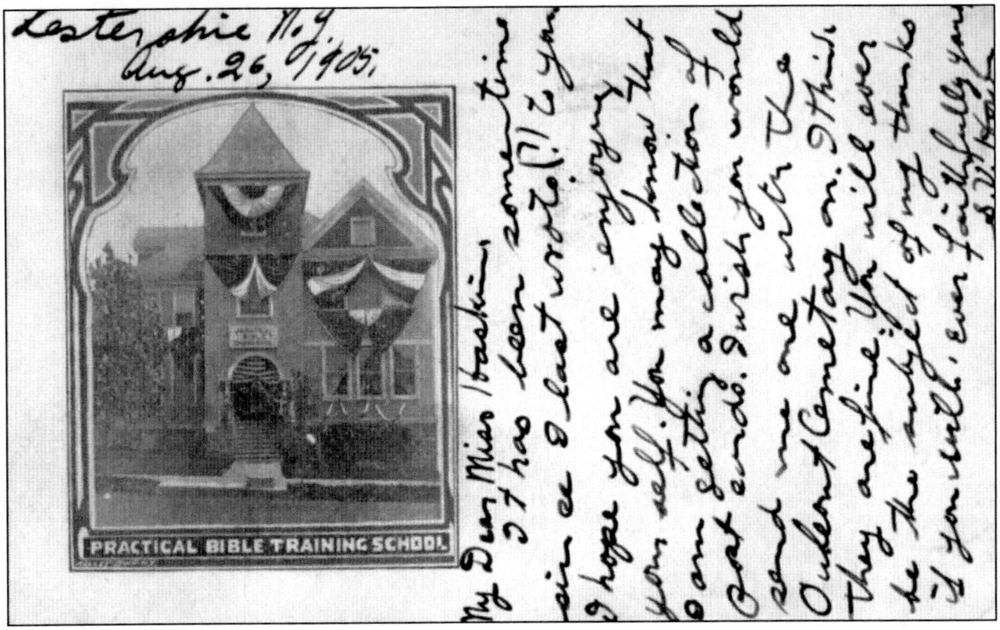

The Practical Bible Training School was incorporated in 1900 and occupied this building in Lestershire until expansion became necessary. In 1911, Dr. Charles S. Wilson purchased the building for use as the Lestershire Hospital. Note the message on this postcard of 1905, requesting postcards for a collection.

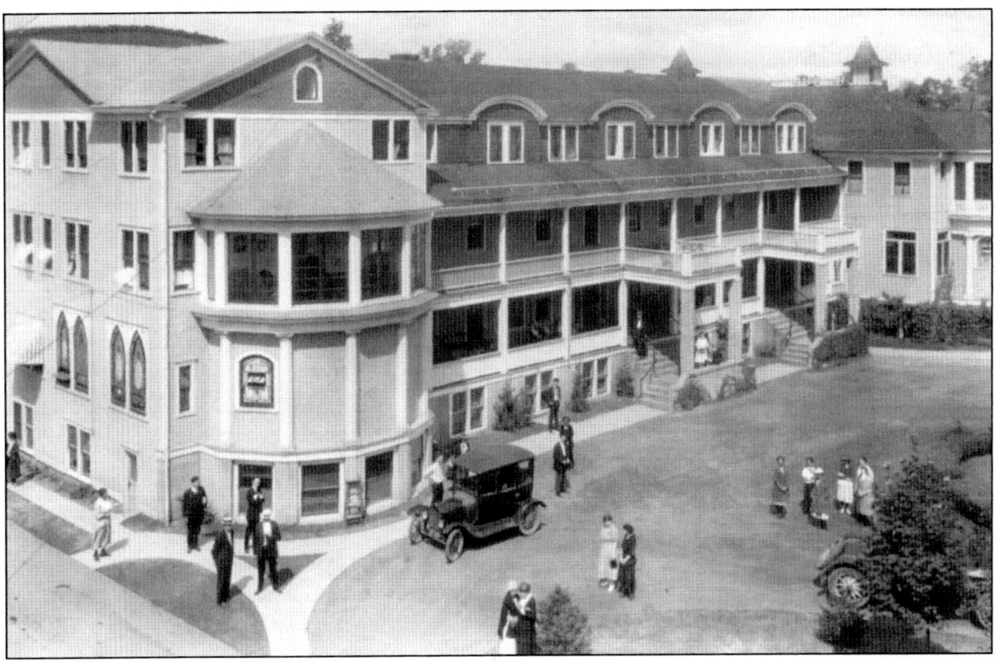

Bible School Park came into existence in 1911 to fill the growing need of the Practical Bible Training School for a larger campus. It replaced a notorious amusement park, White City, on Riverside Drive in Lestershire. This real photo postcard was made in the 1930s.

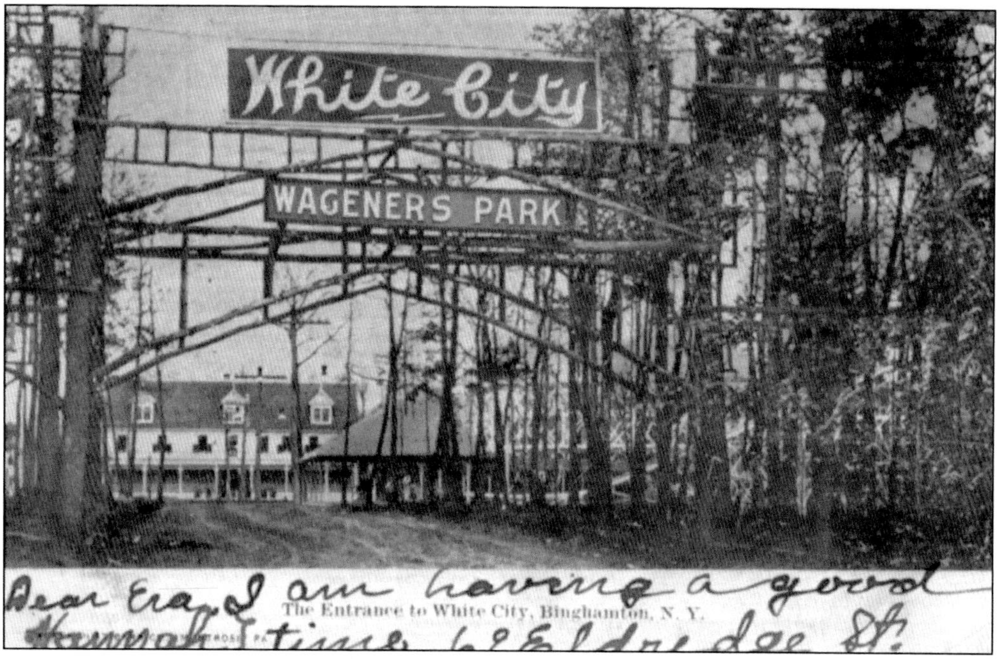

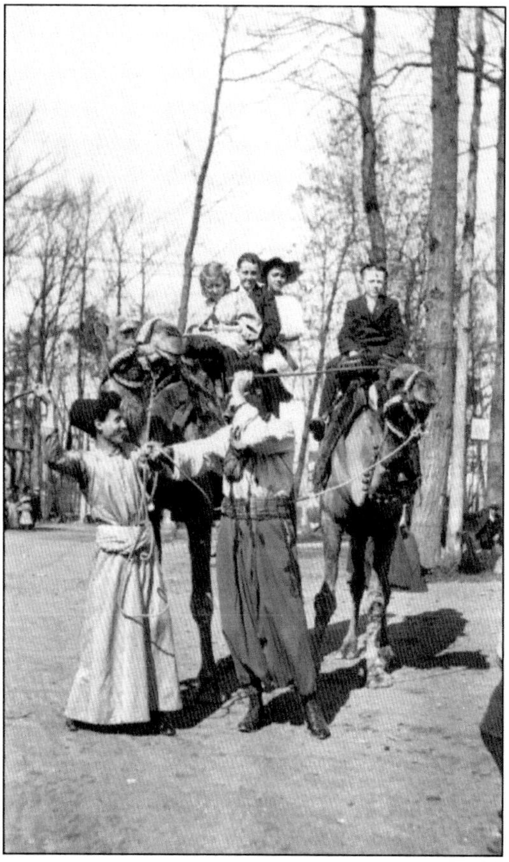

White City, also known as Wagner's Park, opened for business in 1902 on Riverside Drive in Lestershire, overlooking the Susquehanna River. It was originally designed for family entertainment, with one of the largest roller coaster rides in the country, picnic facilities, boats, swimming, camel rides, and midway entertainment. This postcard showing the park entrance was mailed in 1906. The camel ride real photo postcard at left was taken in 1908.

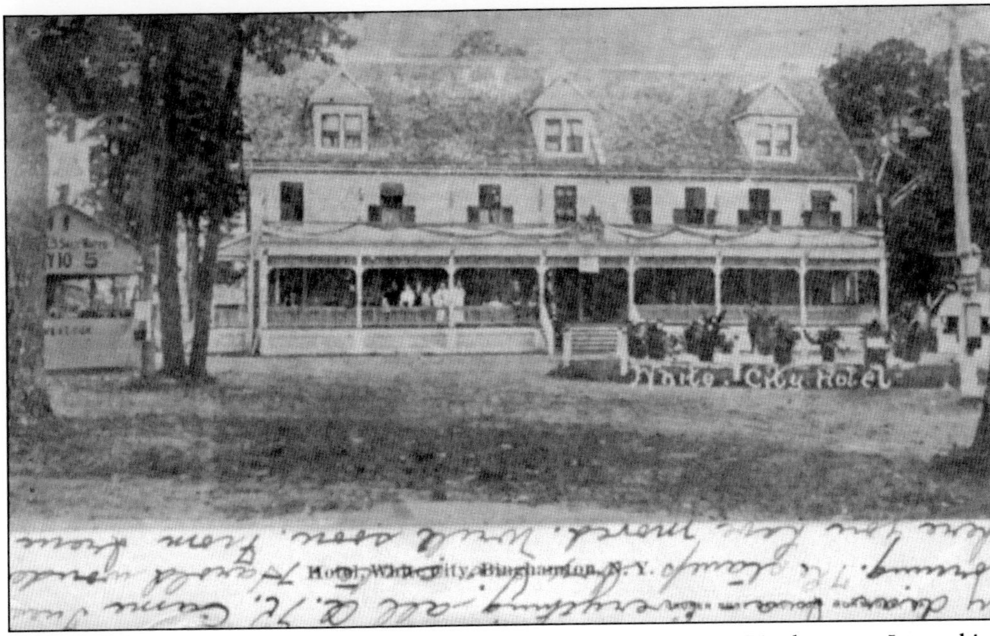

Although postcards of the day listed the location of White City as Binghamton, Lestershire was happy not to be known as home to the park. The entertainment deteriorated—gambling, drunkenness, moral depravity, and corruption made it necessary to build an on-site jail. Sin ruled the nights at White City, and it became unsafe for respectable citizens. From playground to den of iniquity, constables traveled in groups, trying to stem the spread of crime. It was a great relief to the community when the property was sold and the buildings were torn down. The White City Hotel postcard, above, was mailed in 1906, and the Creation Cave real photo postcard, below, was made in 1908.

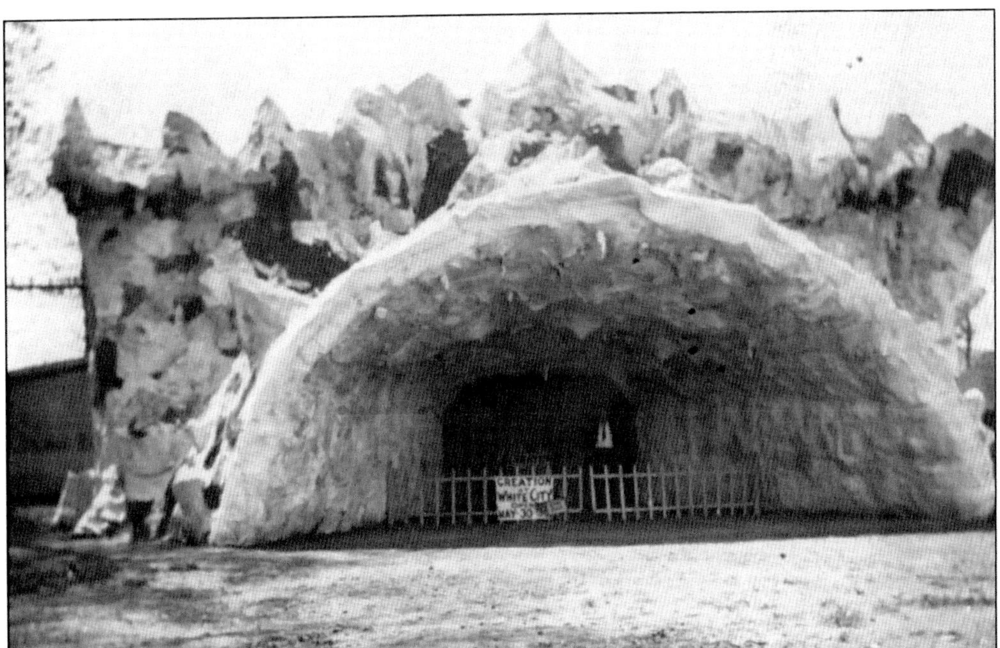

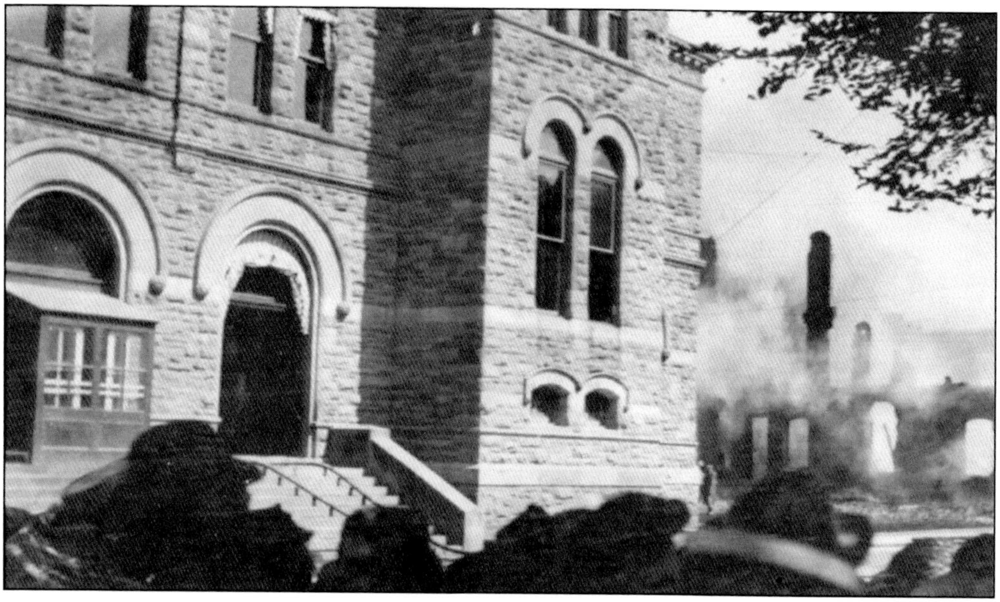

In 1913, a fire devastated the Binghamton Clothing Company on Wall Street in Binghamton. Smoke and burning walls can be seen in this photo postcard. The four-story brick building turned into a raging conflagration in just 20 minutes. The fire took the lives of 32 people; 22 of the unidentifiable victims are buried in a mass grave in Spring Forest Cemetery.

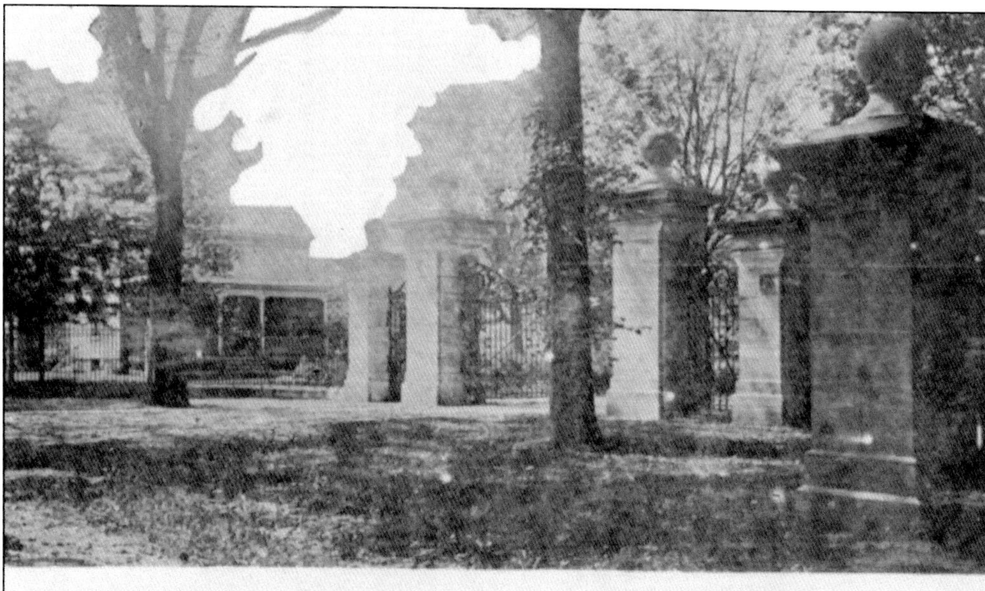

Entrance to Spring Forest Cemetery, Binghamton, N. Y.

Spring Forest Cemetery was organized in 1853 on a 42.7-acre site in Binghamton. The first burial in the Silent City was an Angel: Mrs. Azariah Angel. Some stones may predate Spring Forest's founding, as the directors welcomed displaced cemeteries, relocated because of environmental or development concerns. Architect Isaac Perry designed the entrance gates but did not live to see them finished. He was carried through the portals and buried in a nearby grove.

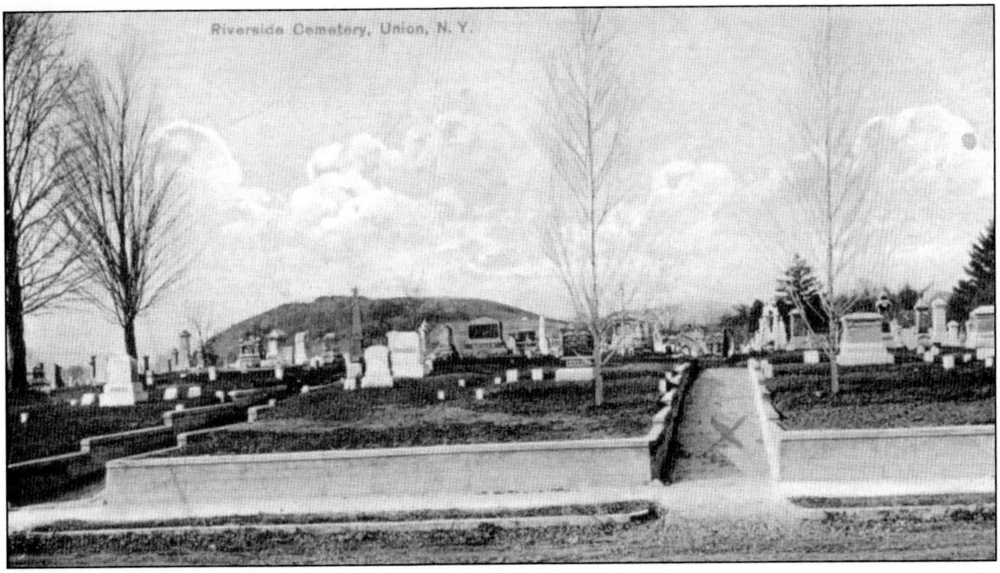

Riverside Cemetery in Union was the site of what was probably the first church constructed in Broome County. The Dutch Reformed church was erected in 1791. In the second part of the 20th century, the location was known for its proximity to Pat Mitchell's Ice Cream Shop. On nice days, the walls along the cemetery became lined with patrons of the sweetshop, enjoying the famous cones of cream.

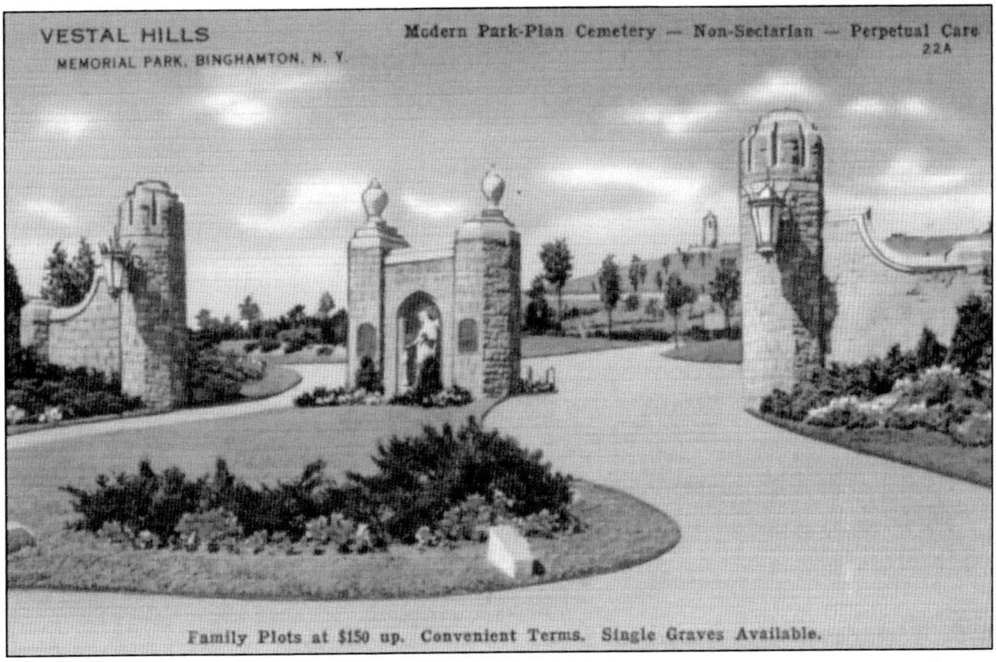

Vestal Hills Memorial Park was established in 1931. The beautifully landscaped grounds are unmarred by any stone monuments. Bronze plaques mounted in the earth note grave sites and maintain the parklike atmosphere. In other areas of the country, such cemeteries have been referred to as God's Acres or Rest Estates. This postcard from the early days of development has a printed message advising people to "investigate before it is too late."

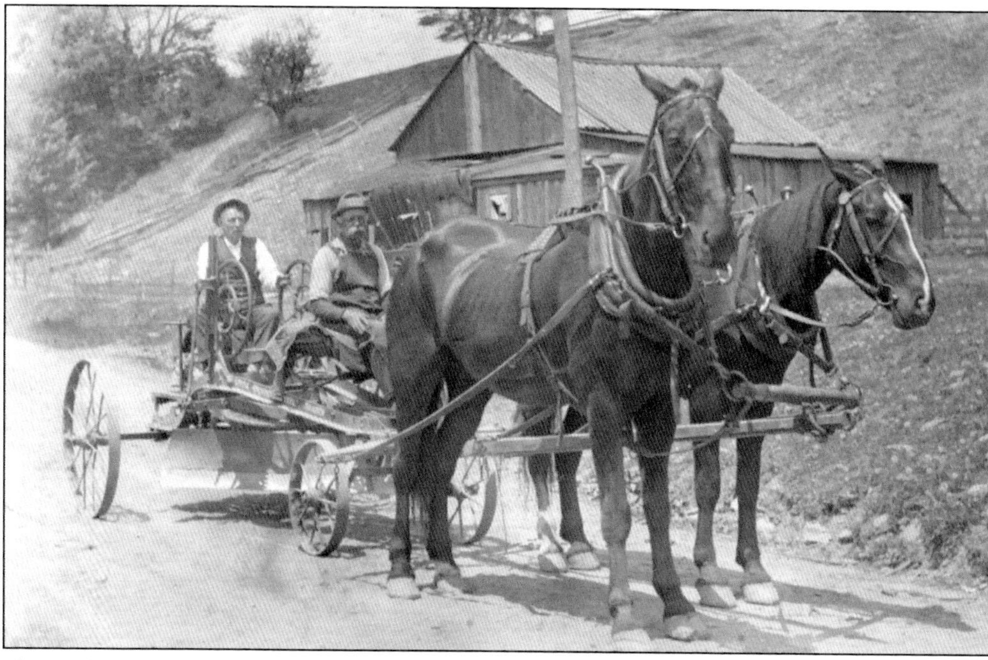

This real photo postcard shows the "Little Victory" road grader. For many years, road care was the duty and responsibility of the ordinary citizen. It was not unusual for substantial landowners to possess their own road maintenance machines.

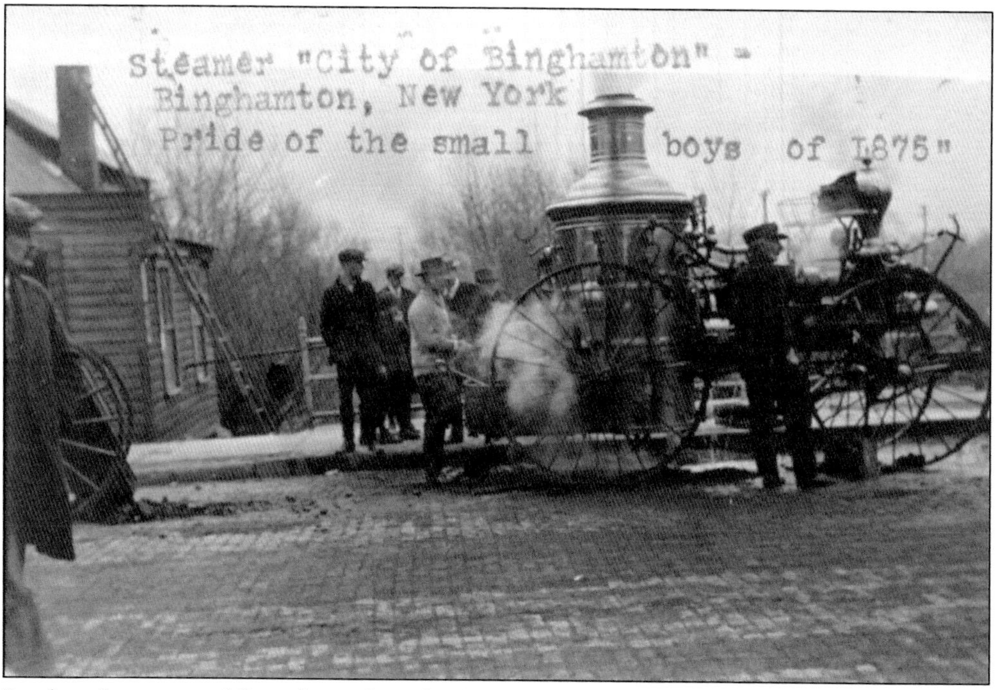

Road work progressed from dirt paths to brick streets, and the horse team was replaced with the "steam team." This postcard dates from 1875.

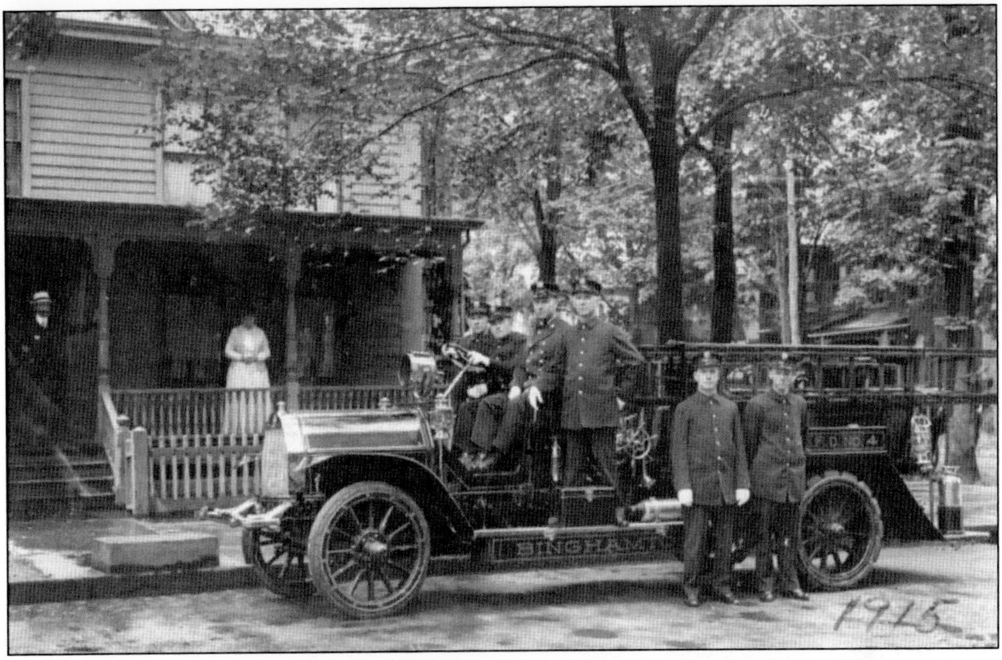

Fire is a frightening part of life, fought diligently by citizen and government. The equipment has changed greatly over the years. However, some fire companies were reluctant to give up the reliability of the horse for horsepower, as is shown in these postcards: in 1915, a motorized version and in 1922, still using steeds in the race to the flames. The 1915 photograph shows what is probably one of the last trucks made with a brass engine cover and brass side lamps. Vehicle manufacturers discontinued the brass fixtures in favor of steel, a stronger product that did not require continual polishing.

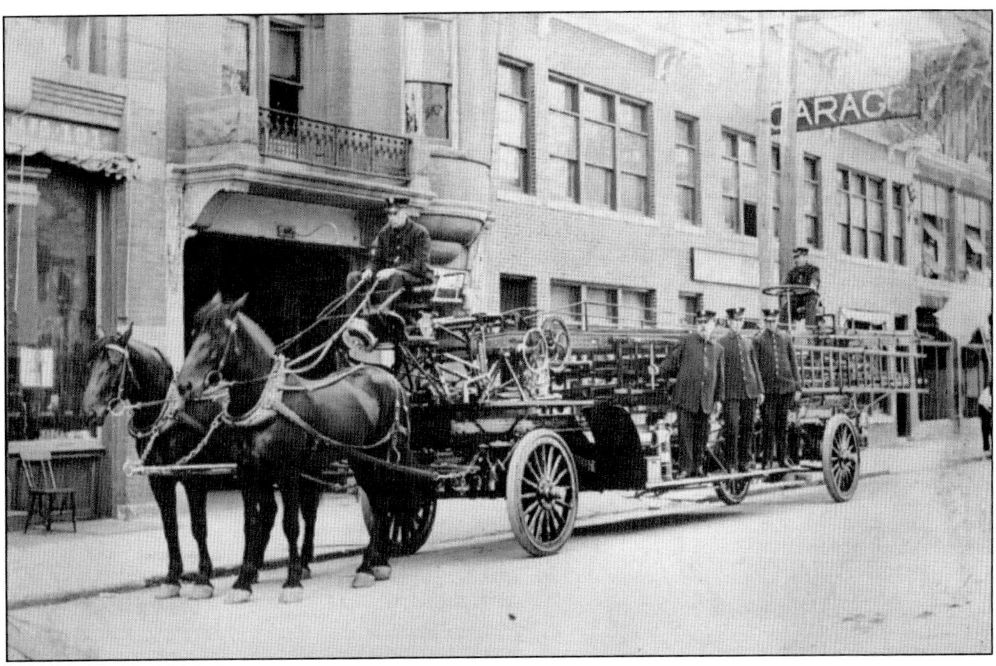

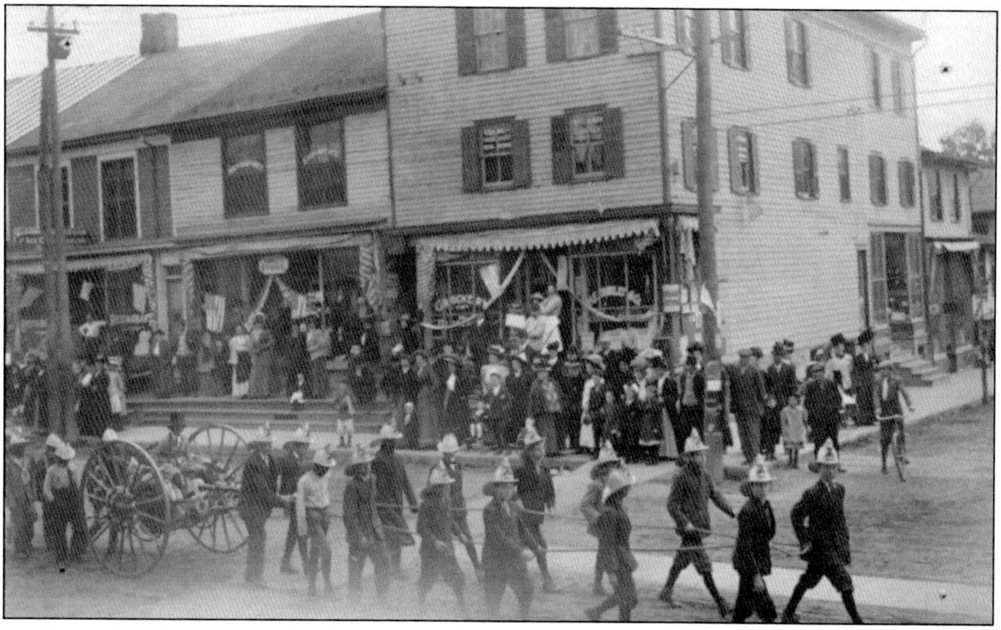

Conflagrations have always been serious situations, and firefighters are recognized as the heroes of flame. This parade to salute fire companies was held in the old Union district *c.* 1898.

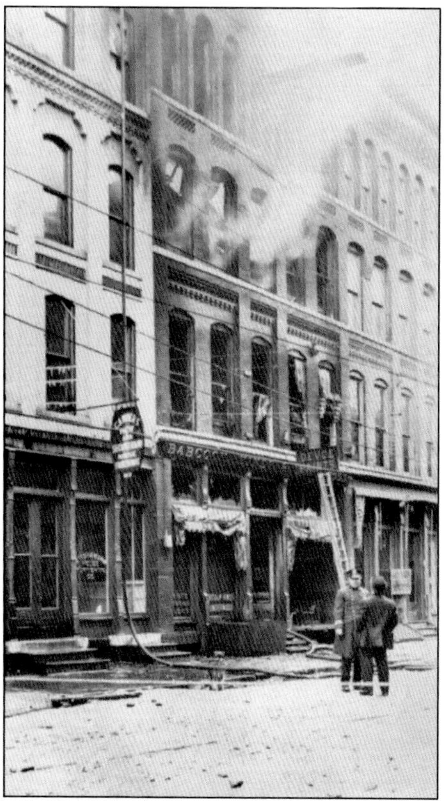

Flames filled the year 1914. This fire was well documented on the back of the postcard: "Fire was at night, 11:30, February 28, 1914, and could have been worse. The building is owned by Lucie Stone Ely, and the building right next door was occupied by the Stickley Brandt Furniture Company."

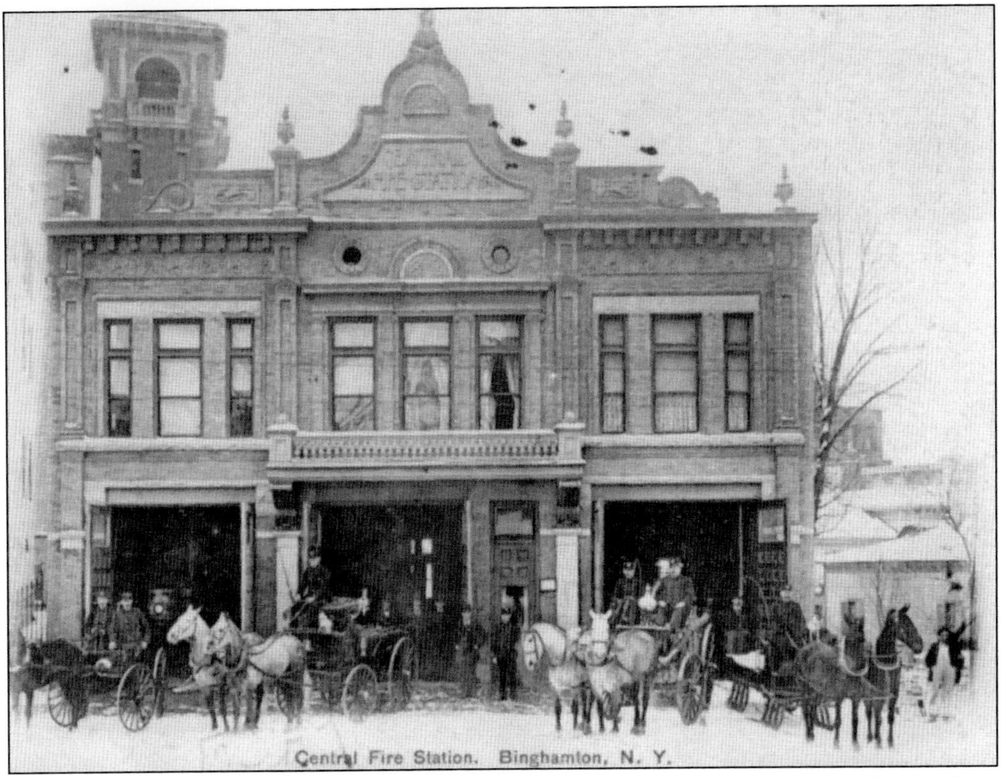

By 1911, the Binghamton Central Fire Station on Chenango Street had grown to house three steam engines and had a paid staff. Firefighters were prepared to put their lives on the line in any weather, as can be seen by the engines with wheels and the one on the right that is fashioned as a sleigh. The postcard was mailed in 1906.

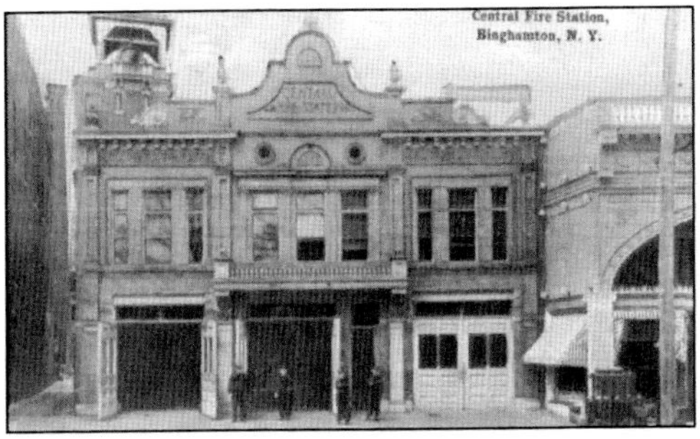

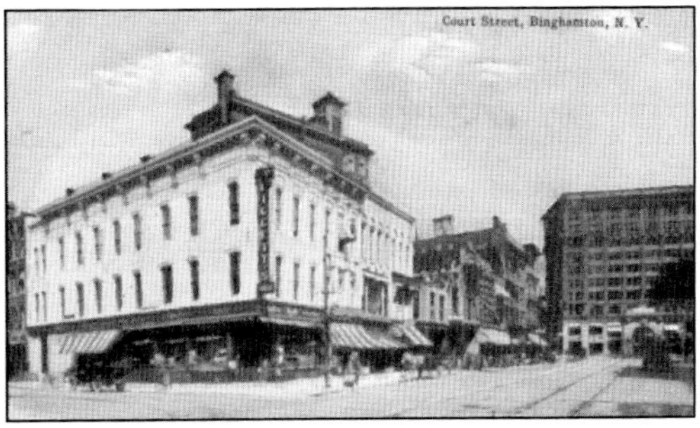

Another view of the same fire station is shown on a postcard that measures only 3.5 inches by 2 inches but is designated on the reverse side an "official postcard." The other miniature postcard is an early-1900s view of Court Street in Binghamton.

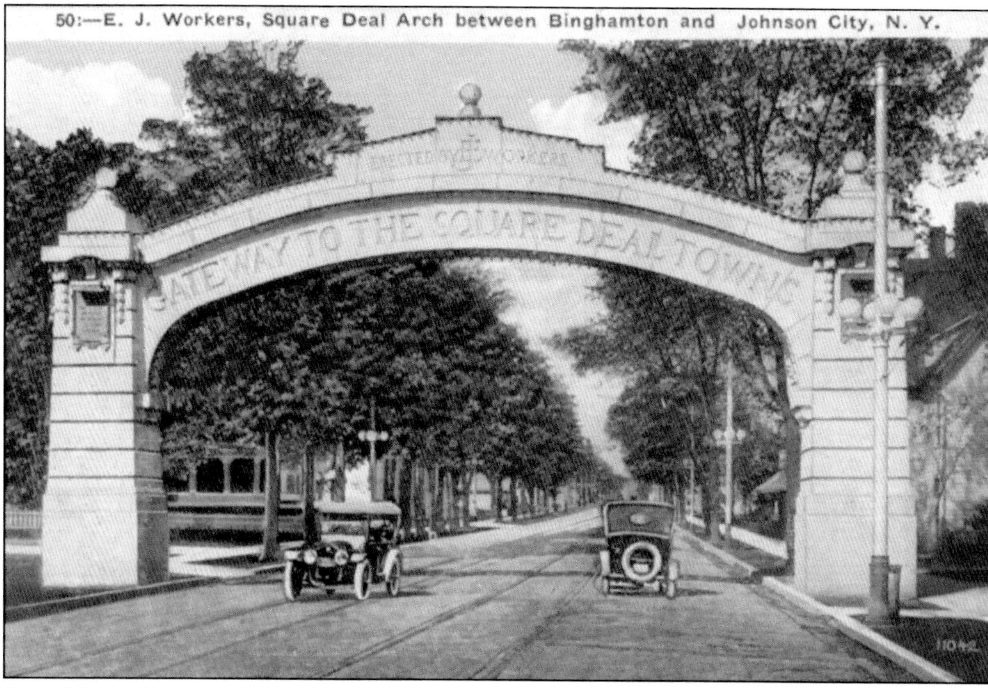

Grateful employees of the Endicott Johnson Corporation donated funds to construct two stone arches in the 1920s. The monuments span the main thoroughfare at the border between Binghamton and Johnson City and between Endicott and the old Union district. The arches symbolize the policies of fairness and generosity and the long memories of citizens who benefited from the opportunity to pursue the American dream through corporate largesse.

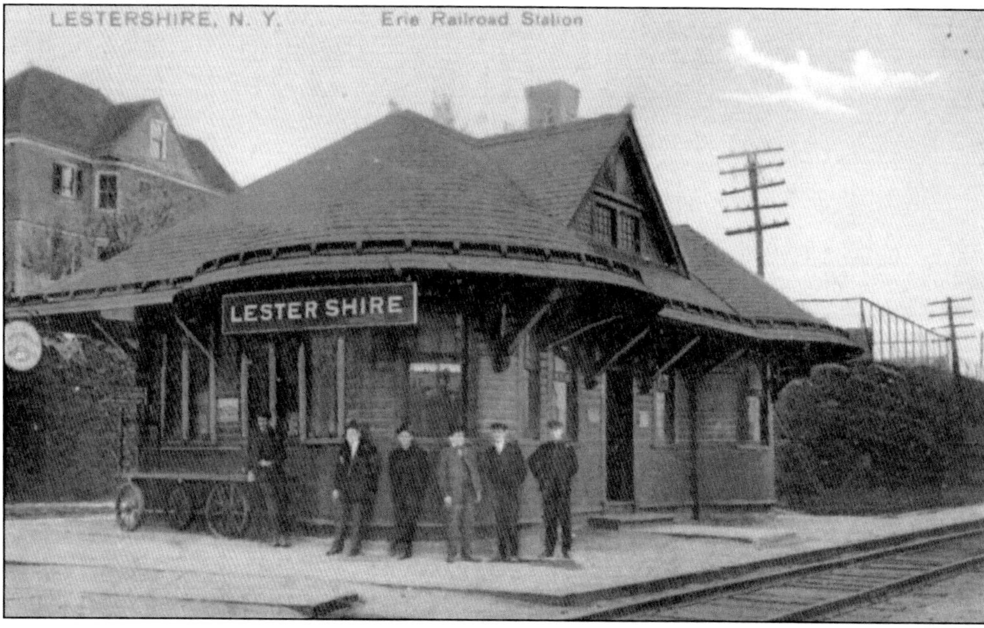

In 1890, the first Erie Railroad station was built in Lestershire. This location met the need for efficient transportation for the local shoe factories. This postcard was mailed in 1909.

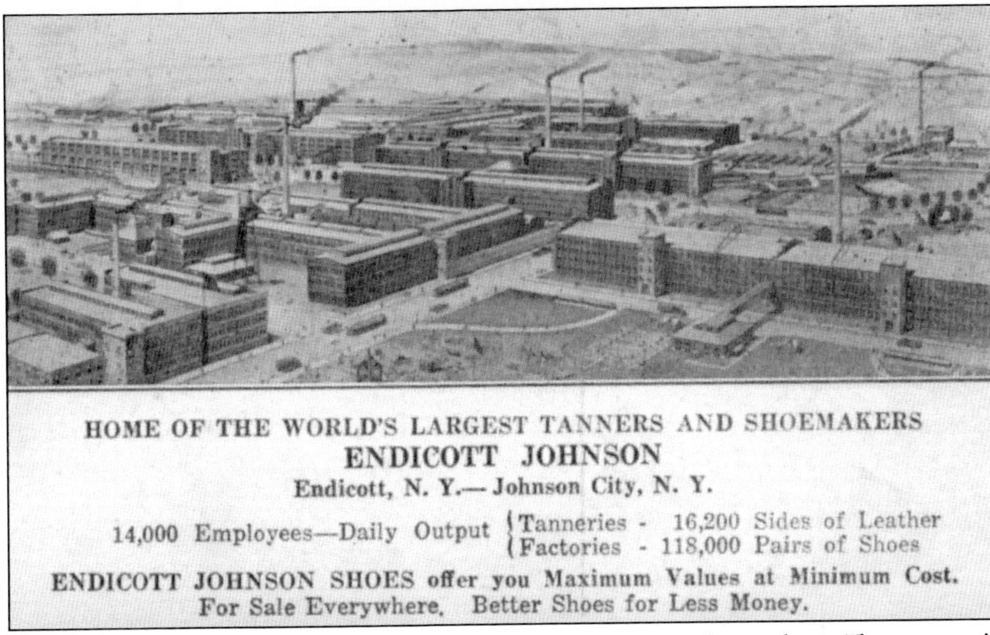

The Endicott Johnson advertising postcard from the early 1900s is shown above. The company's shoe factories put the Triple Cities on the national map of recognition. Endicott Johnson was the home of the "square deal," a cooperative venture between labor and management. Run as a company city, Endicott Johnson provided schools, stores, churches, parks, carousels, homes, and free shoes for all schoolchildren once a year. Unquestioning loyalty was an employee requirement, which remained evident long after the factories closed. The postcard below was mailed in 1917 and was used by Endicott Johnson for acknowledging accounts. It shows a drawing of one of the park areas that the company provided for the community.

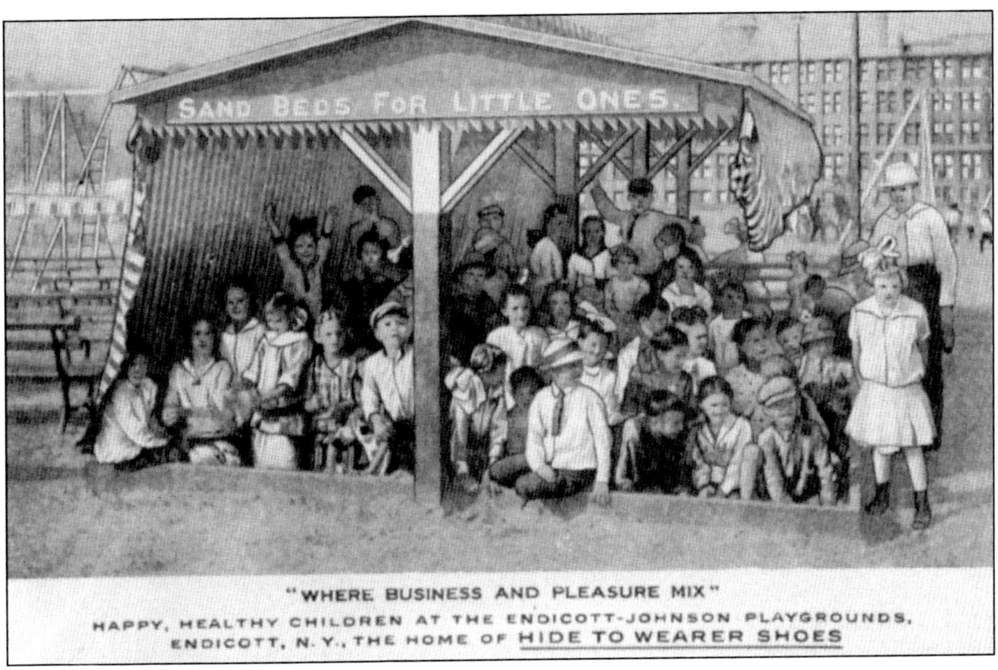

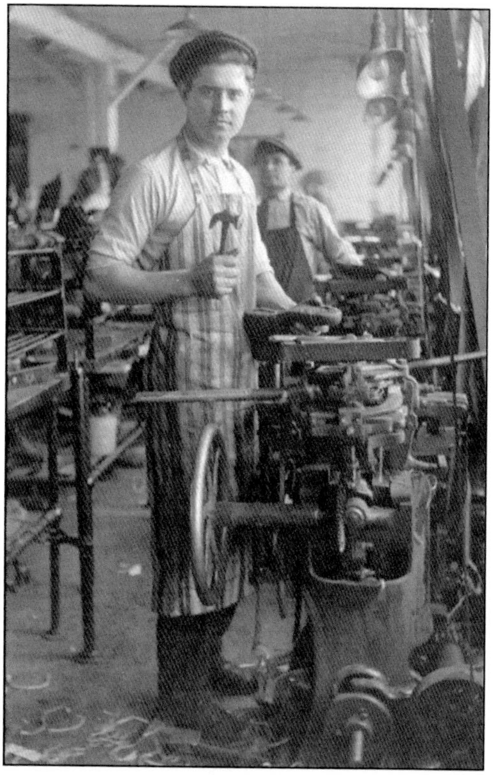

Endicott Johnson depended on the skills of immigrant workers. Most of the employees spent a lifetime on piecework, earning a living for their families. Workers were grateful for the opportunity of steady employment and generous benefits. This postcard is dated 1920.

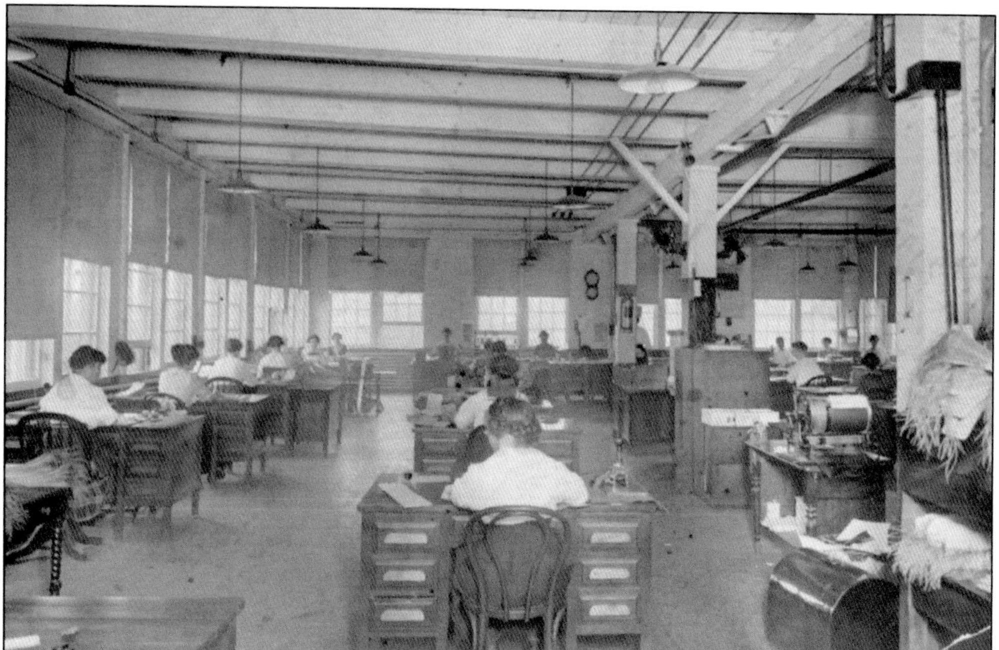

Shown is a typical shoe factory office in the early 1900s. Women were beginning their entry into the world of commerce.

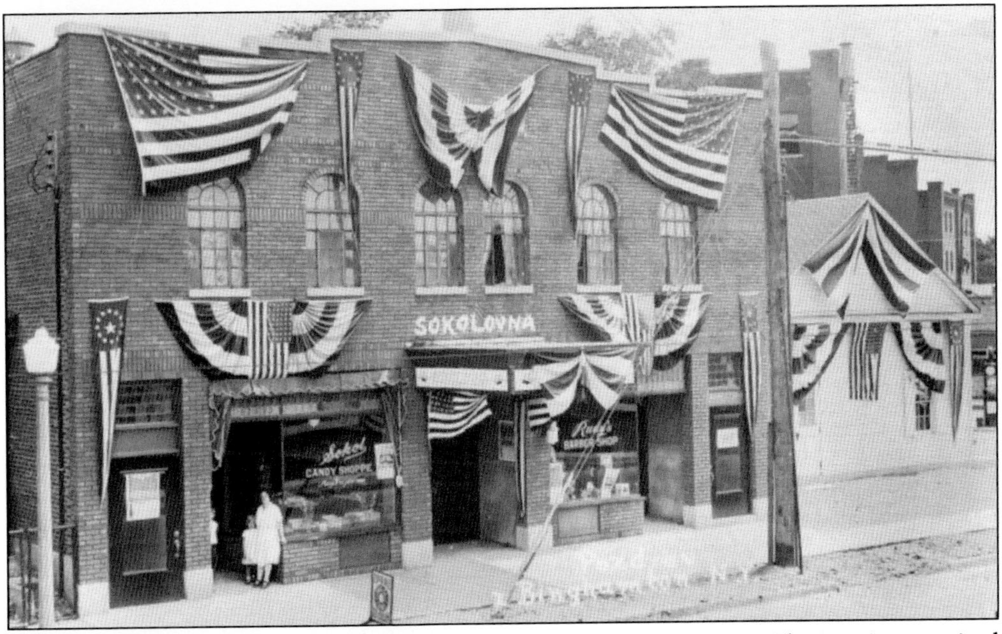

Ethnic clubhouses were a common sight in most Broome County towns. The area is comprised of hundreds of nationalities, each bringing talents and heritage to share with the community. This building is the Sokol Hall of the 1930s, located on Clinton Street in Binghamton. It now serves as a senior citizen center.

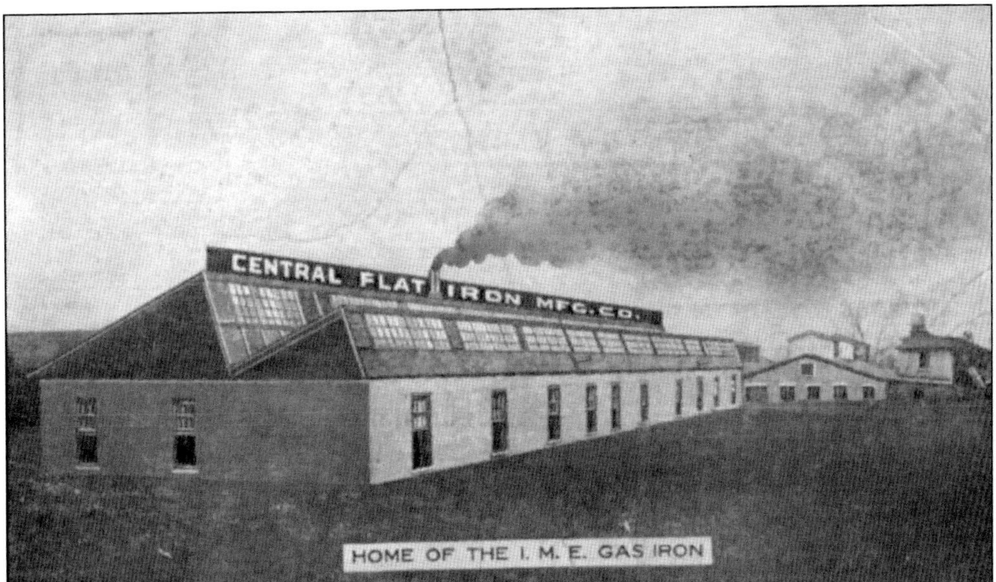

The Central Flat Iron Manufacturing Company was located in Lestershire. It made electric and gas irons. Advertisements in the 1920s promoted a "double point iron, with two hot spots."

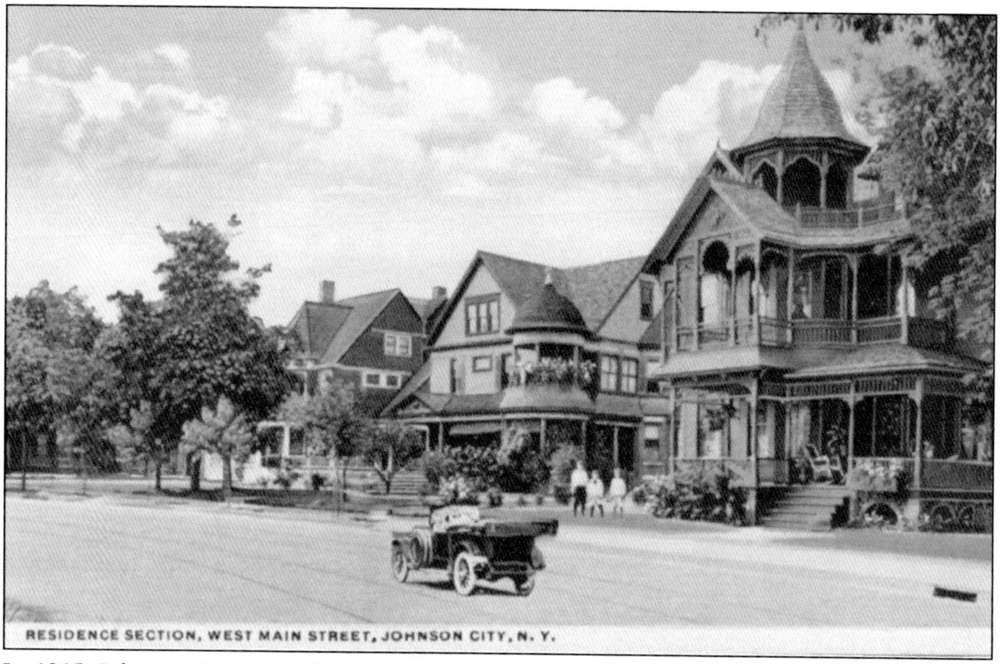

In 1915, Johnson City was still known as Lestershire, and its Main Street was one of the first roads in New York State to have electric lighting, thanks to the efforts of the Endicott Johnson Corporation. This scene has been altered to appear several years later: the automobile looks as if it has been inserted, and the power lines have been erased with an airbrush.

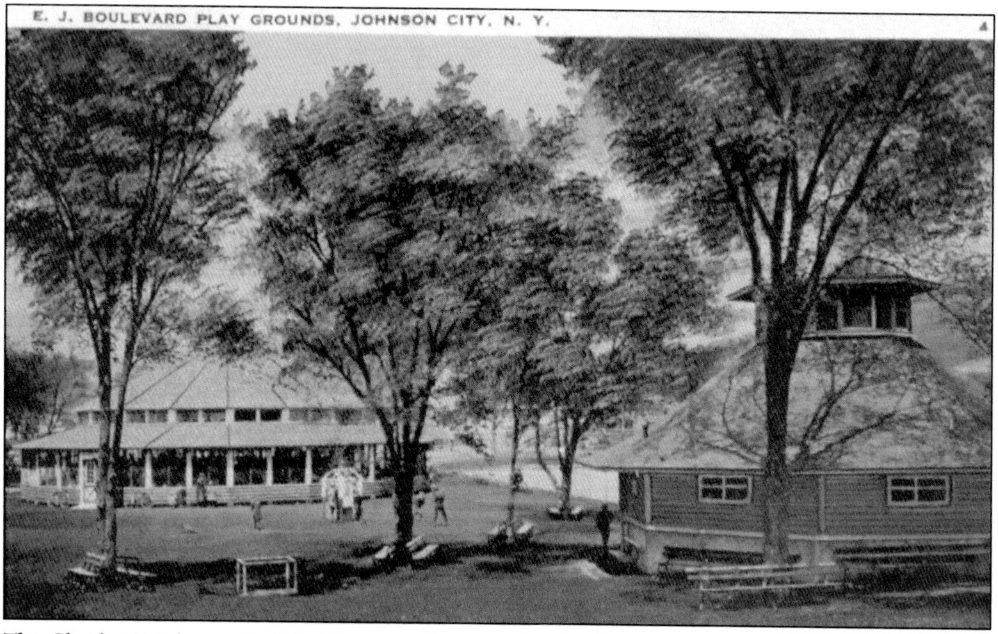

The Charles F. Johnson Park in Johnson City contains the largest carousel of the six in the Triple Cities. Donated by the Endicott Johnson Corporation in 1927, it has four rows of jumping figures, seventy-one horses, and one zebra. Completely restored, the carousel has been placed on the New York State Register of Historic Sites.

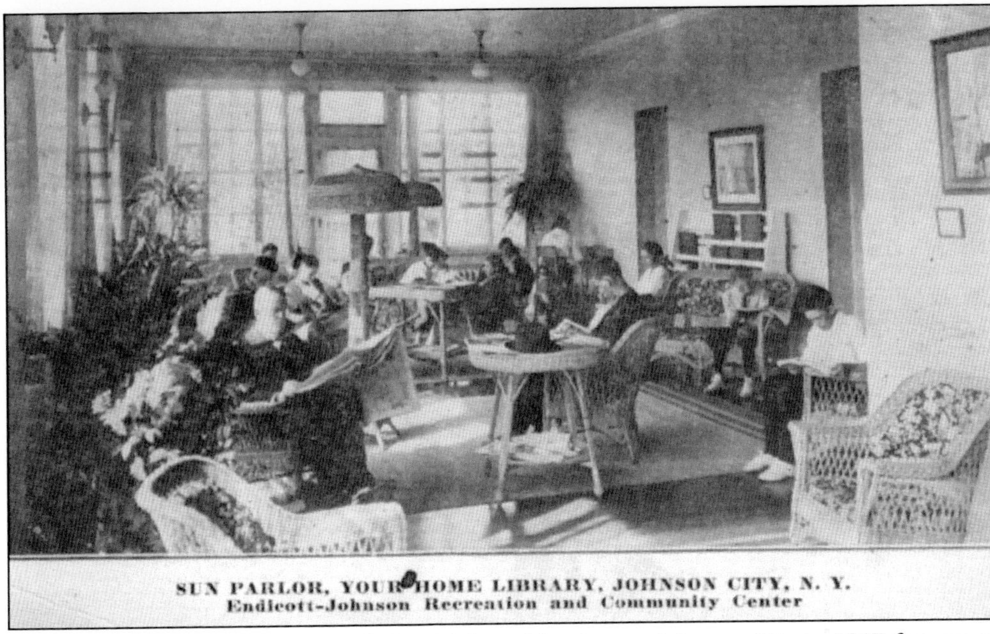

When George F. Johnson donated the Brigham Mansion to Johnson City in 1917 for use as a library, it was designed to encompass the needs of all the local inhabitants and serve as a welcoming community center. Therefore, the building was furnished with comfortable chairs, tables, and lamps for leisurely reading and gatherings, as can be seen in this rare view of the sun parlor. The postcard was mailed in 1926.

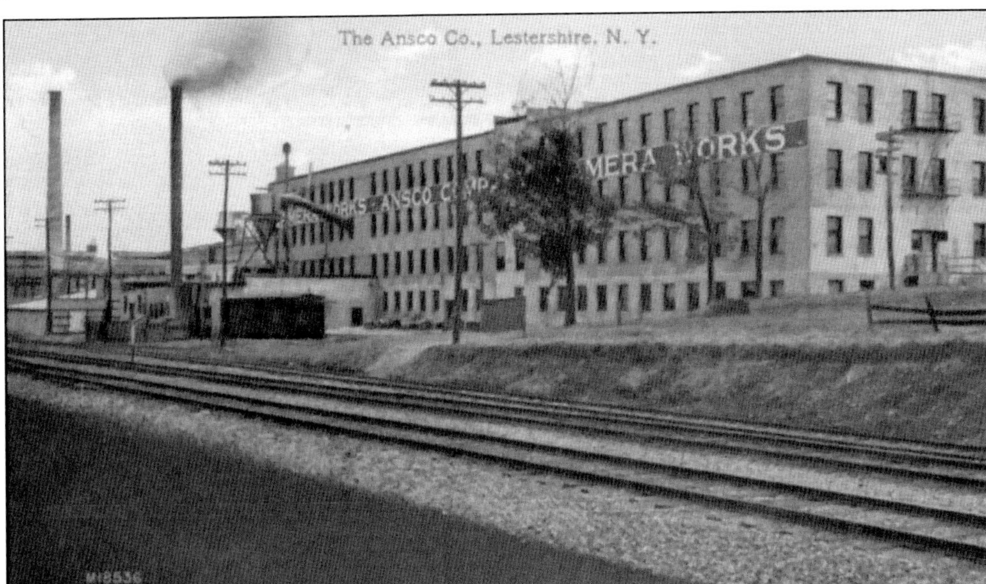

The Ansco Camera Works, located in Binghamton and Johnson City, was a descendent of the earliest pioneers in the photographic industry. Corporation roots date to E & H.T. Anthony and Company of 1842 and the Scoville Adams Company of 1856. Purchased by a German industrial cartel in the 1920s, Ansco was the largest industry nationalized by the U.S. government during World War II. The company was later acquired by Eastman Kodak.

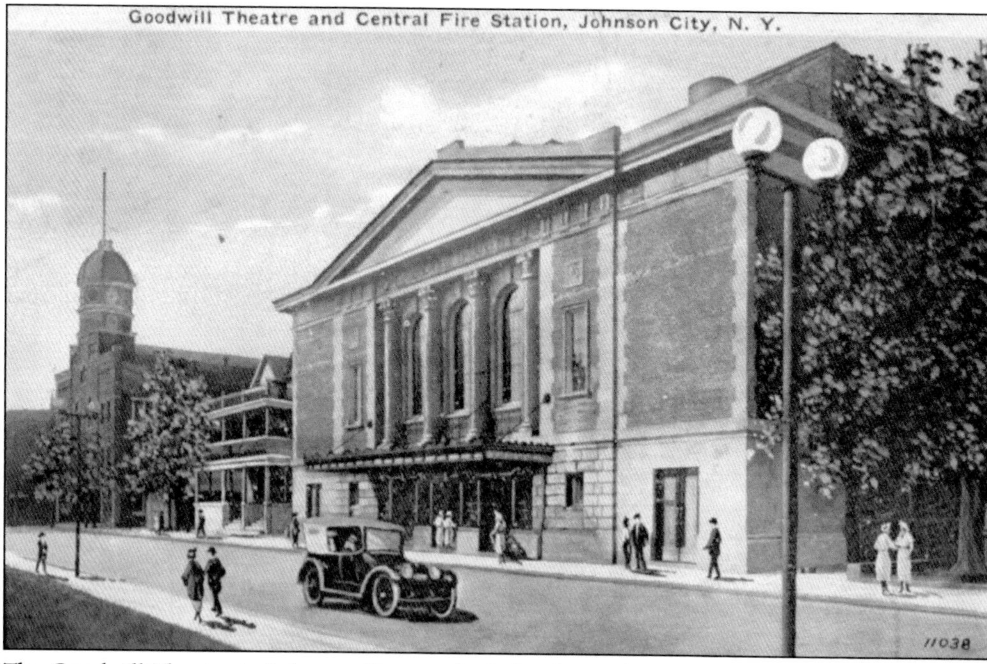

The Goodwill Theater in Johnson City was built by the Endicott Johnson Corporation in 1921 for the benefit of the community. It included a Binghamton-manufactured pipe organ and percussion system, which were needed to augment stage, film, and vaudeville presentations. In later years, the name was changed to the En Joie Theater. This postcard was mailed in 1936. On the far left is the Johnson City Fire Station.

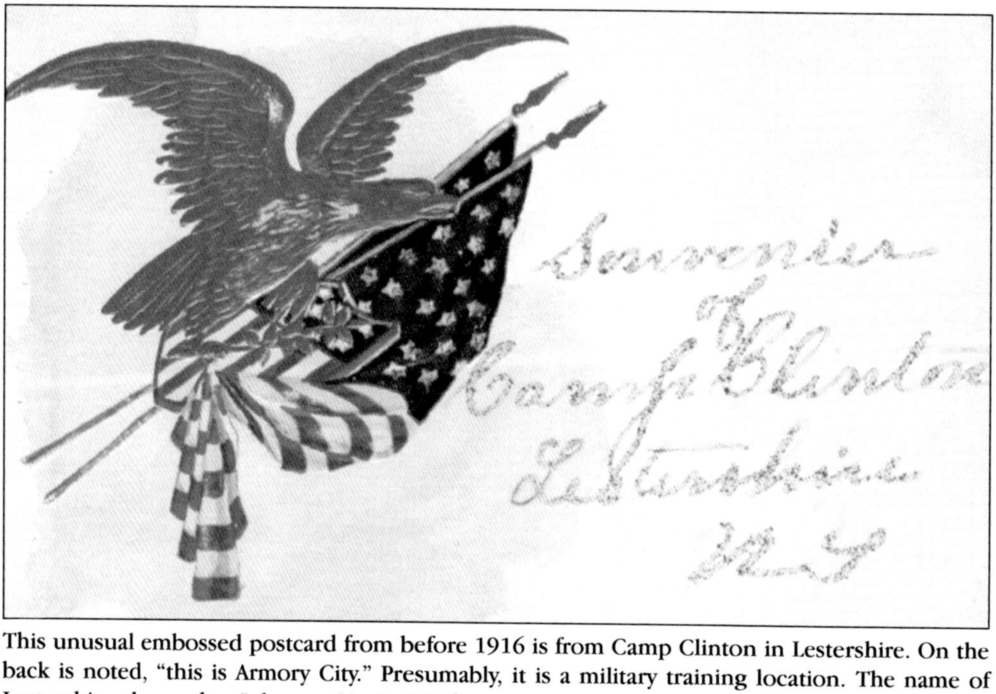

This unusual embossed postcard from before 1916 is from Camp Clinton in Lestershire. On the back is noted, "this is Armory City." Presumably, it is a military training location. The name of Lestershire changed to Johnson City in 1916.

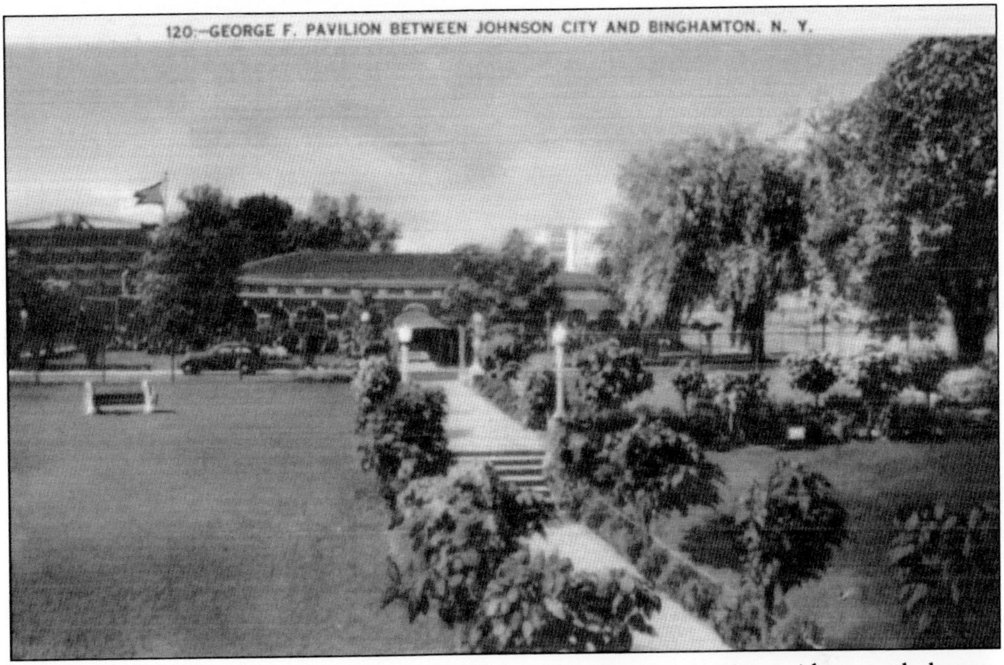

In 1926, the George F. Johnson Pavilion was built in Johnson City to give residents a wholesome place for evening entertainment. Some of the best-known big bands of the 1930s and 1940s came to Broome County. Glenn Miller, Benny Goodman, and Guy Lombardo played to packed houses on the weekends.

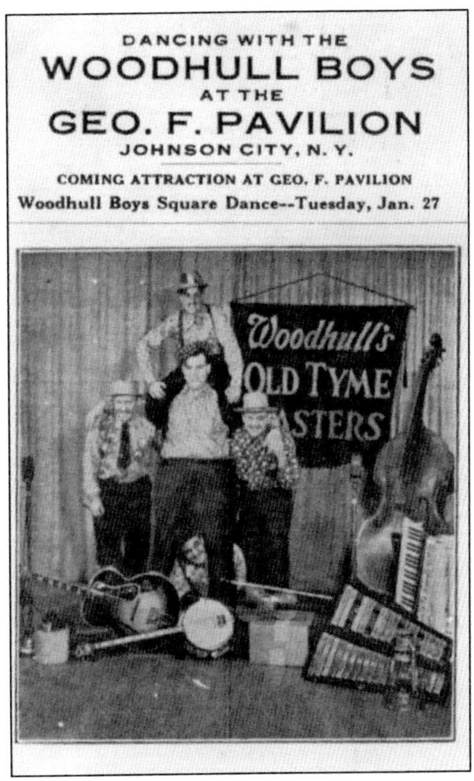

Local bands kept the dance floors full during the week, when the cost of admission was only 25¢. This postcard was sent in 1942, encouraging attendance for the Woodhull Boys performance. Binghamton native Stewart Foster (Tamer Aswad) got his start in show business as a performer at the G.F. Pavilion; he went on to national fame, singing with some of the most popular bands of the day.

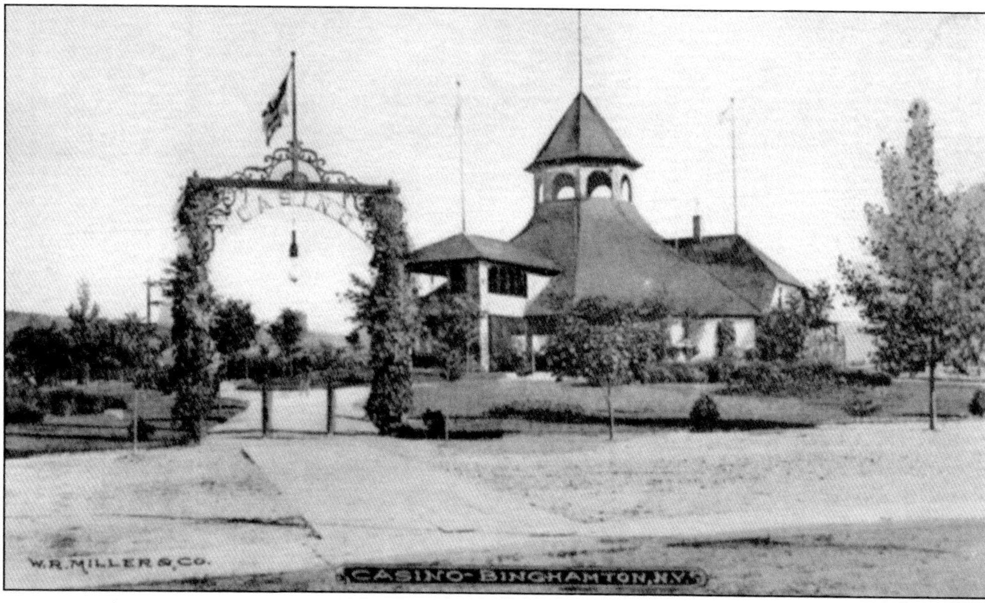

Casino Park opened in 1896 at the end of the trolley tracks in Endicott. It was an investment by the rail company to encourage travel to the "pleasure grounds." Summerhouses, a racetrack, a community house, a dance floor, baseball diamonds, golf facilities, and lush landscaping made the park attractive for family outings. The pavilion burned down in 1948, and the name was changed to Ideal Park and then to the En Joie Health Park. By the 1960s, the Herschell carousel that had been donated by Endicott Johnson was moved to Highland Park in Endwell and the entertainment fields ceased to exist. The postcard above, showing the Casino Park gates, was mailed in 1915. The postcard below shows the bandstand and crowds of visitors at the park sometime after the name had been changed to Ideal Park.

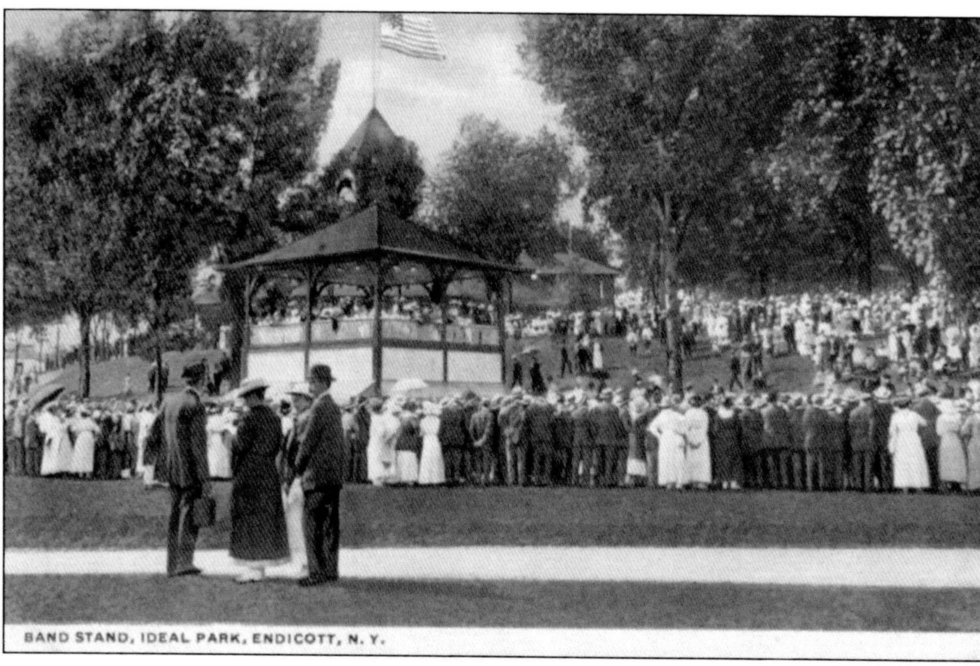

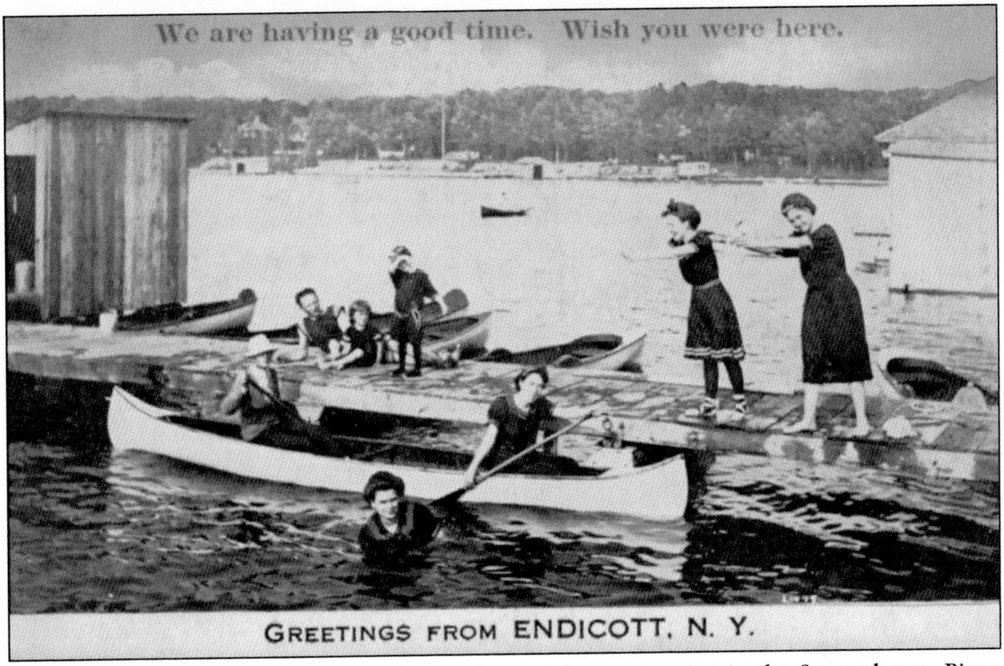

In 1919, this was the accepted garb for modest maidens swimming in the Susquehanna River. Exposed limbs were not encouraged at a public beach. This is an example of a generic postcard, photographed at another location and labeled "Endicott" for the tourist trade, rather than for historical accuracy.

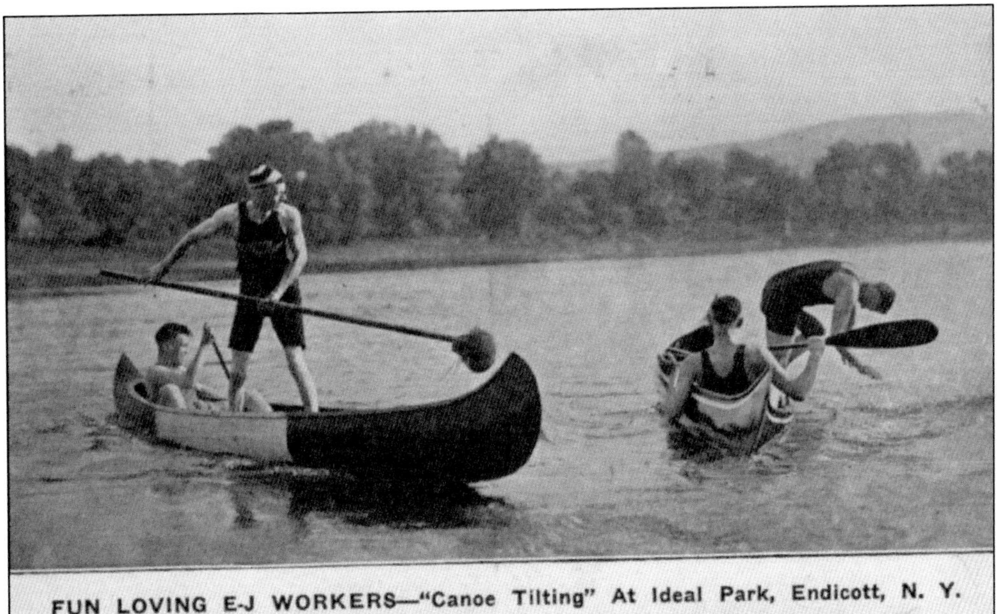

A tilting event is under way on the Susquehanna River at Ideal Park in 1920s. The men really did not want to be pushed into the water, as their bathing suits were made of wool, which became very hot, heavy, and itchy when wet.

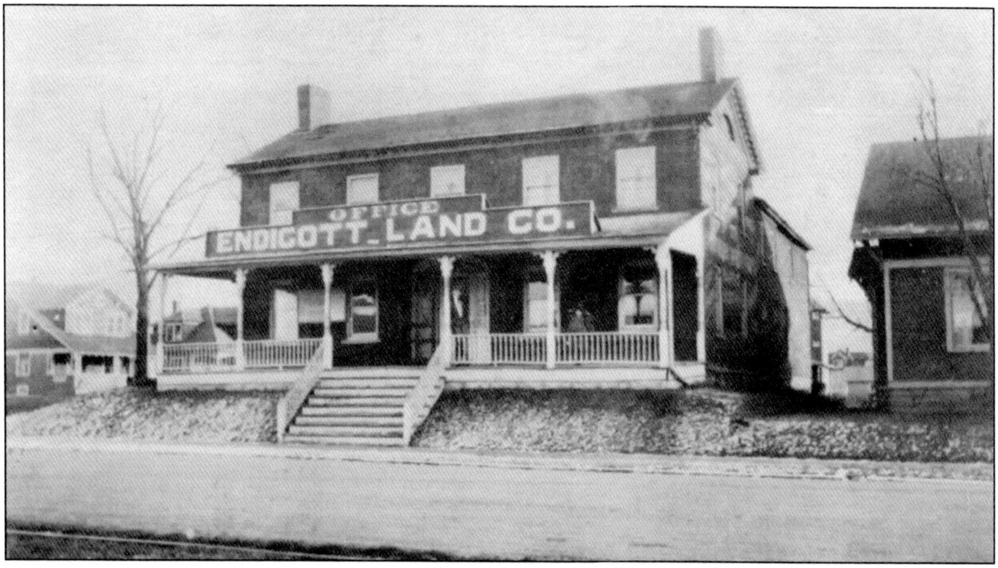

John D. Mersereau lived in this stately Federal-style house in 1825. Located at the corner of Main and Roosevelt Streets in the town of Union, the building was considered a prime site for a real estate development office. In 1901, an office devoted to promoting the growth of Endicott was established here. The building was torn down in 1938.

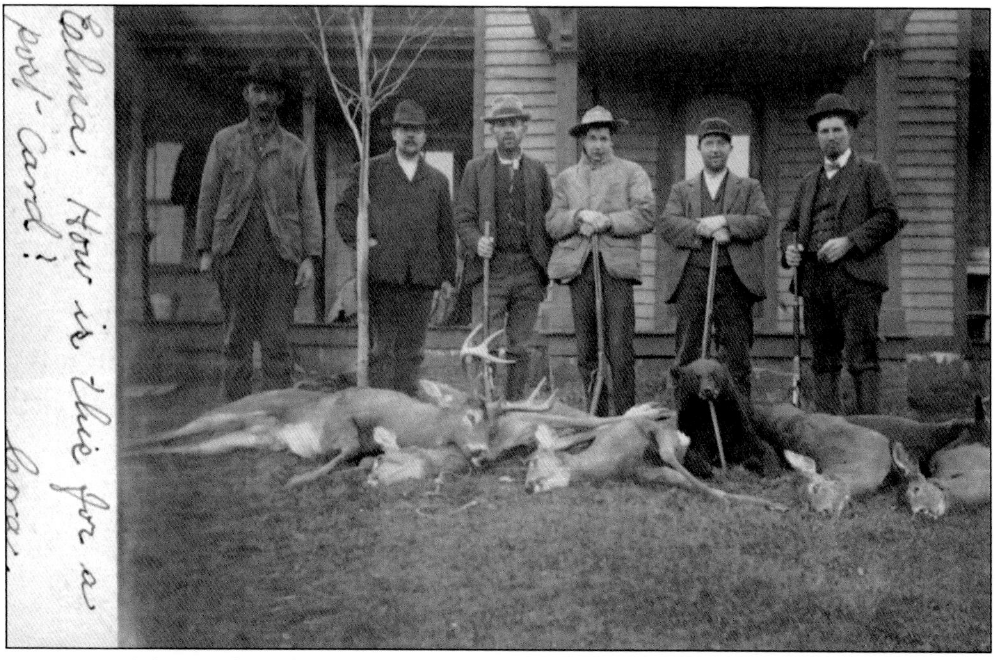

Hunters with hats and manly stances survey the casualties in the early 1900s. This real photo postcard was mailed to a Union resident for a collector's album.

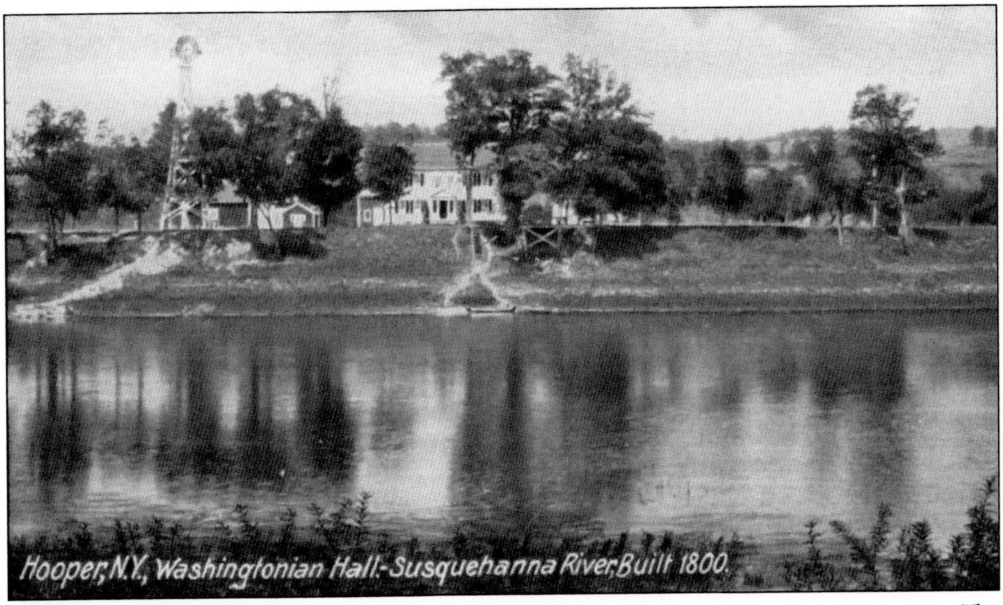

Washington Hall was built in 1799 by one of Union's earliest settlers, Amos Patterson. The house was built without nails; only wooden pegs were used. Years later, when it was used as an inn and meeting place for a local temperance group called the Washingtonians, the group's name was painted on the outside walls. The residence still stands. It is privately owned and has recently been placed on the National Register of Historic Homes. This view was taken from the Susquehanna River.

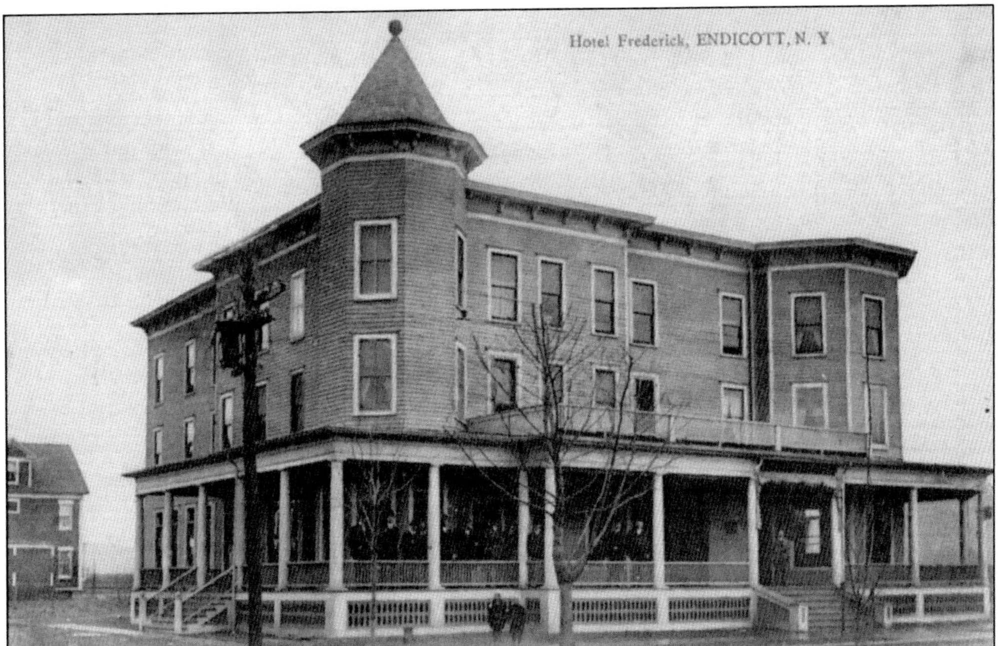

The Endicott Johnson Corporation opened the Hotel Frederick in 1906 to provide good accommodations for visitors to the new community. It was located on Washington Avenue, a site now abounding with fast-food establishments.

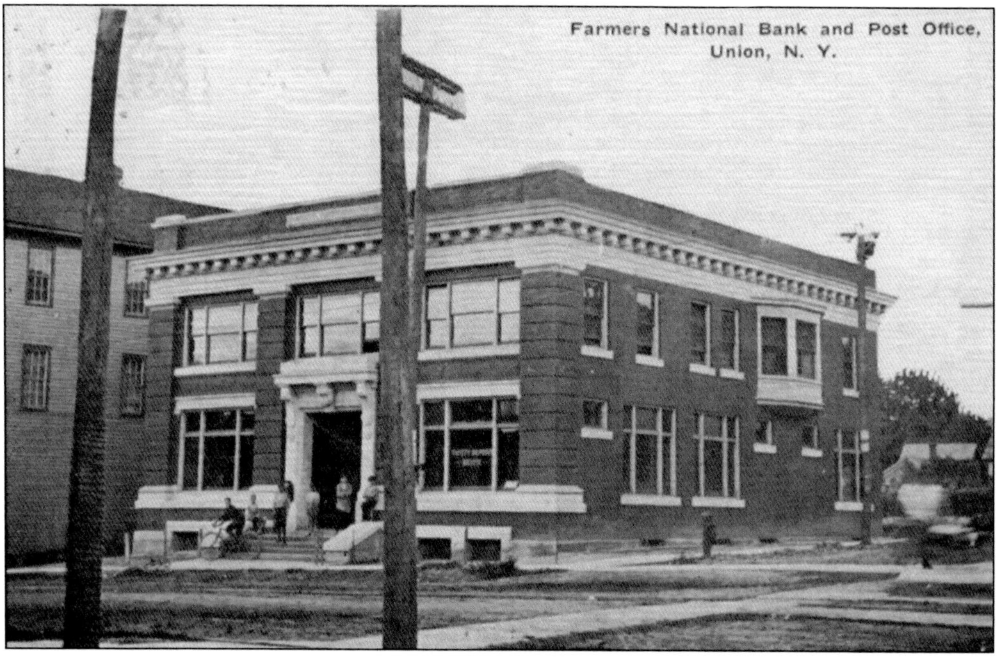

Once upon a time, in 1910, a beautiful brick building was constructed on the corner of Nanticoke and Exchange Streets in the old Union district of Endicott. Created as the Farmers National Bank, the structure survived many uses, retaining its original architectural magic throughout each incarnation. Now the bank remains only in memories and on postcards as a symbol of lost elegance and a lost battle for its preservation in 1996.

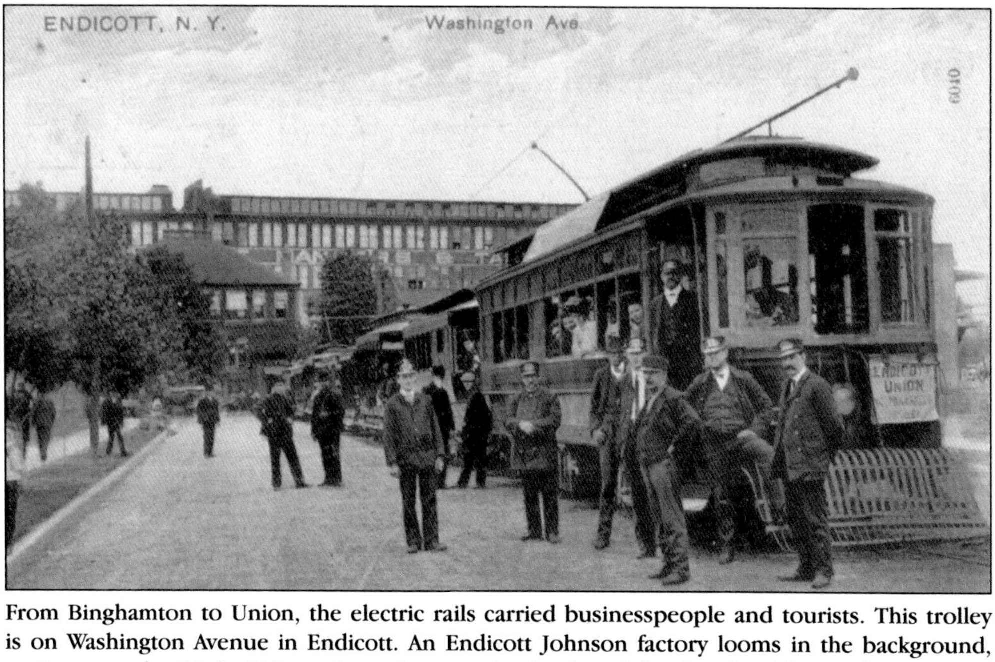

From Binghamton to Union, the electric rails carried businesspeople and tourists. This trolley is on Washington Avenue in Endicott. An Endicott Johnson factory looms in the background, casting over the Triple Cities a glow of prosperity that lasted for decades. This card was posted in 1908.

The demise of the canal system began when the iron horse first made its appearance. The Erie Railroad laid tracks starting in 1835 in Deposit. By 1869, most of Broome County was connected economically with population centers across the country.

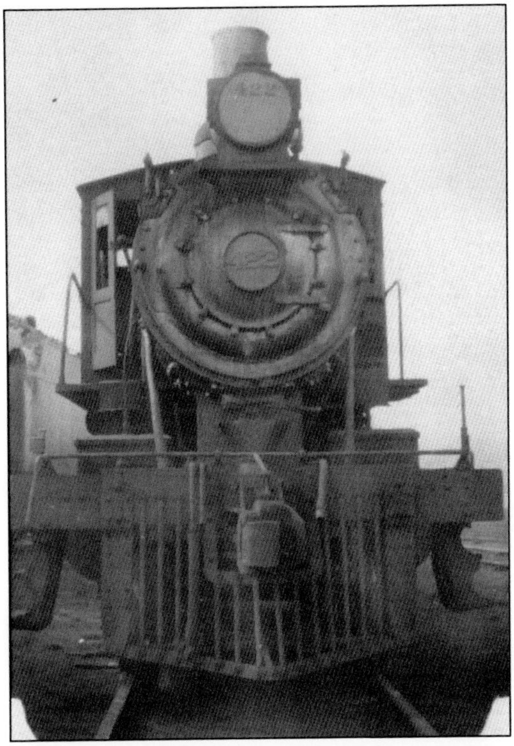

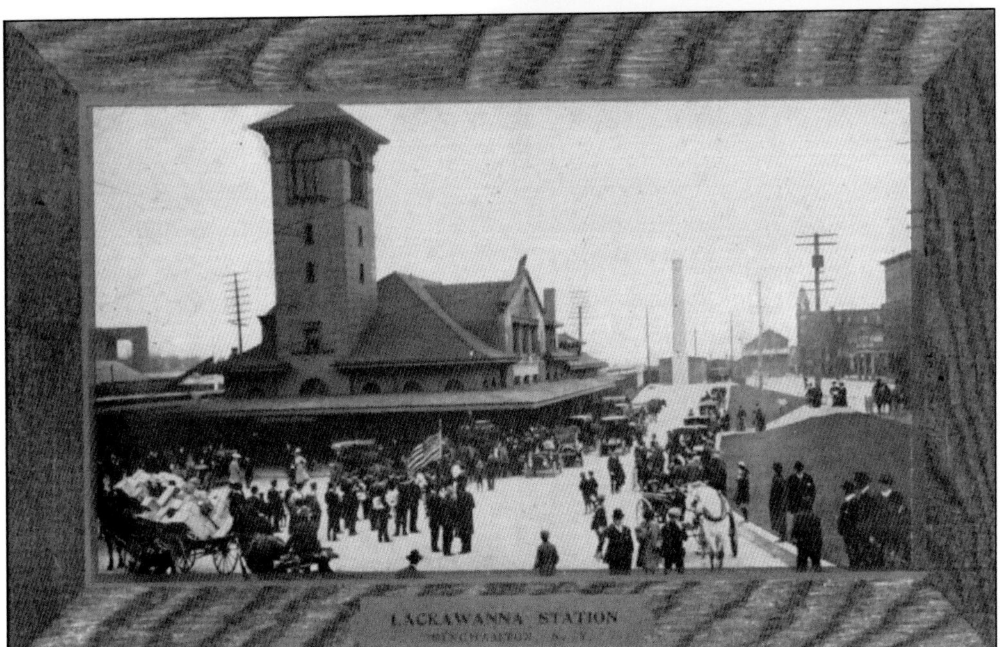

The Delaware Lackawanna and Western Railroad station was built in 1901 in Binghamton. Designed by New York City architect Samuel Huckel, the building still stands. Although trains no longer stop along the tracks near the landmark, the building still stands, privately owned since 1985. It used to house small businesses.

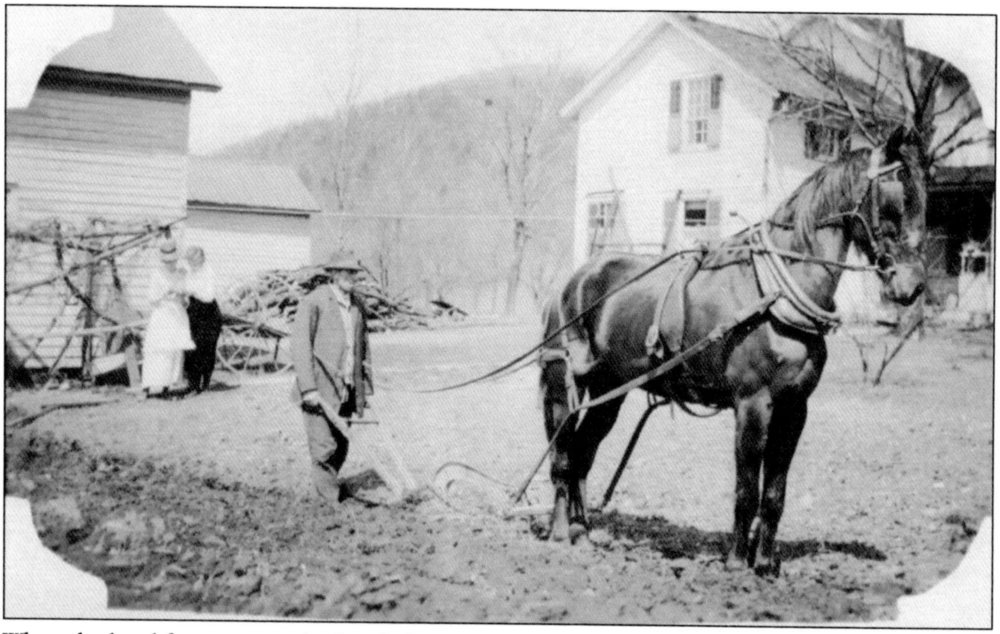

When the local forests were depleted, the economy changed from mostly lumbering businesses to farming. The first Farm Bureau in the United States was organized in Broome County in 1911. With the hills behind and the rock-strewn soil below, gardens such as this one being plowed by Mr. Burgett were a rough row to hoe.

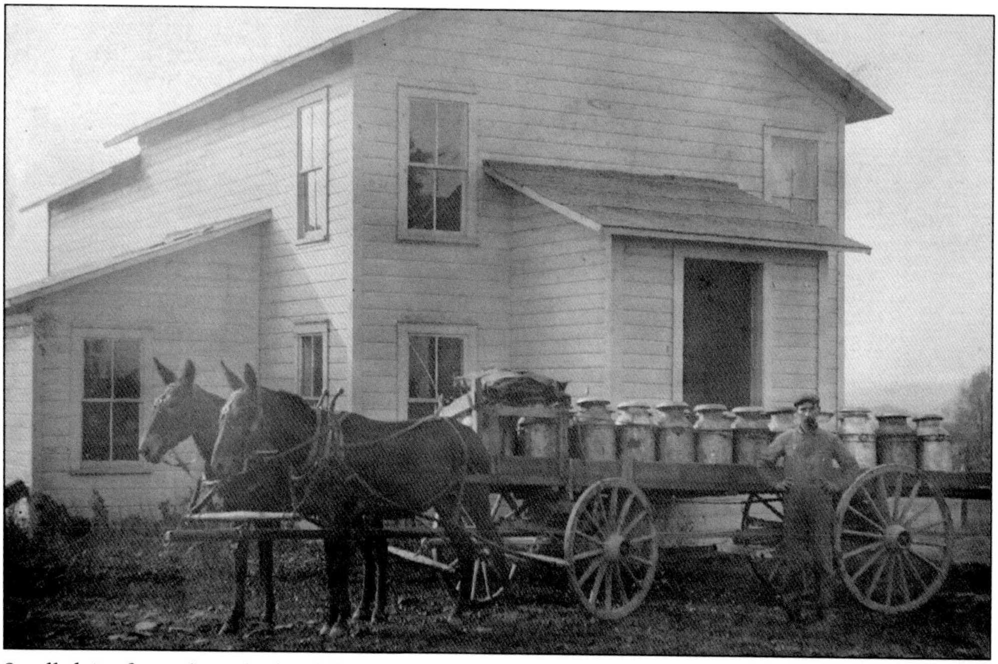

Small dairy farms have had a difficult past. After the milk strikes of 1916 and 1919, most of the local dairy farmers joined the Dairymen's League, which succeeded in obtaining a guaranteed minimum price from dealers for raw milk. This real photo postcard was mailed as a Christmas greeting in 1912.

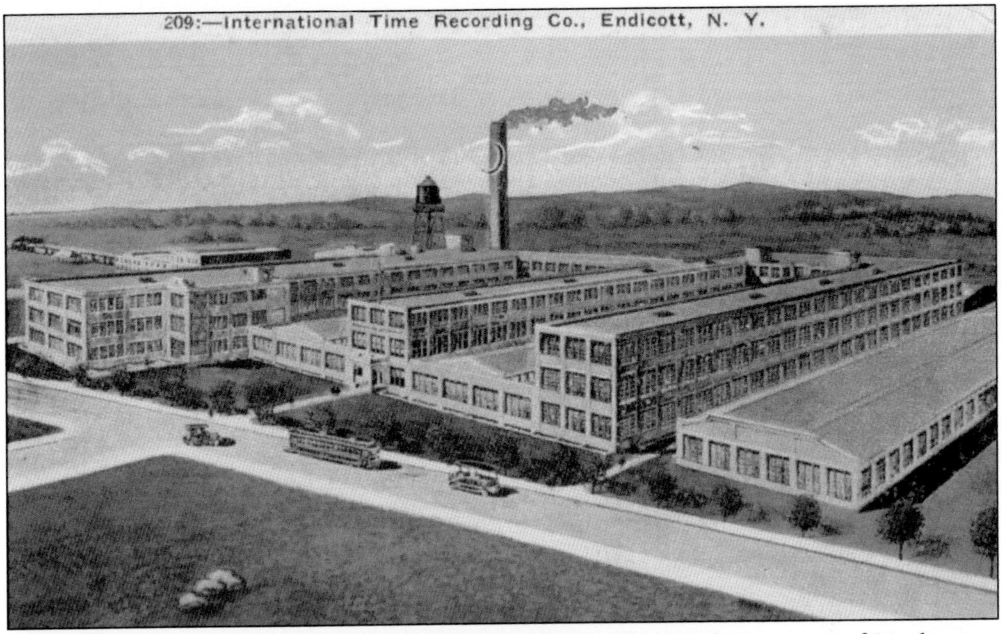

The computer age in Broome County began in Endicott. The Bundy Company of Binghamton moved to Endicott and became ITR in 1906. The name was changed to CTR in 1911 and finally became the industry giant International Business Machines (IBM). The corporation brought high technology to the world and prosperity to local inhabitants.

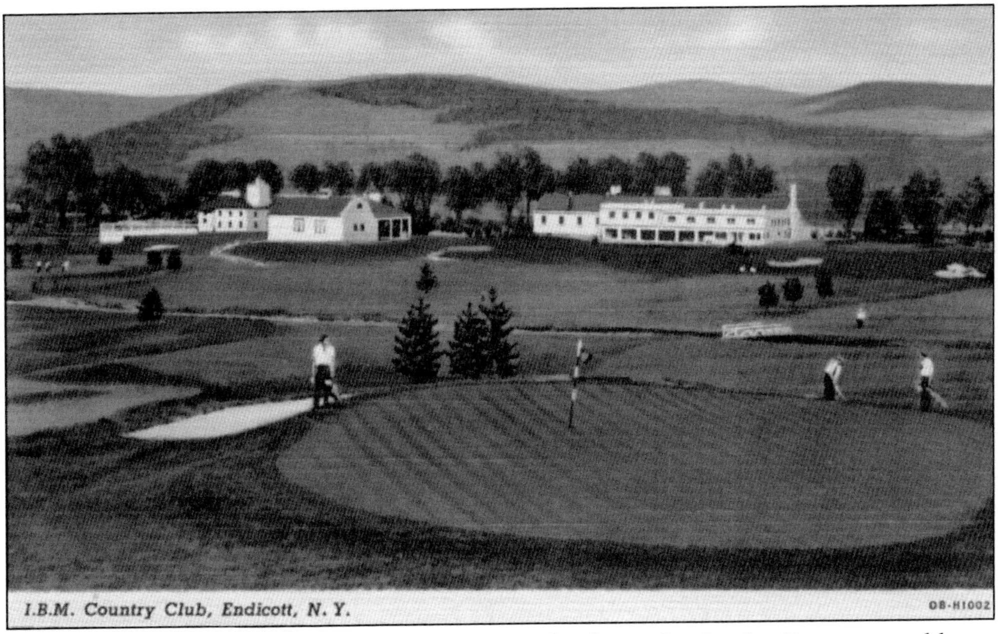

The IBM Country Club on Watson Boulevard in Endwell was the Crocker Estate, owned by an early settler in the town of Union. As a special benefit to workers, the property was purchased in 1931. It was the first employee-only country club for IBM. Due to economic challenges, the site has now been put under private management and is open to the public as the Heritage Country Club.

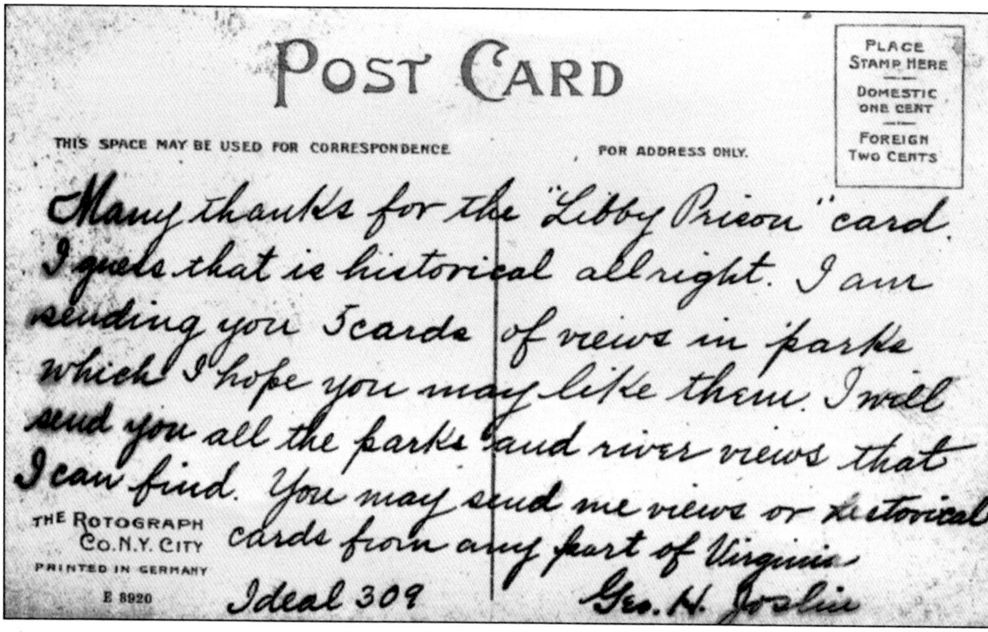
POST CARD

PLACE STAMP HERE

DOMESTIC ONE CENT

FOREIGN TWO CENTS

THIS SPACE MAY BE USED FOR CORRESPONDENCE

FOR ADDRESS ONLY.

Many thanks for the "Libby Prison" card. I guess that is historical allright. I am sending you 5 cards of views in parks which I hope you may like them. I will send you all the parks and river views that I can find. You may send me views or historical cards from any part of Virginia.

Ideal 309

Geo. H. Joslin

THE ROTOGRAPH CO. N.Y. CITY

PRINTED IN GERMANY

E 8920

The message on this postcard mailed in the 1920s shows the interest in collecting and trading postcards. The photograph on the front is an early view of Ross Park in Binghamton.

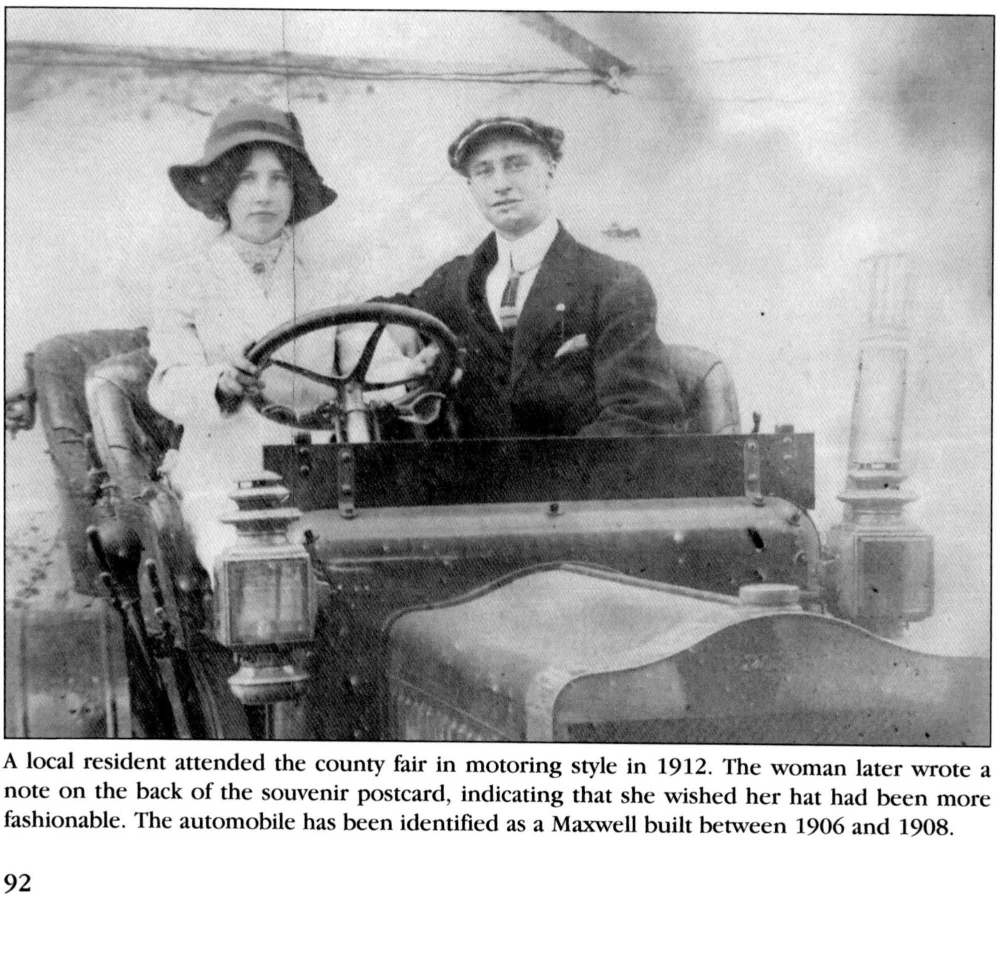

A local resident attended the county fair in motoring style in 1912. The woman later wrote a note on the back of the souvenir postcard, indicating that she wished her hat had been more fashionable. The automobile has been identified as a Maxwell built between 1906 and 1908.

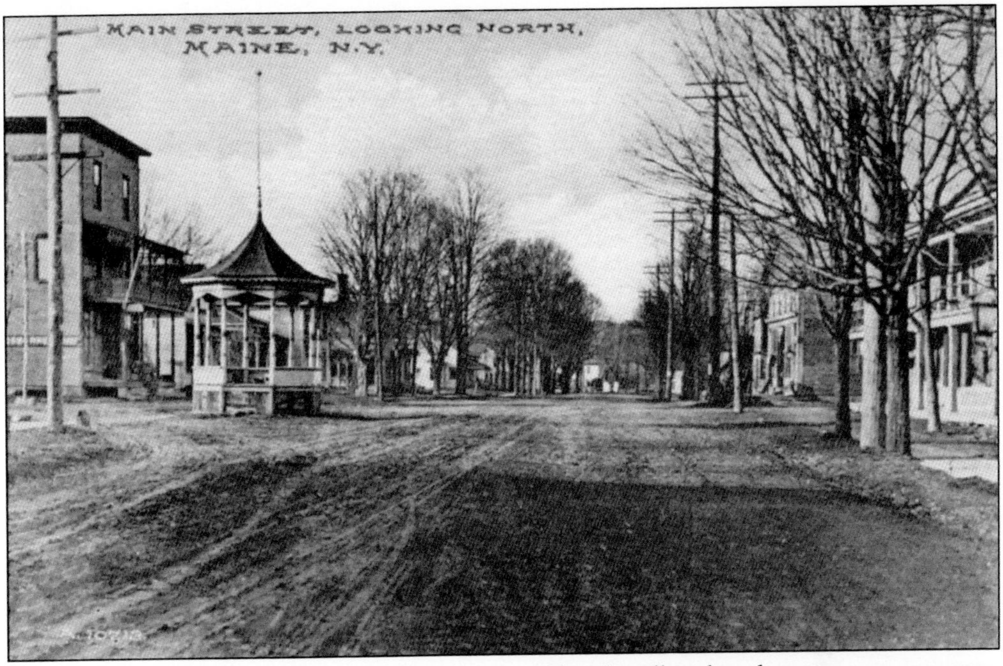

The township of Maine was formed from Union in 1848. The village has chosen to preserve many of its historic buildings, and it remains a charming and interesting place to visit. This postcard was mailed in 1908.

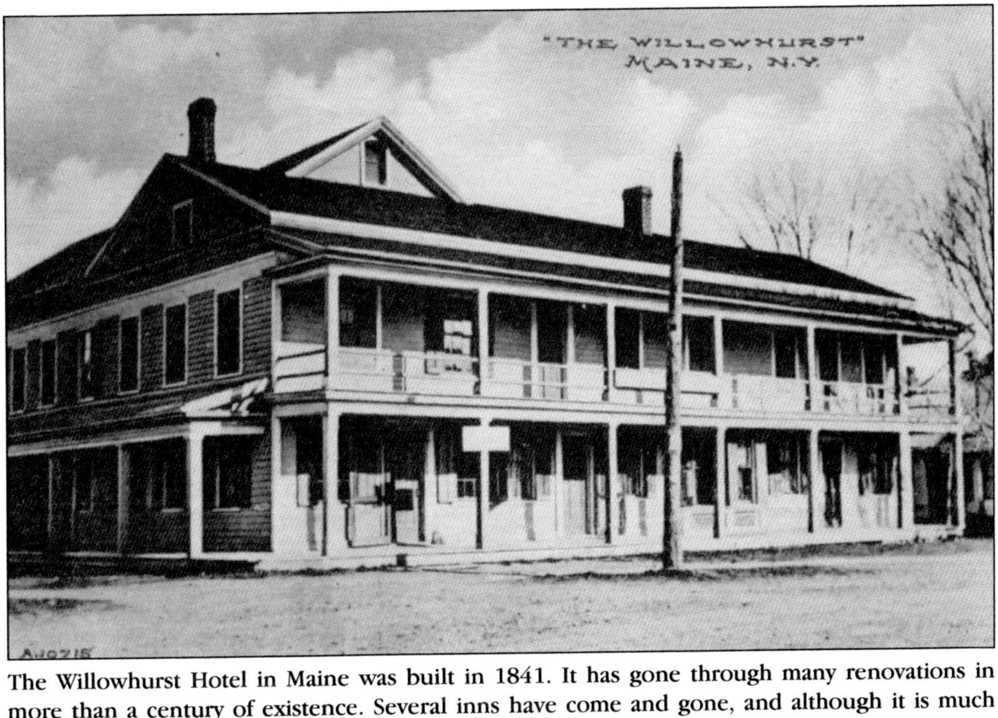

The Willowhurst Hotel in Maine was built in 1841. It has gone through many renovations in more than a century of existence. Several inns have come and gone, and although it is much remodeled, the building still stands, currently owned by the Catholic Church.

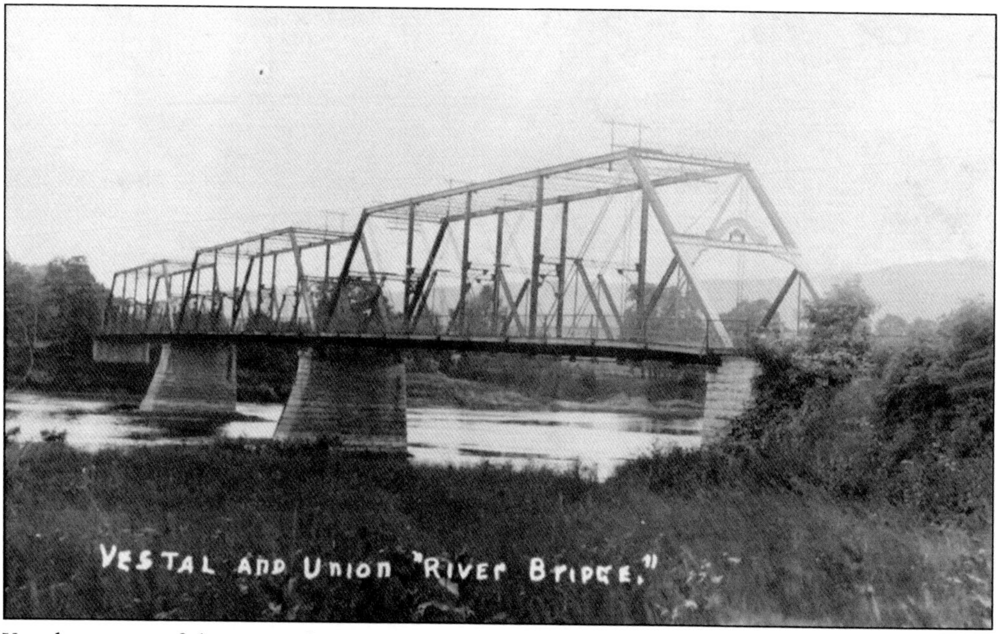

Vestal was part of the town of Union until 1823, and the only way to cross the river was a ferry service run by Jonathan Crane. Vestal, known as Crane's Ferry and then as Vestal Mills, began with settlers purchasing land for ten shillings an acre. This bridge was constructed in 1895. A sign advised users of the bridge that "anything faster than a walk" would result in a $5 fine.

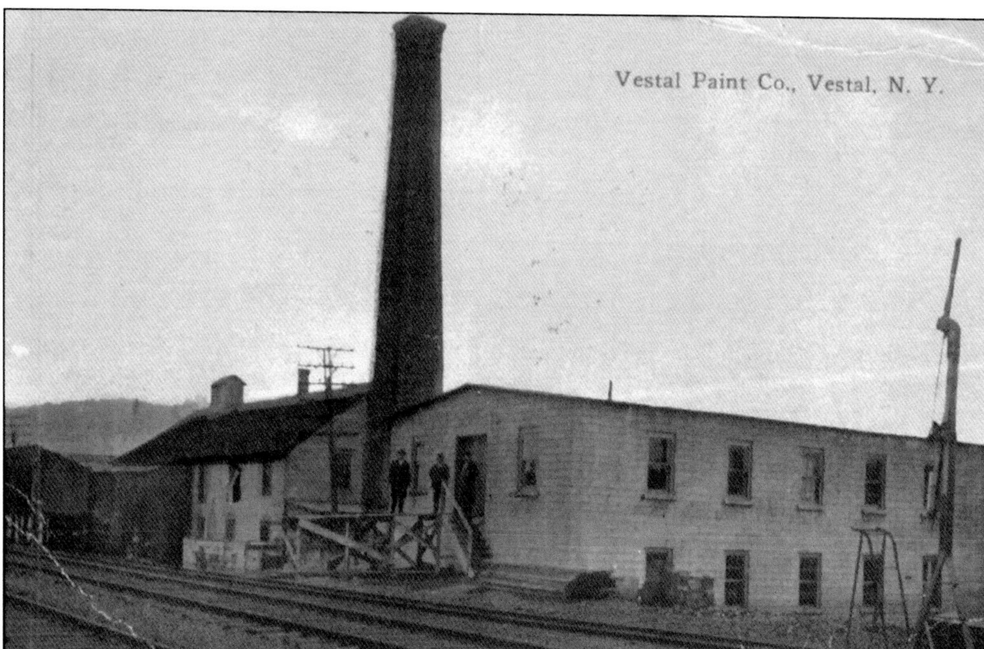

Hoping there would be a demand for paint made from the clay found along the banks of the Choconut Creek, Jake Crane opened the Vestal Paint Company in 1900. However, the No Sale sign rang too often, and the company was out of business by 1910. The same site housed another unsuccessful enterprise, the manufacturer of a new style of safety pin.

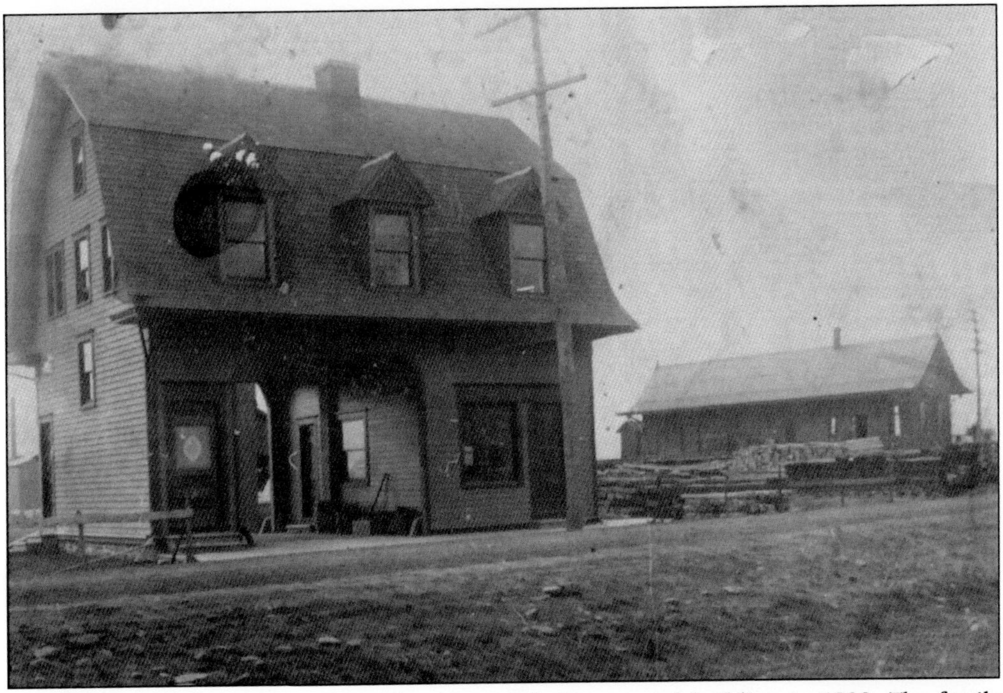

The Rounds Coal Company of Vestal constructed this unusual building in 1908. The family had been selling coal since 1881 from the railway station, located in the right background. The original platform scale in the center of the building, to weigh truckloads of fuel, dates to the early 1800s, and a similar scale is still in use.

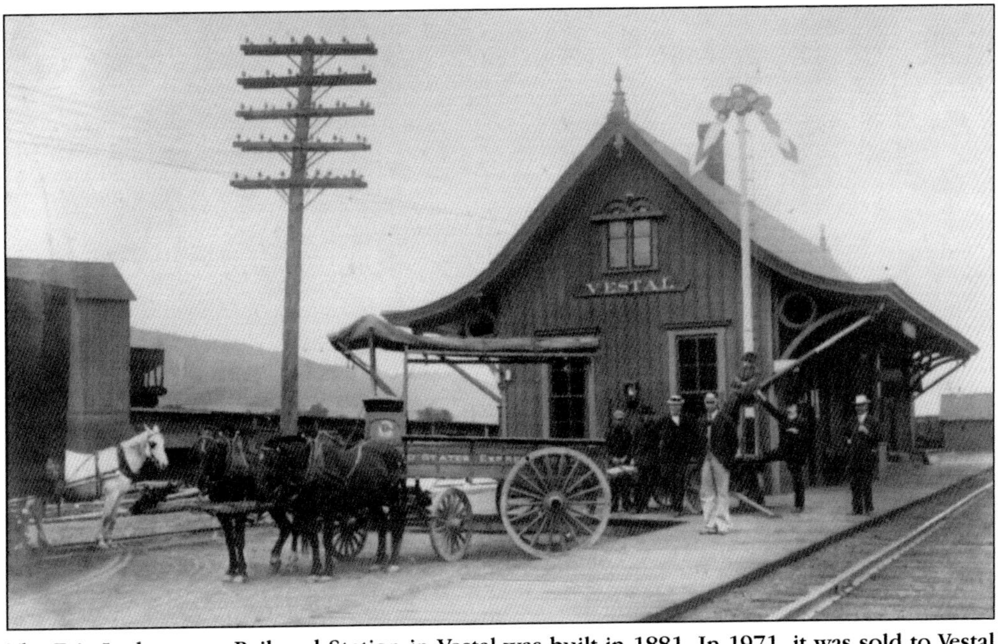

The Erie Lackawanna Railroad Station in Vestal was built in 1881. In 1971, it was sold to Vestal and was moved to the library parking lot on the Vestal Parkway. It now serves as the home of the Vestal Museum and Historical Society.

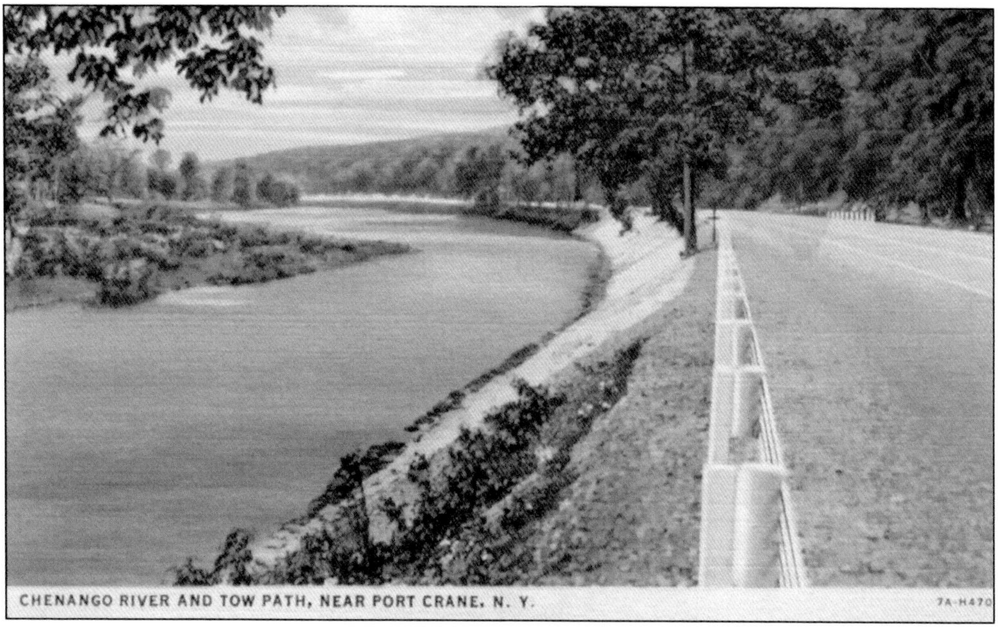

Port Crane, a hamlet located in the town of Fenton, was an important stop on the Chenango Canal in the 1800s. The remnants of the towpath can be seen along the roadway. The trail where mules once pulled packet boats is slowly eroding into the flowing waters. Originally, the whole town was Port Crane, but it was renamed in 1867 to honor Gov. Reuben Fenton.

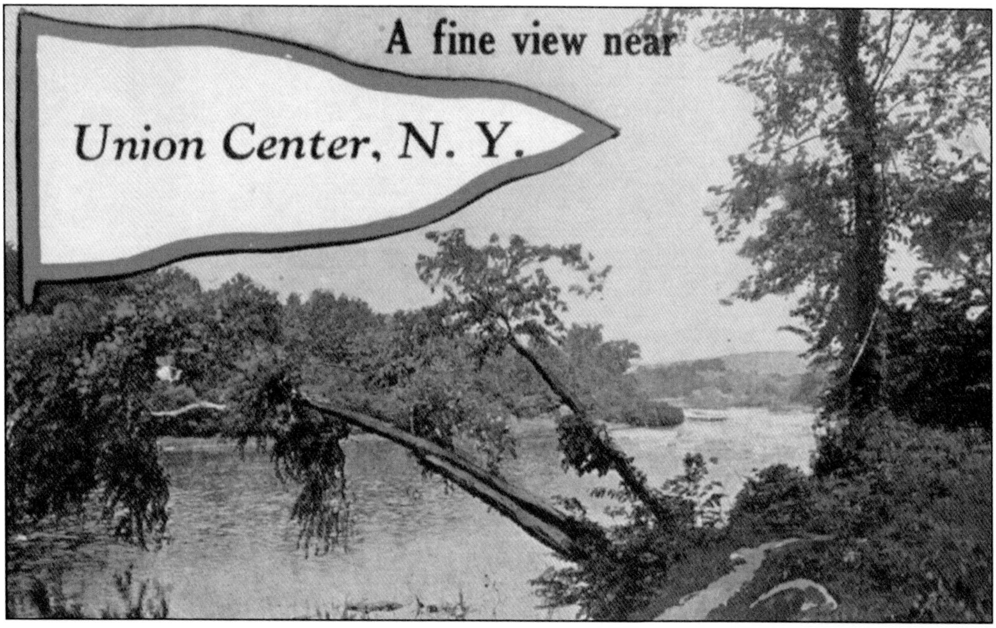

Union Center was sparsely settled *c.* 1792 near the north line of Union on the Nanticoke Creek. By 1848, a post office was established. It is an interesting note on small-town cooperation that there was no public transportation in the 1930s between Endicott, where many of the residents worked, and Union Center. The locals got together, purchased a bus, and rotated driving duties. This postcard is a 1914 view.

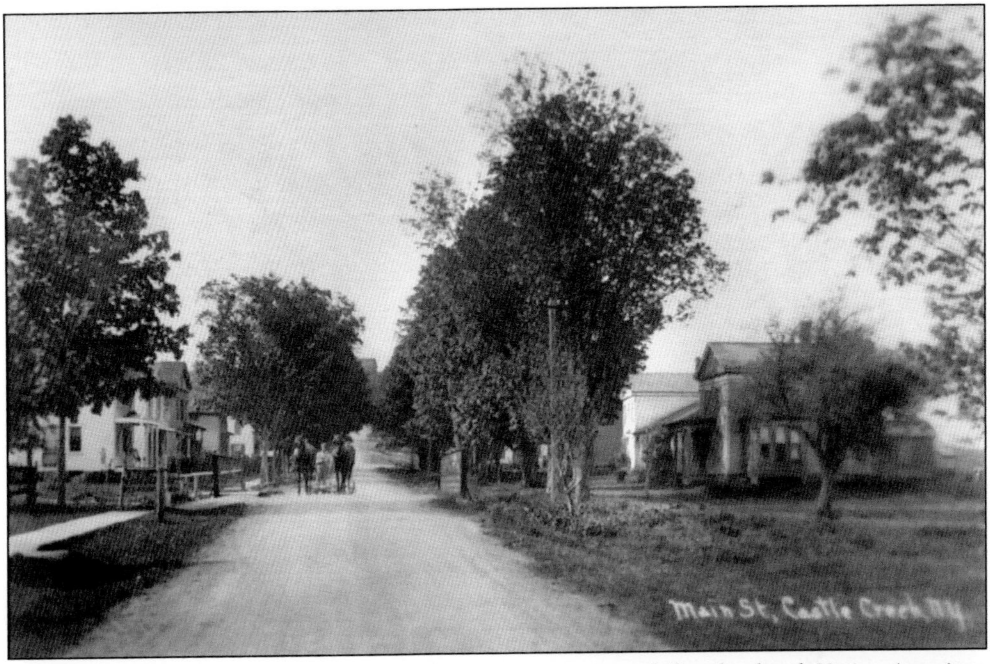

Castle Creek, located in the town of Chenango, was named for the local Native American settlement that was surrounded by a stockade resembling a castle. In 1792, an unscrupulous trader named Patterson obtained title to the 160-acre "Castle Farms." Pretending to offer the Native Americans an ornate silver mounted rifle in trade for pelts, Patterson instead drew up a bill of sale for their land. He was later killed by the victims after the fraud was discovered.

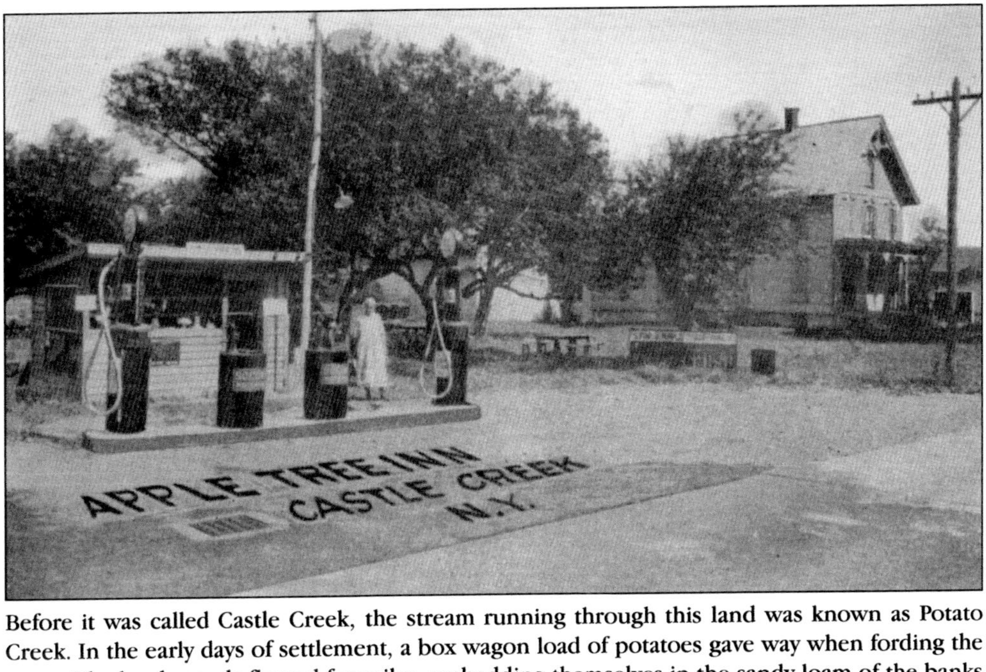

Before it was called Castle Creek, the stream running through this land was known as Potato Creek. In the early days of settlement, a box wagon load of potatoes gave way when fording the water. The hardy spuds floated for miles, embedding themselves in the sandy loam of the banks along the way. The next spring produced a bumper crop of potatoes for miles downstream.

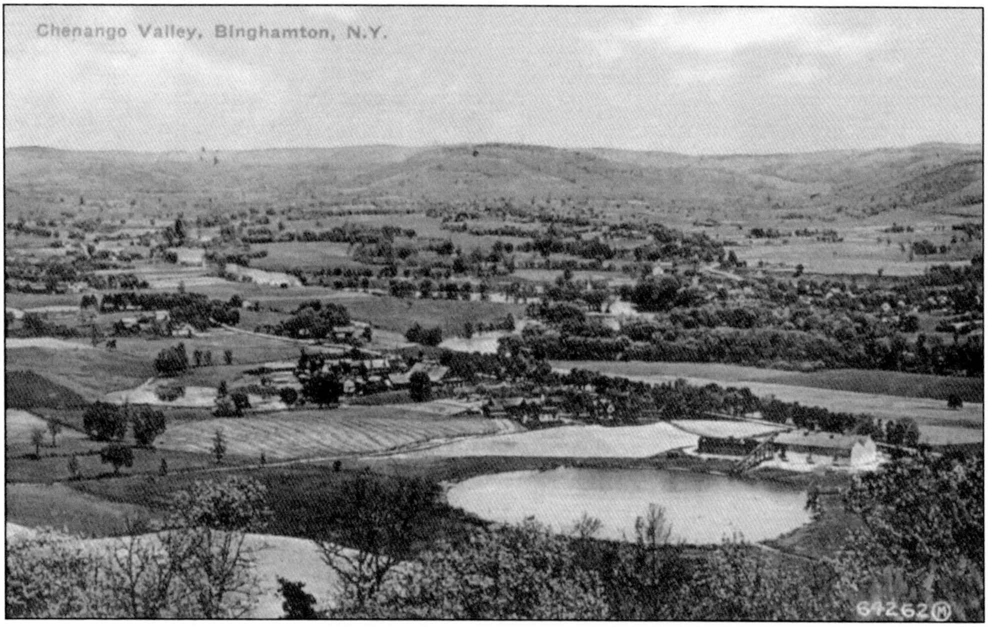

This view shows Chenango Valley near the reservoir. Chenango was settled *c.* 1787 and was officially established as a township in 1791. It was one of the original towns in Tioga County. This postcard was mailed in 1911.

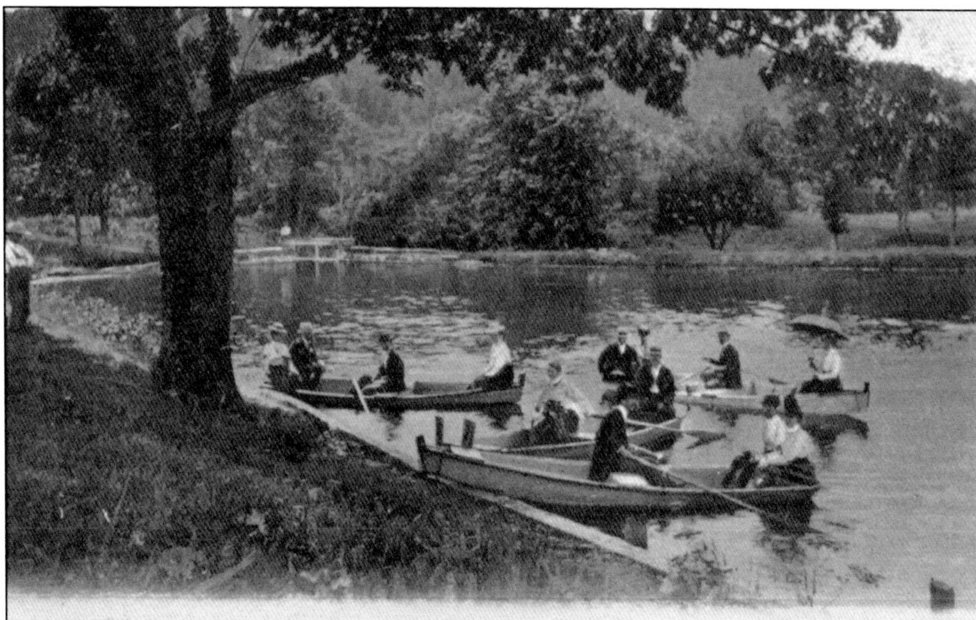

In a setting of woodland harmony, a small kettle lake exists, created thousands of years ago during the Ice Age. In the early 1900s, a boatload of water lily roots were planted in three serene coves on the west side of the lake. The plants thrived and multiplied, providing beauty and giving the lake a name: Lily Lake. The lake is located in the 1,000-acre Chenango Valley State Park.

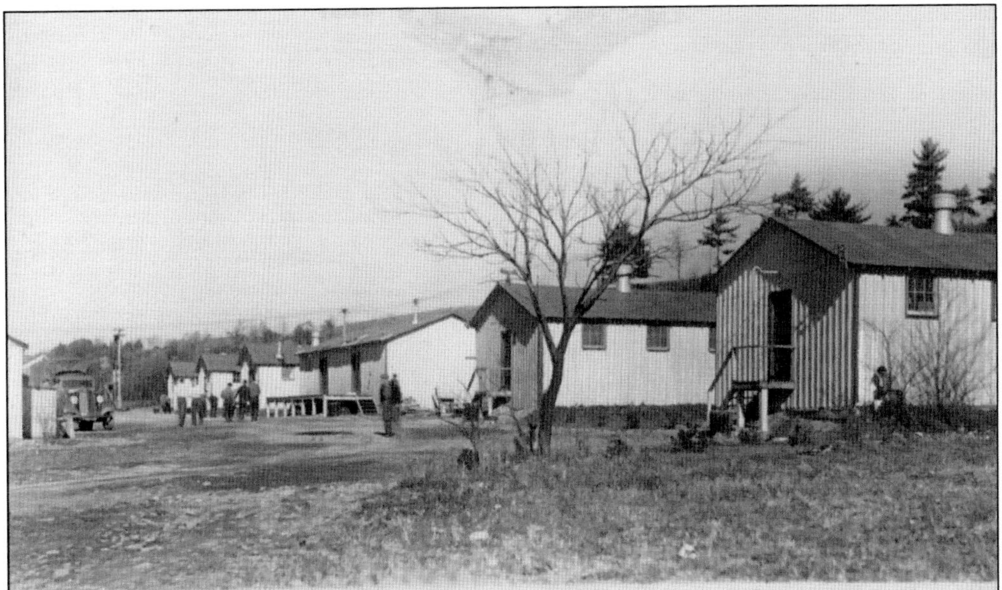

Company 236, Camp 28 C. C. C., Chenango Valley State Park, Chenango Forks, N.Y.

Chenango Valley State Park has a more current history nearly as interesting as the Ice Age that formed the landscape. Black Thursday and the stock market crash of 1929 precipitated the Great Depression that reached into every home in America. By 1933, the destroyed economy had put more than 13 million people out of work. The newly elected president of the United States, Franklin D. Roosevelt, immediately created one of the most efficient relief programs ever instituted by the federal government: the Civilian Conservation Corps (CCC). These views show the CCC camp that was erected near the New York State park and the administration building that the CCC workers built of local stone.

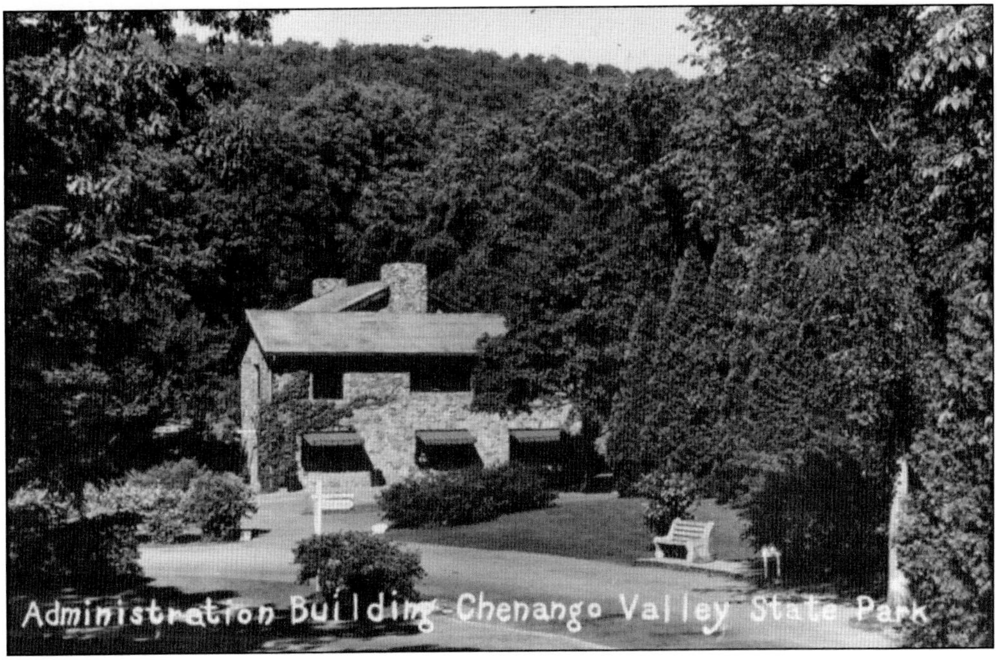

Administration Building-Chenango Valley State Park

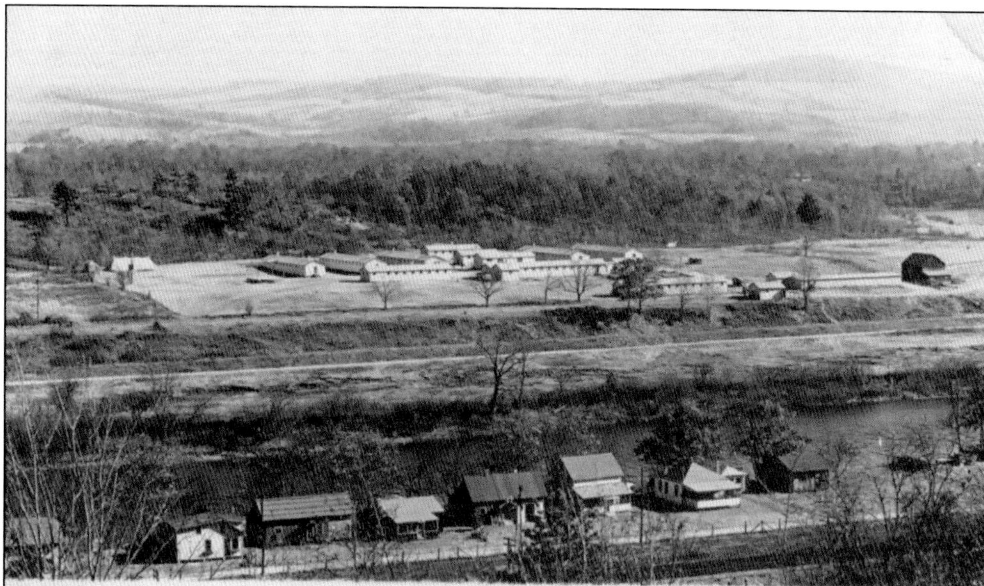

Company 236, Camp 28 C. C. C., Chenango Valley State Park, Chenango Forks, N.Y.

The Civilian Conservation Corps enrolled nearly 500,000 youths to work in forests, parks, and rangelands. Often called the "soil soldiers," the young men had to be unemployed, unmarried, under 25, and come from families on relief. All the solid stone buildings, the beaches, the bridges, and the roads of Chenango Valley State Park were worked on by CCC enrollees. Each youth earned $30 a month, $25 of which was sent home to his family. All the necessities of everyday life were provided by the government, including clothing and the option of attending classes. The postcard above shows an aerial view of the CCC camp. The postcard below shows one of the park's stone bridges that is still in use.

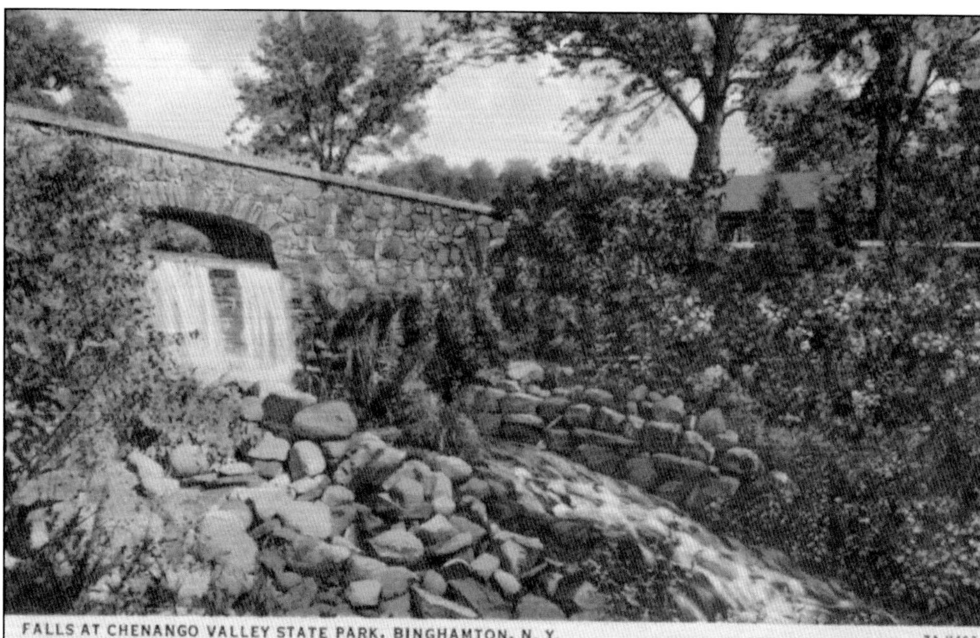

FALLS AT CHENANGO VALLEY STATE PARK, BINGHAMTON, N. Y. 7A-H462

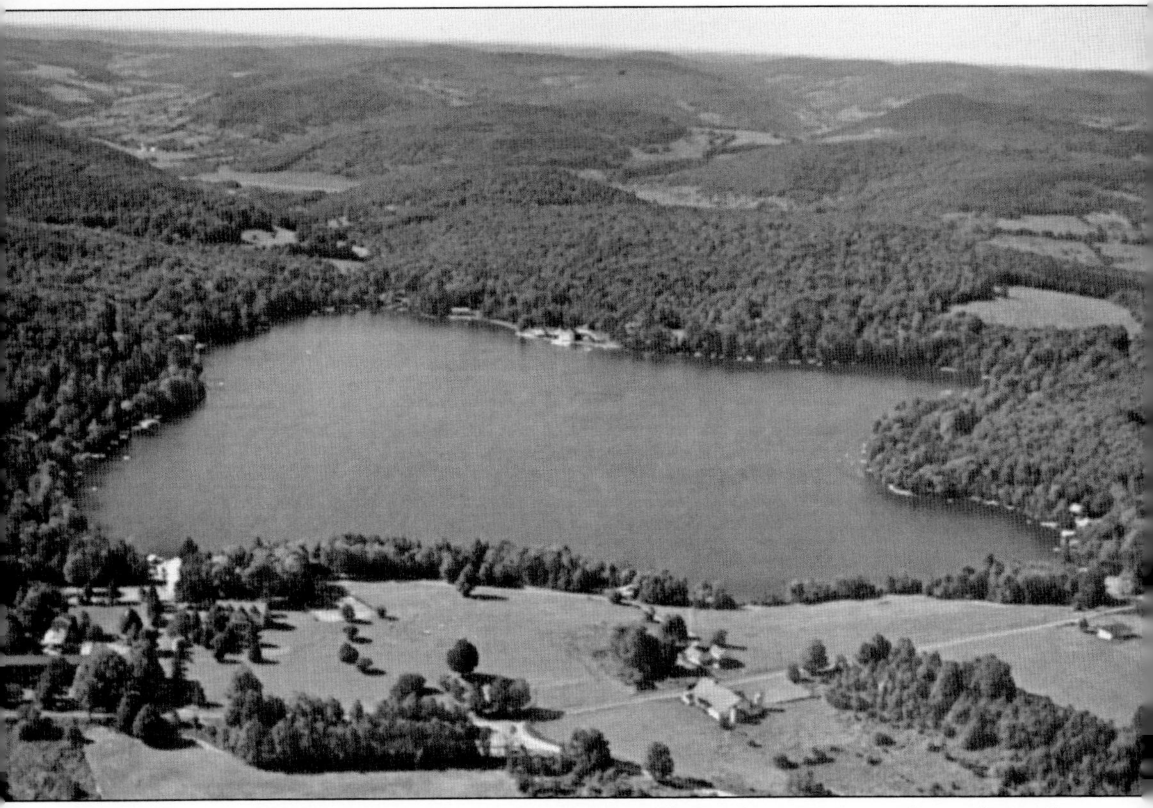

Oquaga Lake was brought fourth eons ago by volcanic and glacial energy. Located on a forested mountaintop near Deposit, the lake is an icy spring-fed lake about one mile long and three-quarters of a mile wide. In some places, the clear frigid pools reach 180 feet in depth, and in other areas traditional methods of measurement have failed to locate the bottom. The name comes from the Indian word *oghawagah,* meaning huckleberry or clear water, depending on which old text is to be believed. The peaceful, ancient surroundings have been a popular resort since the days when the horse and buggy offered the only access to the mountain retreat.

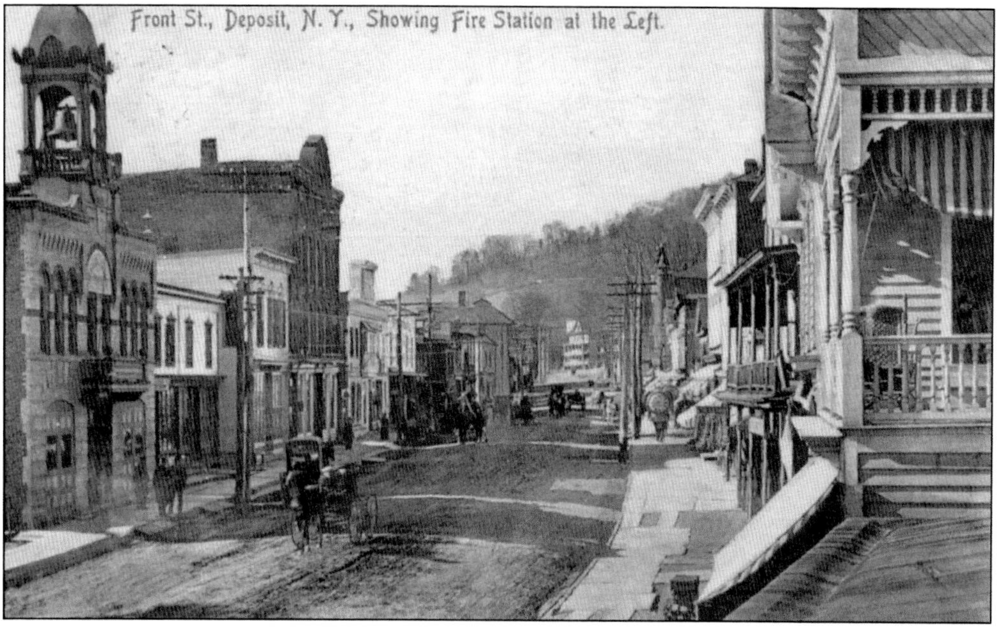

Incorporated in 1811 in the township of Sanford, Deposit is the oldest village in Broome County. Part of the village is in Delaware County. Its name was derived from early lumber industries, which deposited logs into the river to be rafted to market. When the town was formed, there were not enough freeholders to comprise a jury, so an act was passed proclaiming that any male resident could be called for duty. This postcard is from 1909.

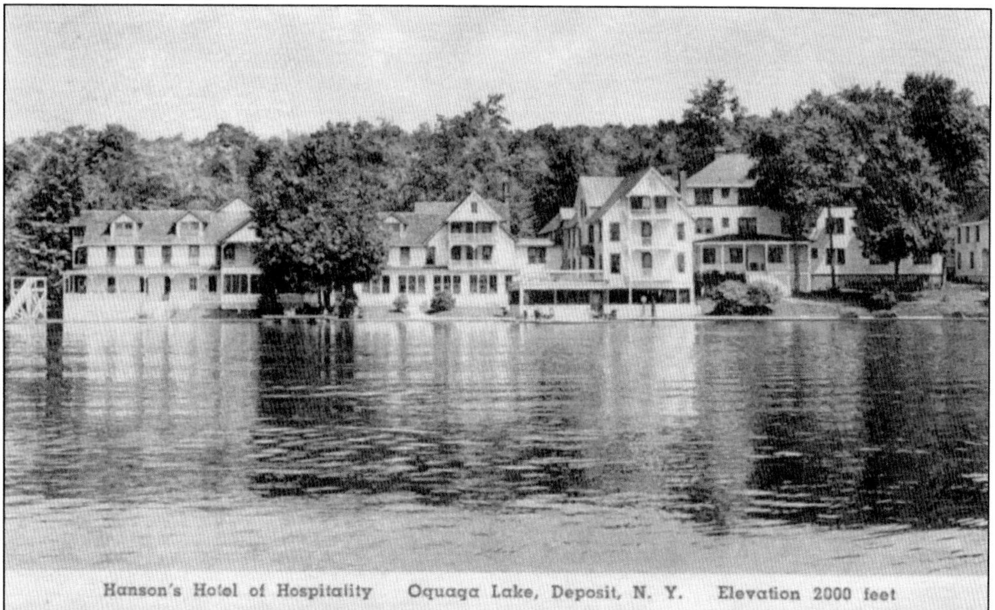

Hanson's Hotel was originally known as the Retlaw, which was the owner's last name spelled backwards. A popular resort on Oquaga Lake in Deposit, it is 2,000 feet above sea level. In 1947, when this postcard was mailed, the hotel boasted fresh air, boat rides, an abundance of fishing, and no mosquitoes.

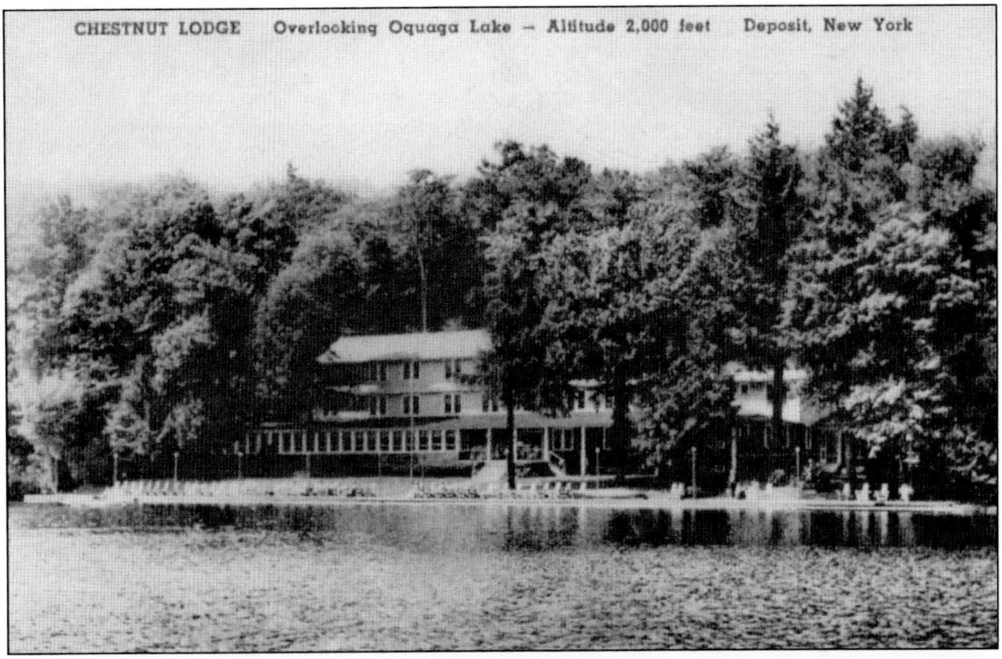

Construction of the Chestnut Inn on Oquaga Lake was started in 1924 and completed in 1929. It is built of North American chestnut harvested from the surrounding forests. All the paneling, moldings, trim, and even closets are made of this now rare and extinct wood. The inn is still accepting guests and providing interesting accommodations and entertainment.

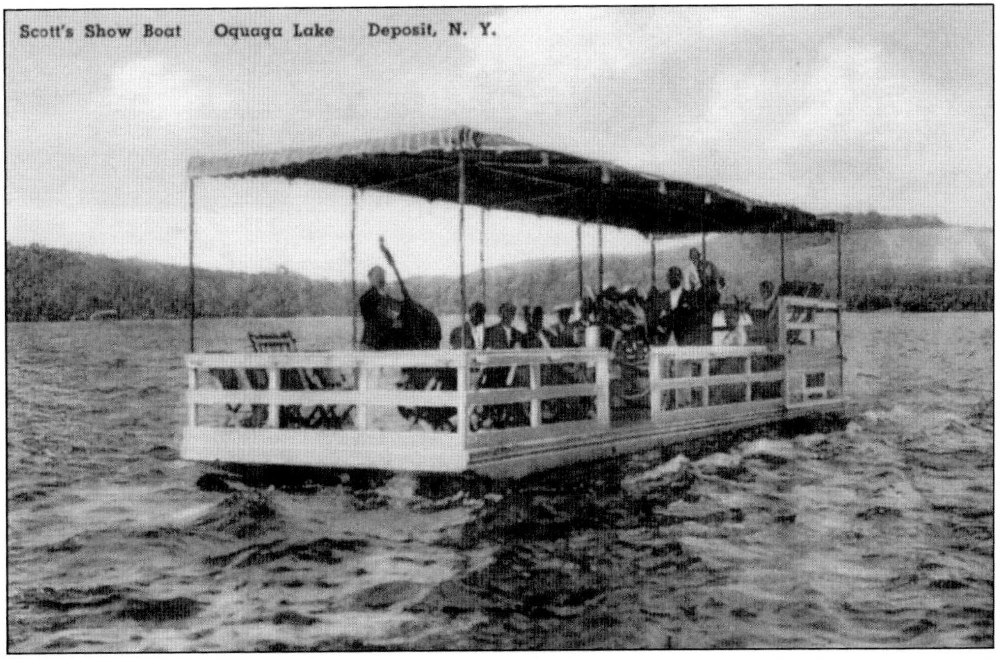

From 1870 to the present day, Scott's Resort on Oquaga Lake in Deposit has been owned and operated by the Scott family. The sixth generation of Scotts are continuing to accommodate the public at a resort that has always been a "dry" establishment.

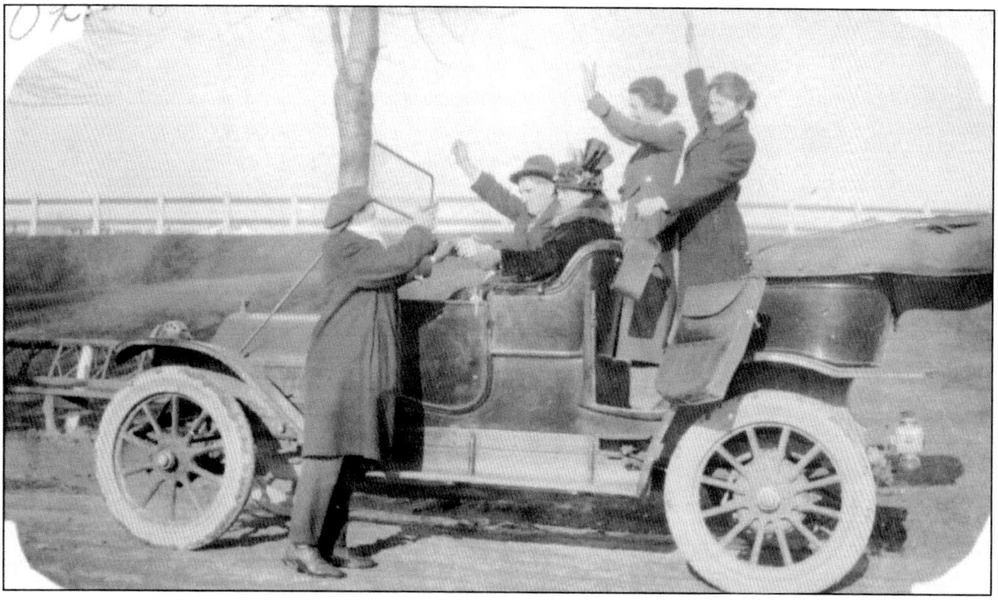

This early-20th-century postcard shows the newest status possession—the automobile—and includes a good example of the humor of the day. The written caption says, "Oh! Say, U-Auto-B-in the holdup with us." The automobile appears to be a 1912 or 1913 model Buick, Cadillac, or Overland.

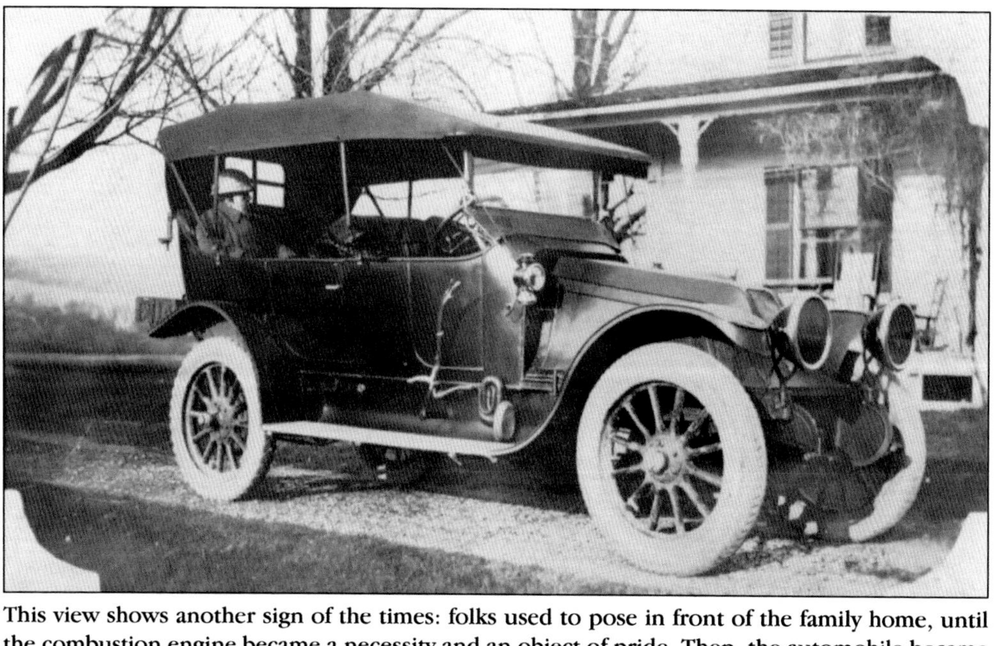

This view shows another sign of the times: folks used to pose in front of the family home, until the combustion engine became a necessity and an object of pride. Then, the automobile became the location of choice for family snapshots. A hand-written note on this postcard indicates that the vehicle was the "last big six Franklin made" *c.* 1915.

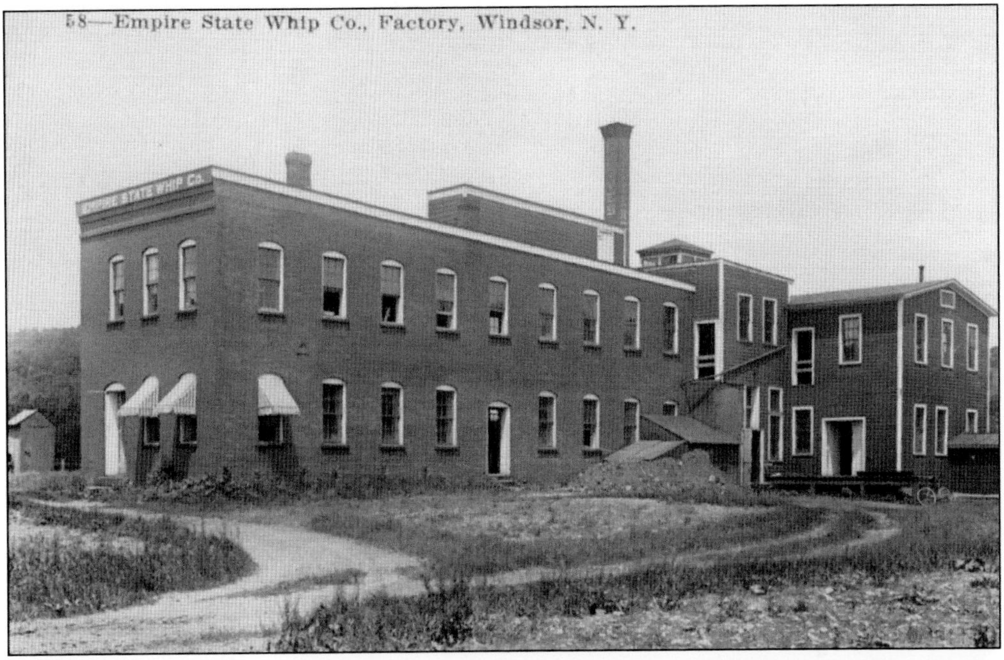

In 1854, Adin W. Coburn, a shoemaker, expanded his business to include the making of buggy whips. From this small beginning, one of Windsor's major industries developed, with several factories devoted to whip production. As horsepower replaced horses, the need for whips declined. By 1924, there were only five buggy whip companies in the United States, and two of them were still located in Windsor. This postcard shows the Empire State Whip Company, *c.* 1908.

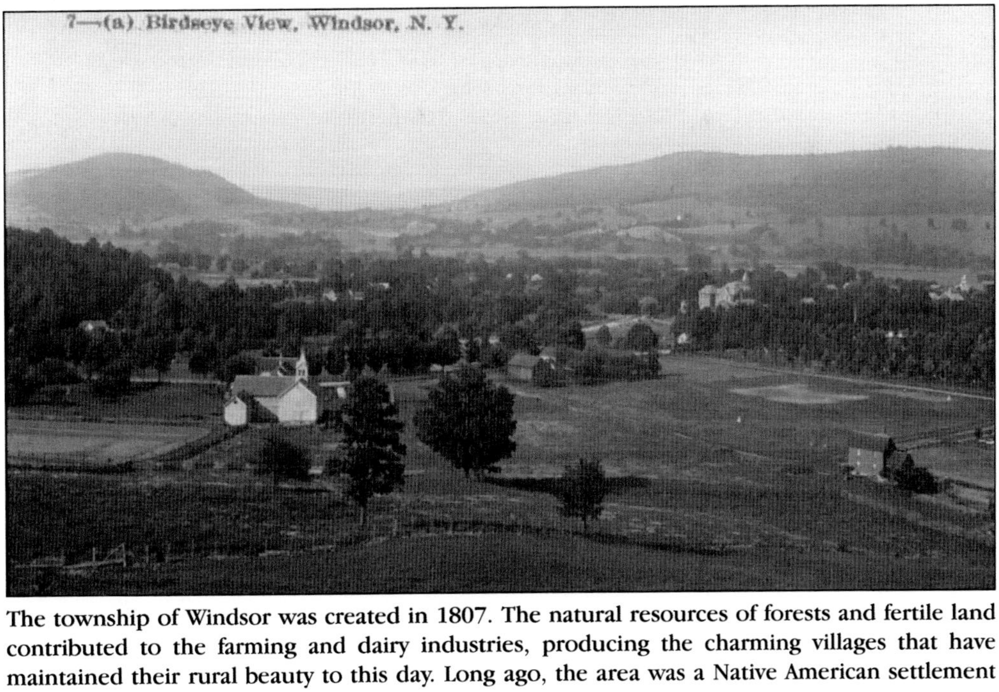

The township of Windsor was created in 1807. The natural resources of forests and fertile land contributed to the farming and dairy industries, producing the charming villages that have maintained their rural beauty to this day. Long ago, the area was a Native American settlement known as Old Onaquaga.

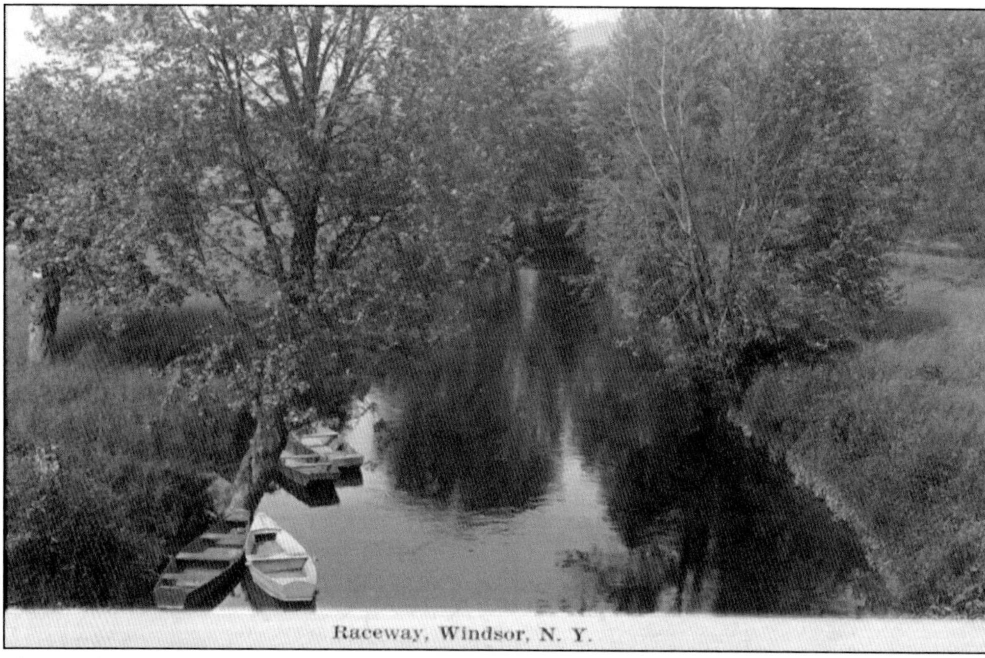

The Windsor Raceway was a beautiful channel, cut from the banks of the Susquehanna River as a course for water to run the local mills. This postcard was mailed in 1910.

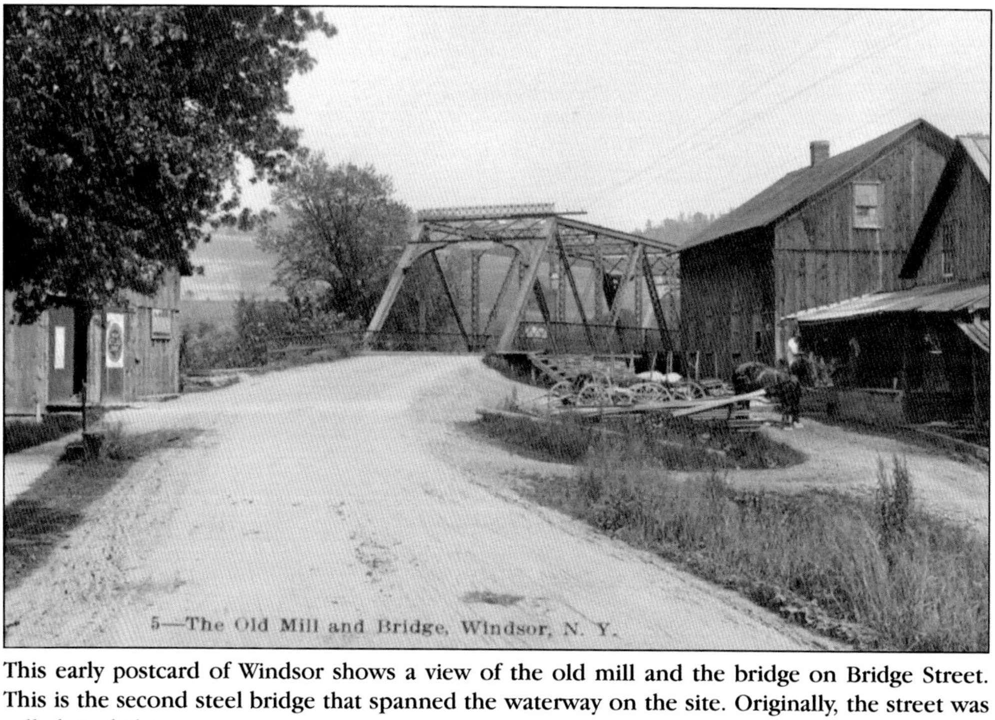

This early postcard of Windsor shows a view of the old mill and the bridge on Bridge Street. This is the second steel bridge that spanned the waterway on the site. Originally, the street was called Mud Flat.

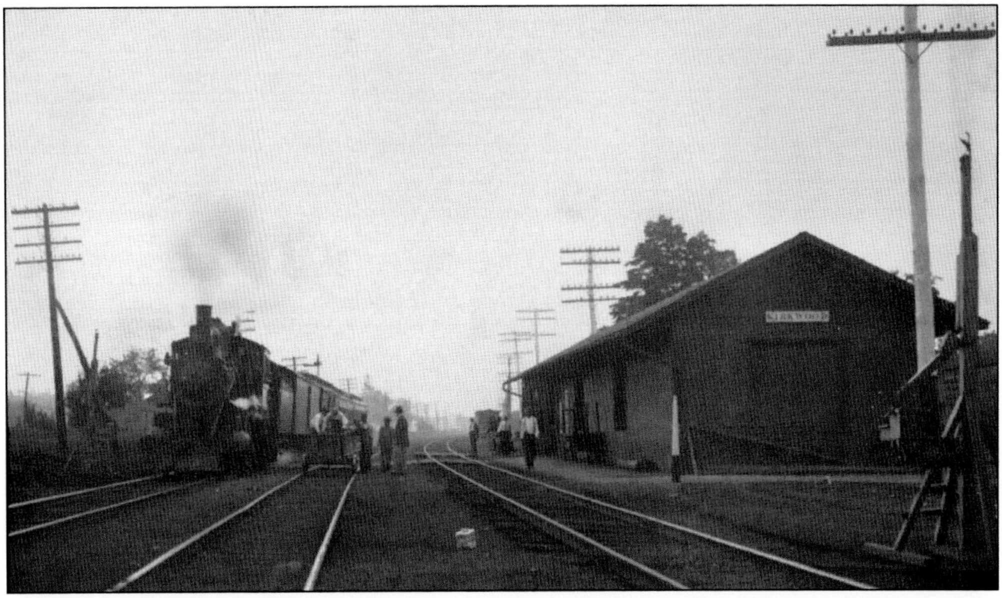

Kirkwood, organized in 1859, is one of the youngest towns in Broome County. For many years, it was on the principal route along the river between Binghamton and Great Bend, Pennsylvania. Kirkwood was noted for public houses so numerous as to be only 3 miles apart, offering stage travelers a surfeit of accommodations and refreshment. When the stagecoach era ended, Kirkwood capitalized on its location along the Erie Railroad tracks.

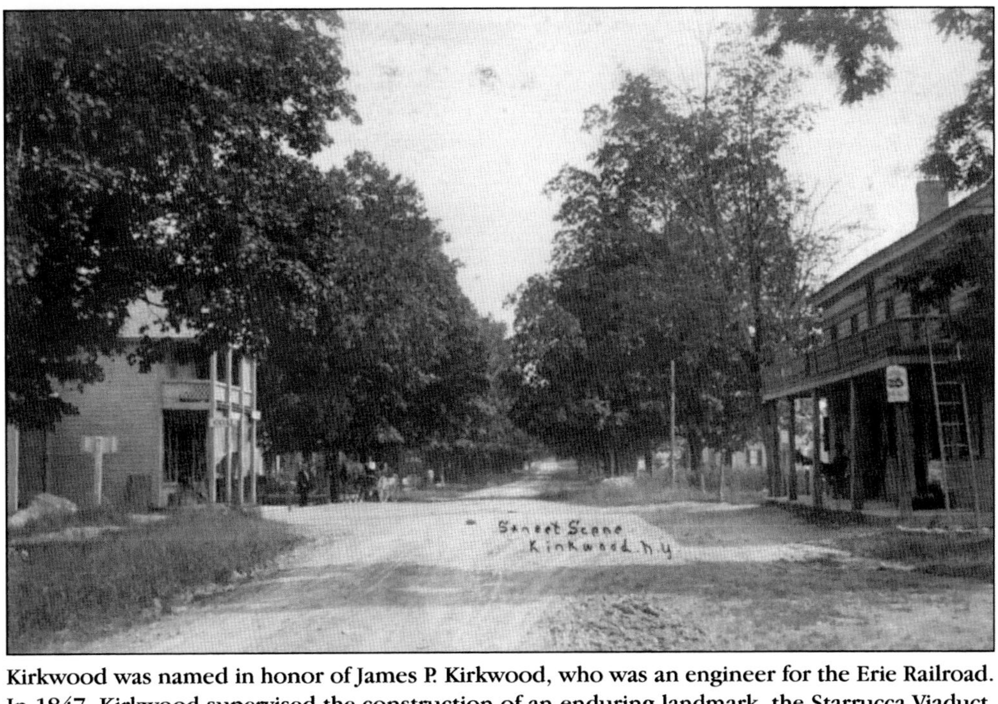

Kirkwood was named in honor of James P. Kirkwood, who was an engineer for the Erie Railroad. In 1847, Kirkwood supervised the construction of an enduring landmark, the Starrucca Viaduct. The first gristmill in the county was erected in this township. The postcard, an early view of a main thoroughfare, was mailed in 1910.

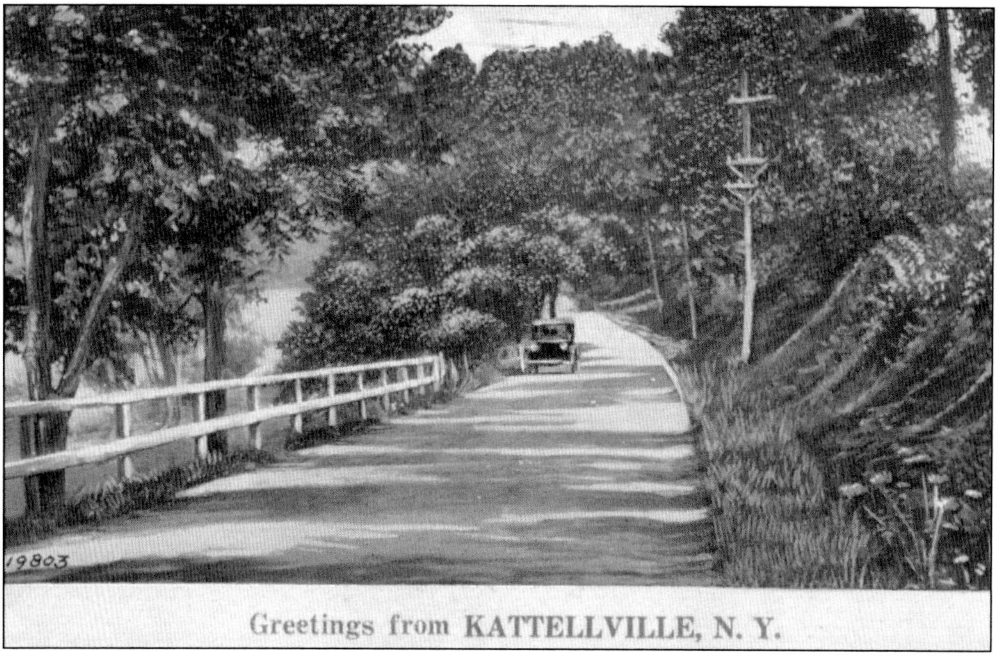

Kattellville in the township of Chenango was founded by Elias Kattell *c.* 1796. On a 1,000-acre tract, Kattell established a family dwelling, a tavern, and a distillery. On the banks of Gilbert's Creek, he constructed two sawmills, and eventually the waterway name was changed to Kattell Creek. This postcard was mailed in 1928.

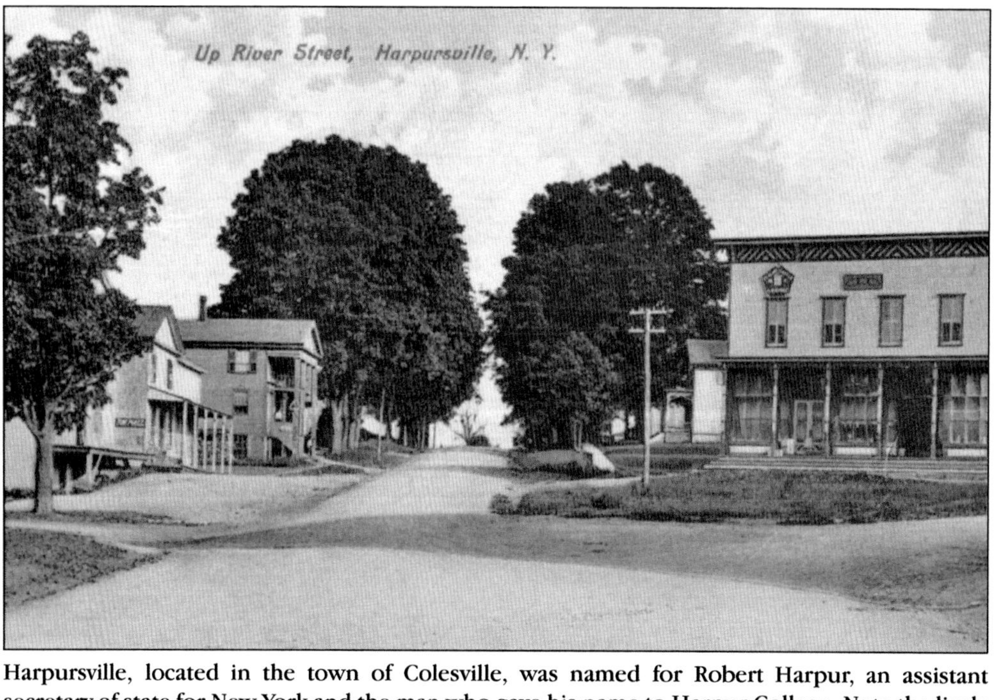

Harpursville, located in the town of Colesville, was named for Robert Harpur, an assistant secretary of state for New York and the man who gave his name to Harpur College. Note the lively mercantile life obvious in this 1910 photograph dating.

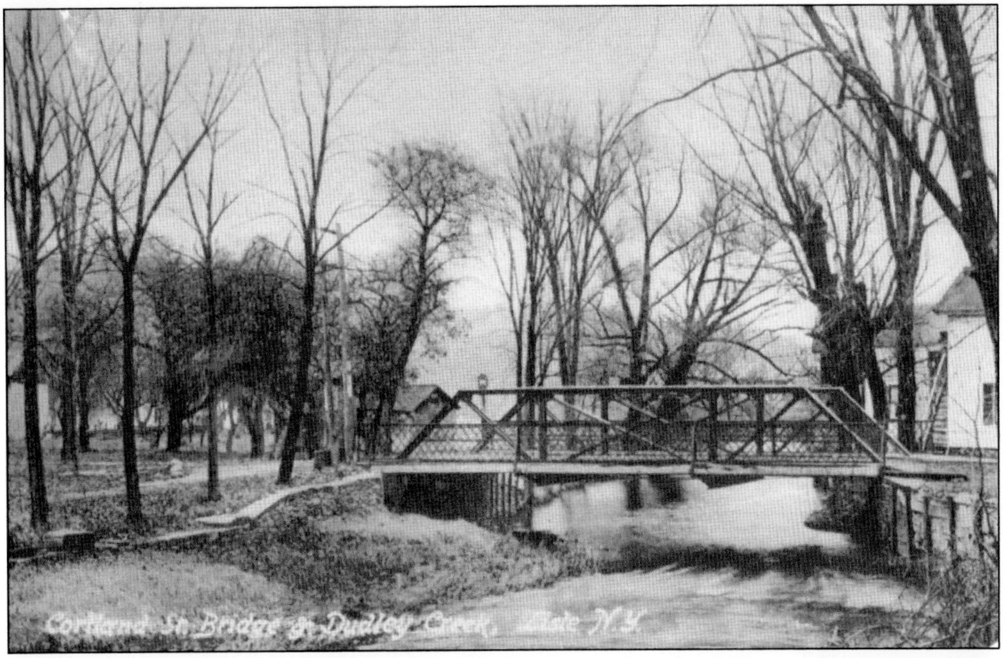

Lisle was first settled in 1791. The old Catskill and Ithaca Turnpike, built in 1796, was one of the most important roadways in this section of the country, and it passed directly through Lyle. The area is probably named for Lisle, France, at the suggestion of the Marquis de Lafayette, according to *Broome County Illustrated*, published in 1895.

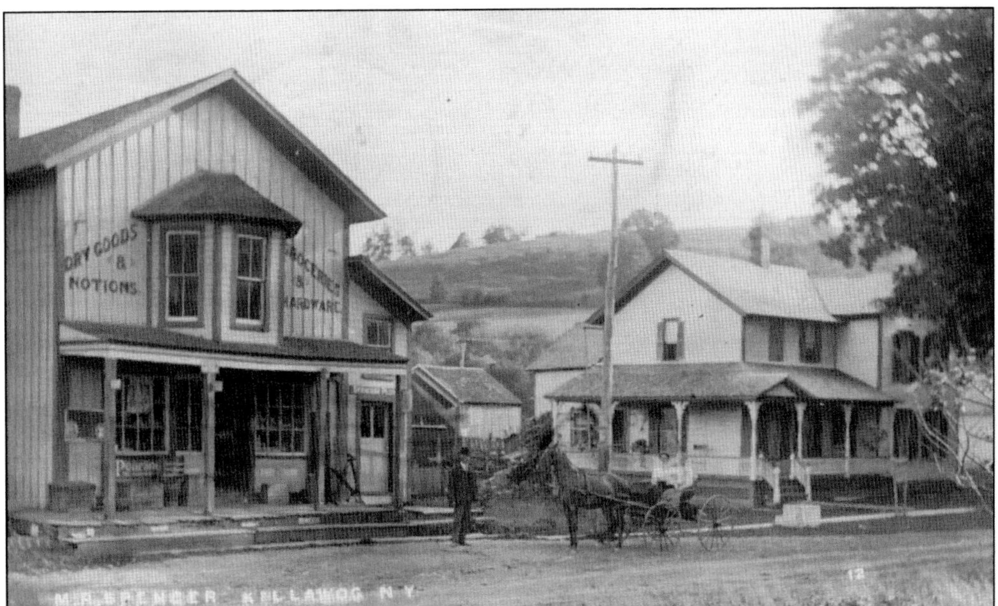

Long ago, Killawog was known as Union Village. *Broome County Illustrated* suggests the new name was considered a memorial for a Native American child named Abel Hartshorn, who was killed in 1810 by a team of horses in the town square. Another story traces the name's origin to the word kill, which in English and the original Dutch means channel or creek.

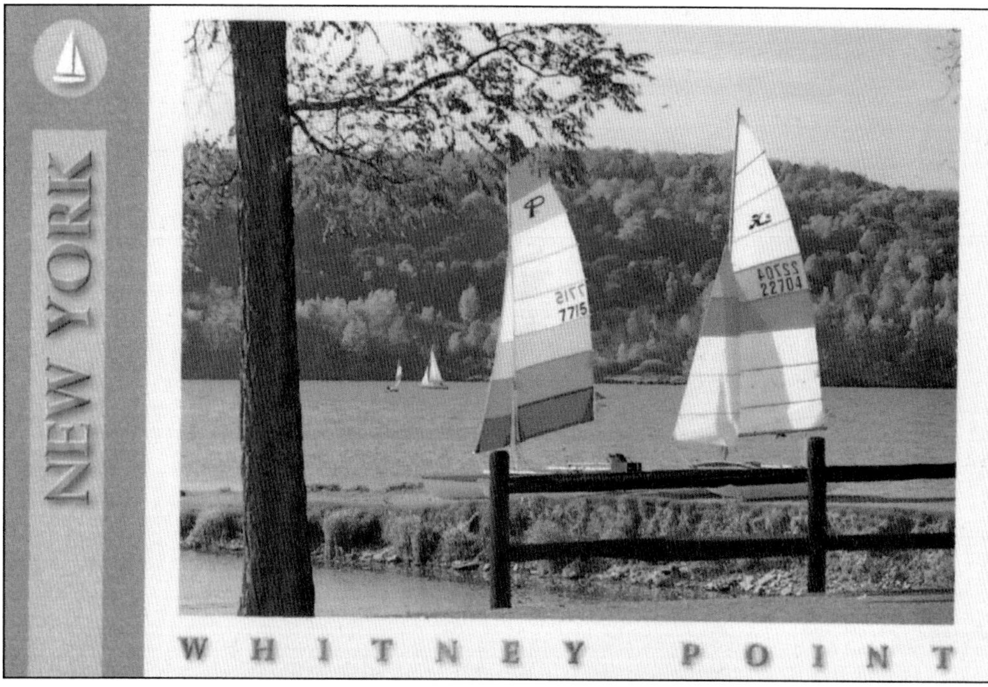

Whitney Point in the town of Triangle was formed from Lisle in 1831. In 1942, the Whitney Point Dam was built to control the power of the Otselic River. Three county parks have evolved around the picturesque reservoir. Ice fishing on the lake inspired the event known as the Almost Yearly Crappie Derby, which attracts hundreds of participants and spectators. This postcard is a modern photograph by Ed Aswad.

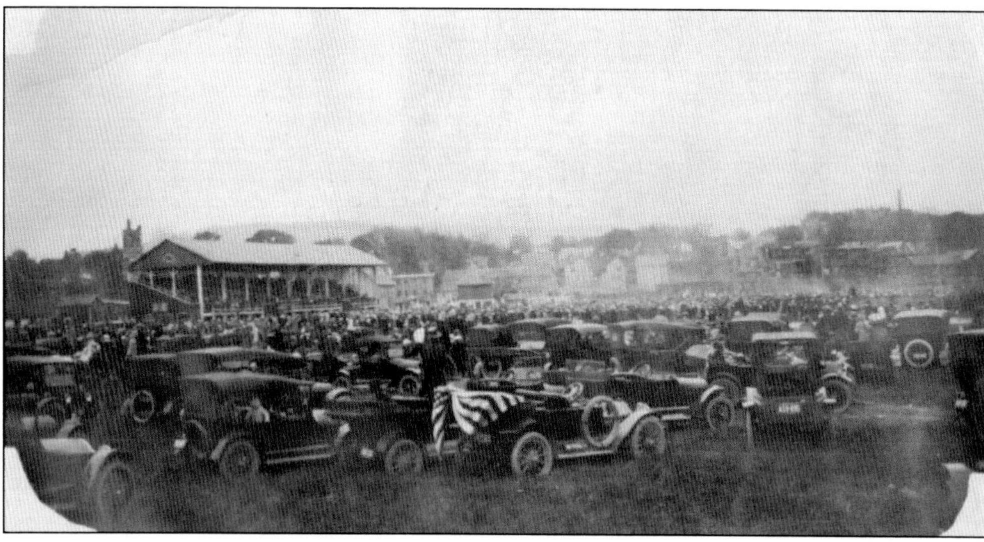

John Patterson settled this land in 1791, and for a time it was known as Patterson's Point. But in 1824, it became Whitney's Point in honor of Thomas Whitney. Since 1871, it has been known as the home of the Broome County Fairgrounds. This postcard shows the fairgrounds in the 1920s. In 1897, the entire commercial center of Whitney's Point was destroyed by fire. The only buildings left standing were churches.

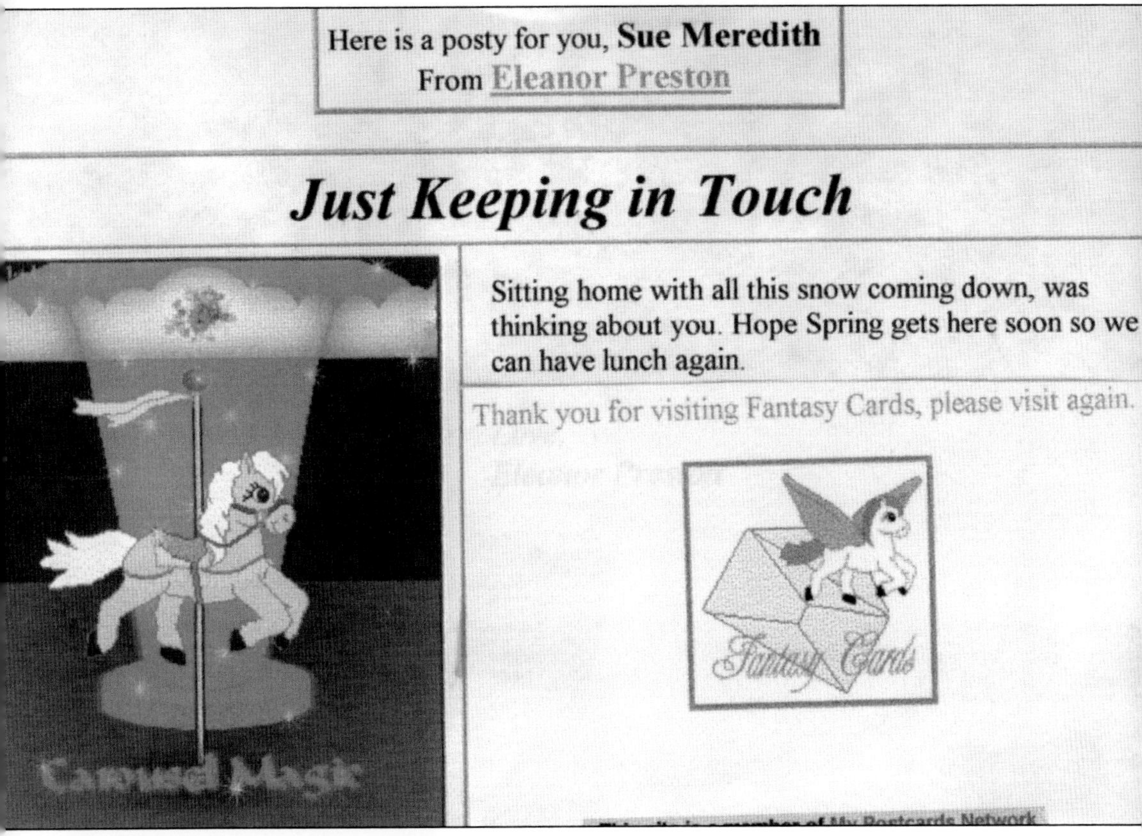

Postcards have gone online. At last count, there were more than 24,000 websites relating to postcards. Postcards can be viewed, traded, bought or sold, all without leaving the keyboard. Postcards are also delivered on the computer, often as singing and dancing figures. Shirley MacKinley operates Fantasy Cards, which offers free electronic greeting cards for all occasions. This carousel horse is from her collection. Sponsor banners that come with each salutation are the advertisements that pay her expenses. Perhaps someday, computer notes will be treasured mementos, and the future may hold even more remarkable changes in greetings. However, many dedicated historians and collectors will always favor the vintage postcards.

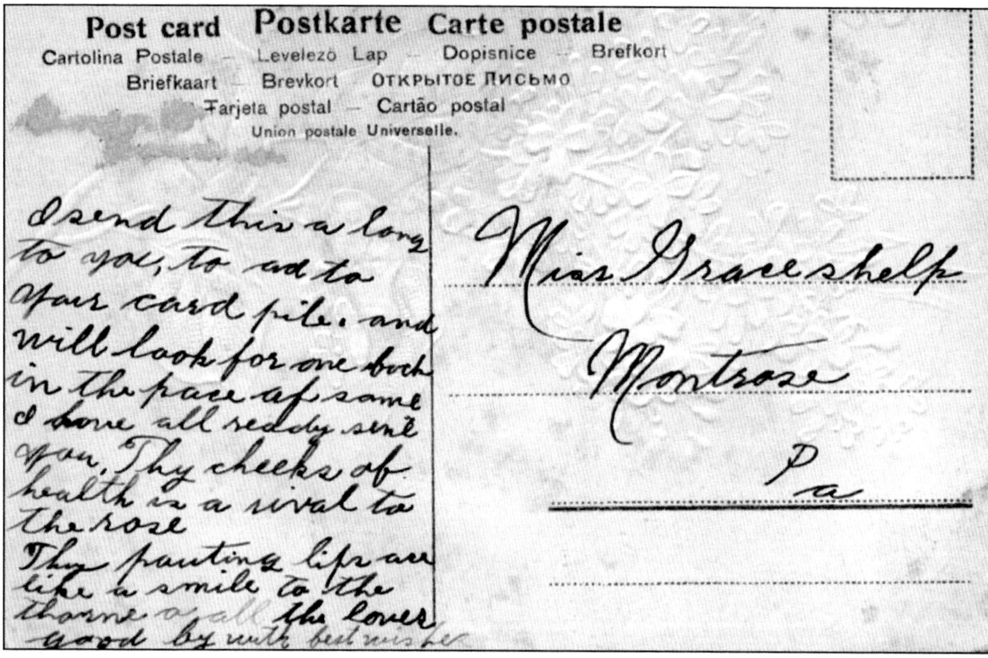

Both of these postcards are interesting because of the information recorded on the back. The first postcard is sent from Binghamton for a lady's postcard collection, and continues with words of love. The second postcard, sent in 1911, records a poignant bit of history as a farm is about to lose 44 head of cattle to a "dreadful disease." Even a payment from the state of New York could not compensate for the heartache of death.

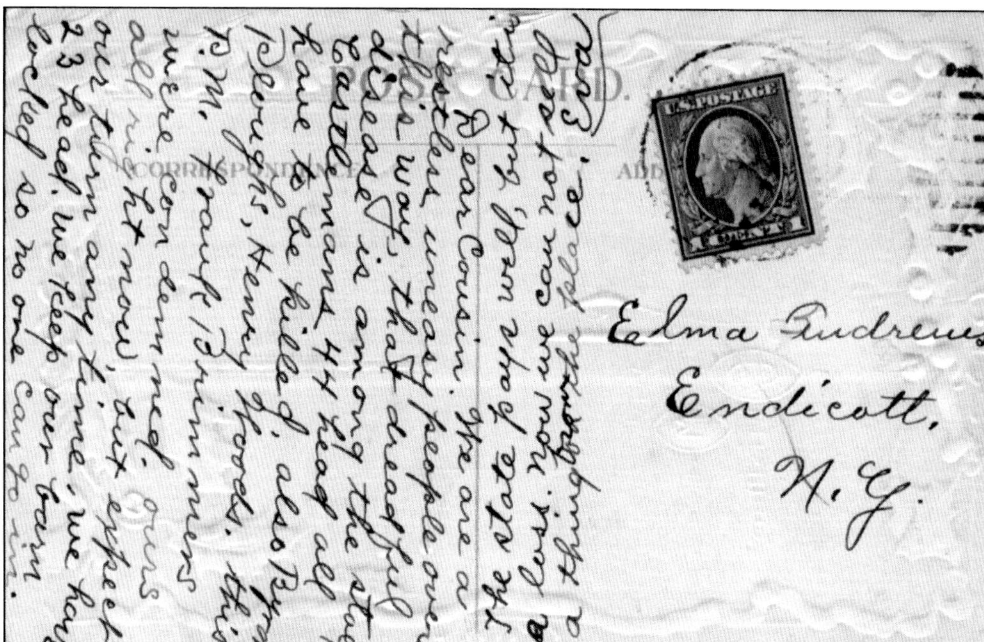

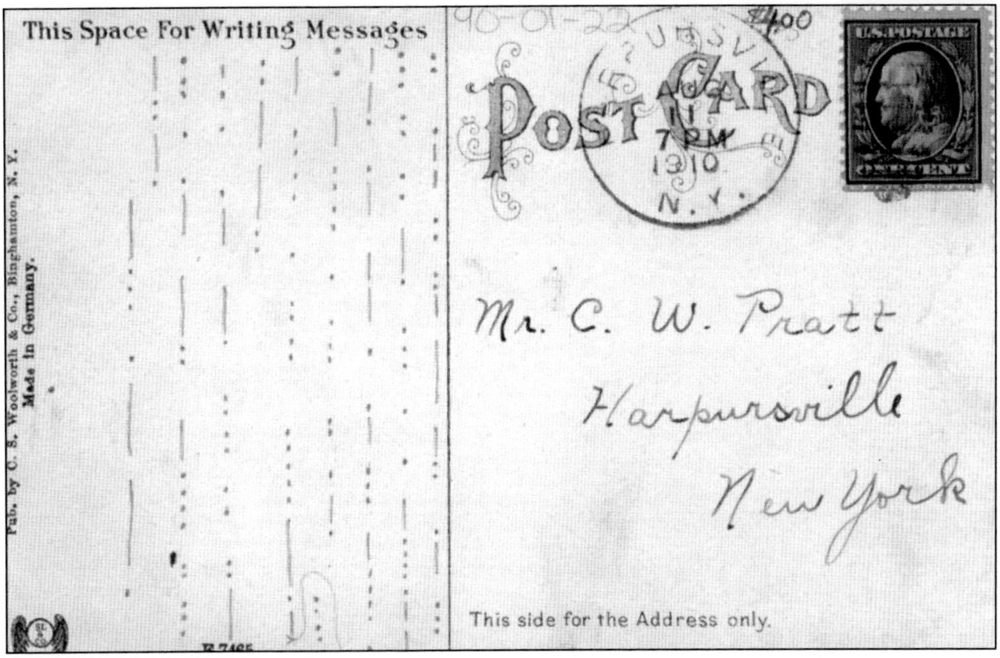

An interesting fact about the postcard above, mailed in 1910, is that its message is written in Morse code. The second postcard, sent in 1912, is also written with many words encrypted for privacy. Anyone who is able to decipher these messages is asked to get in touch with the authors. The information will be included in a subsequent volume, with credit going to the code breaker.

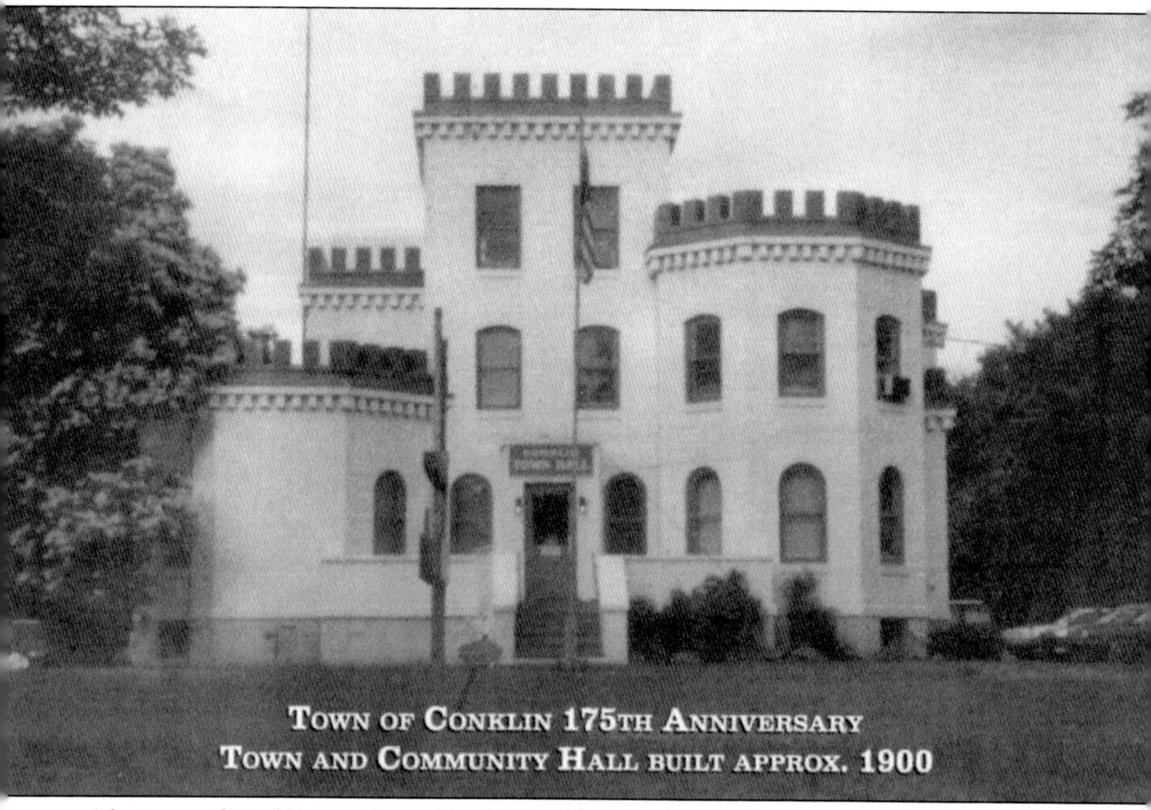

TOWN OF CONKLIN 175TH ANNIVERSARY
TOWN AND COMMUNITY HALL BUILT APPROX. 1900

The town of Conklin was formed in 1824, with the original village named Milburn. The name Conklin was chosen to honor founding settler Judge John Conklin, who arrived to the area in 1817. Divided from Chenango County, Conklin is the second smallest civil division in Broome County. An interesting landmark is the town hall, better known as "the Castle." It was constructed in 1900 by Althus Corby, who was enamored with European castles. As in all buildings that are old and unique, it has a colorful history that includes accounts of a deranged woman being locked in the tower and stories of a well-known ghost. Upon the deaths of the original inhabitants, in 1920, the building became a Universal Spirit Church, owned by a woman whose companion was the shade of Rudolph Valentino. During the Great Depression era, the building provided respite for destitute children. By 1944, George F. Johnson had donated the Castle to the town of Conklin, with the understanding that it would forever remain a stronghold of temperance—no alcohol. Today, it is the location of government offices, the site of community meetings, and the home of the Conklin Historical Society.

Four

Before and After, and Modern Postcards

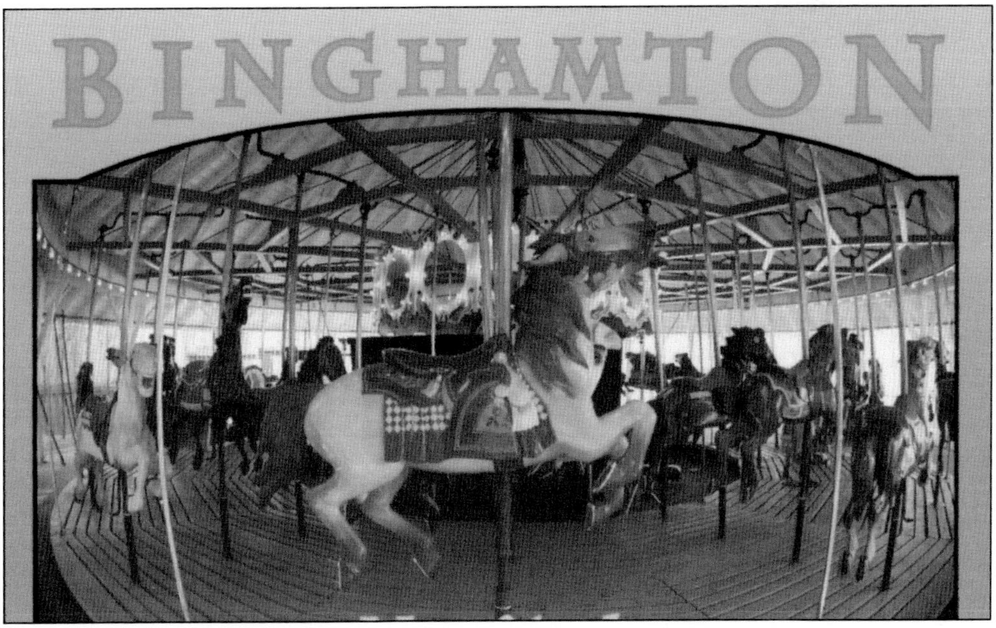

The presence of six Allan Herschell antique merry-go-rounds has earned Broome County the title of carousel capitol of the world. All six were donated by George F. Johnson and family and are located in public parks throughout the area. Built between 1919 and 1934, the machines are constructed in the county fair style. A special feature of these carousels is that they have no stationary animals—all are "jumpers." The carousels have been placed on the National Register of Historic Places. Preserved and operational, carousel rides remain forever free and continue to inspire dreams of beautiful possibilities.

All of the new postcard photographs and the "after" pictures in this chapter are by Ed Aswad.

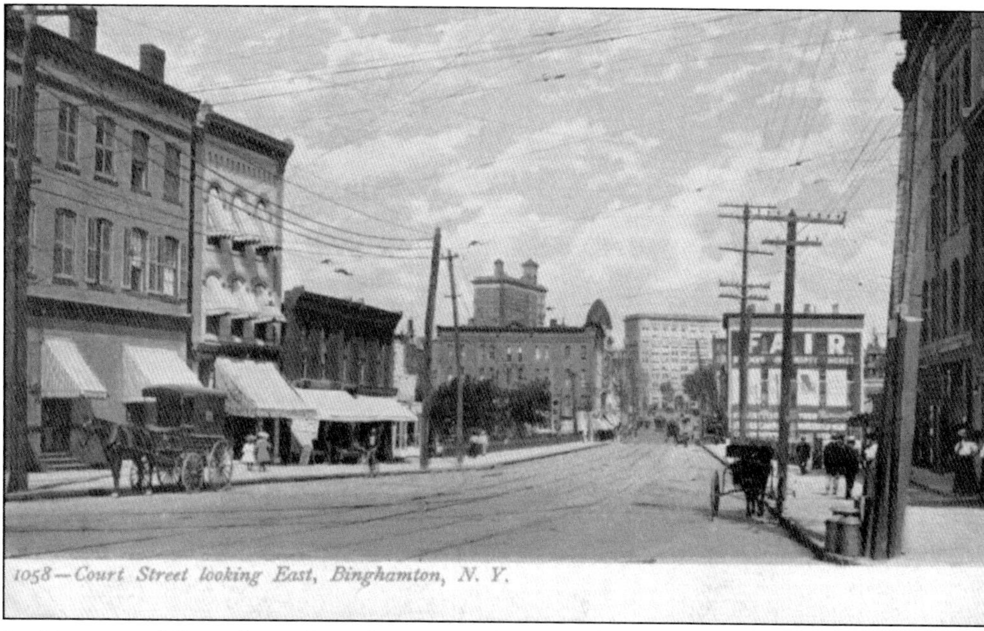

Looking toward Court Street from the corner of Main and Front Streets, the tides of change are very evident. The horse and buggy has disappeared, as has the cleanup crew necessary to remove what the horse left behind. Milk cans no longer sit on the corner. A new bridge spans the river. The building on the left corner was torn down just after the new view was printed.

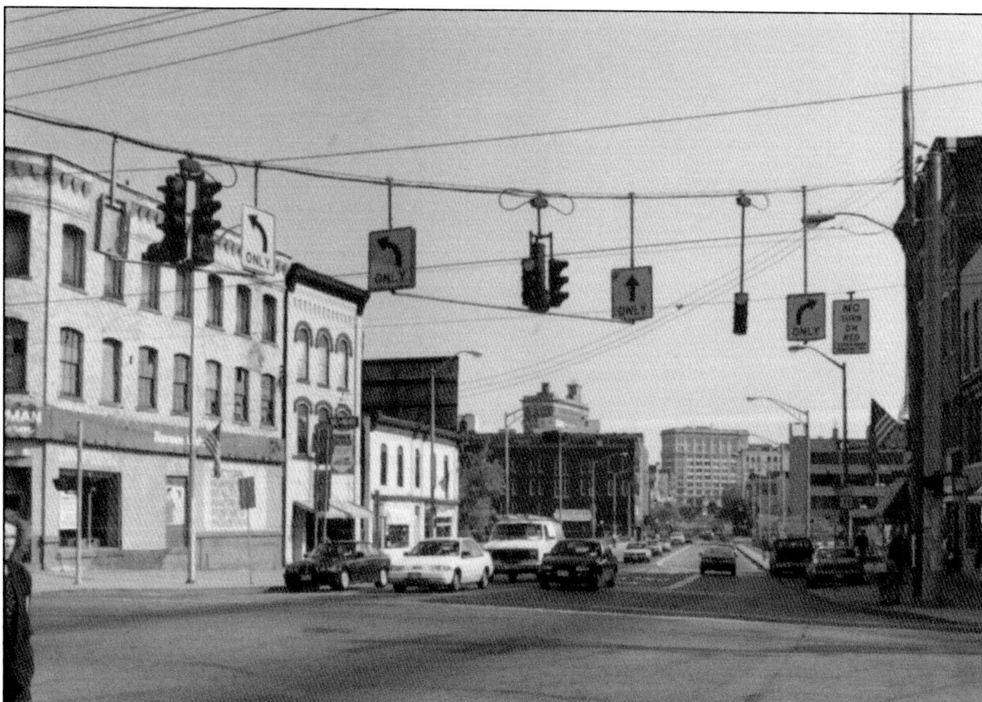

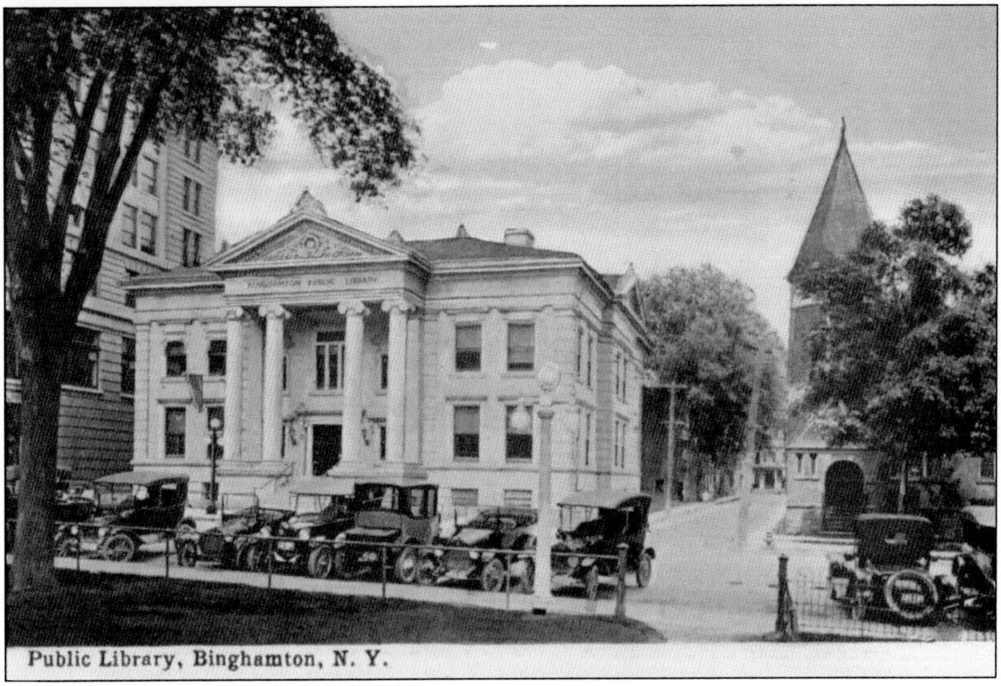

The Binghamton Public Library on Exchange Street was built in 1904 as a gift of Andrew Carnegie. In 1985, it became the Broome County Public Library. In 2000, the library was scheduled to move out of the building and into another space. At that time, plans for the future of the empty library had not yet been made. In the earlier view, the First Universalist Church, built in 1863, stands to the right of the library. The church was demolished in 1929 and the site is now occupied by the Binghamton Savings Bank.

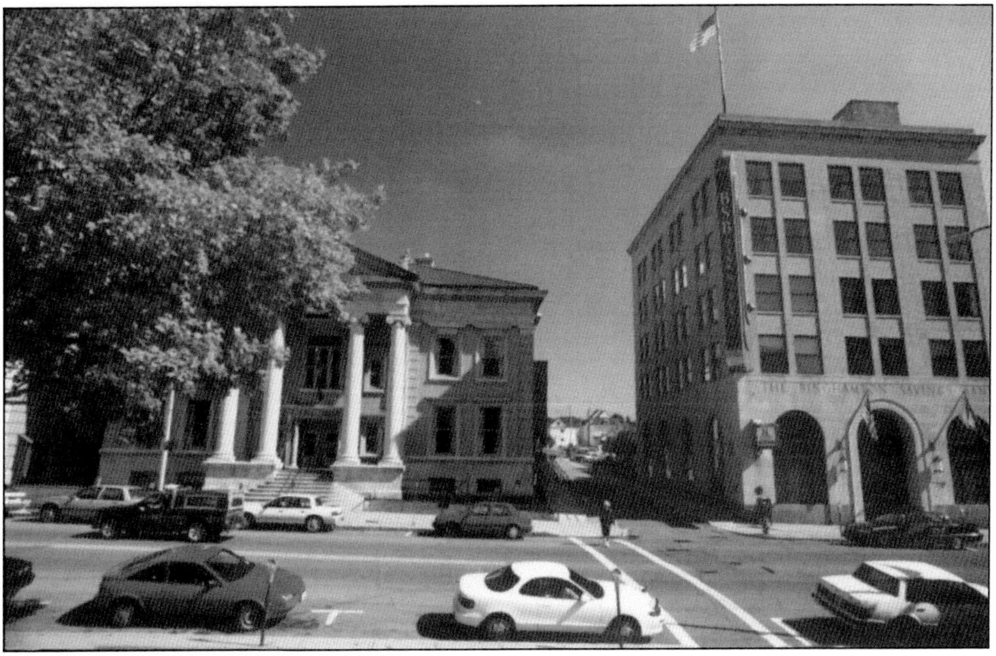

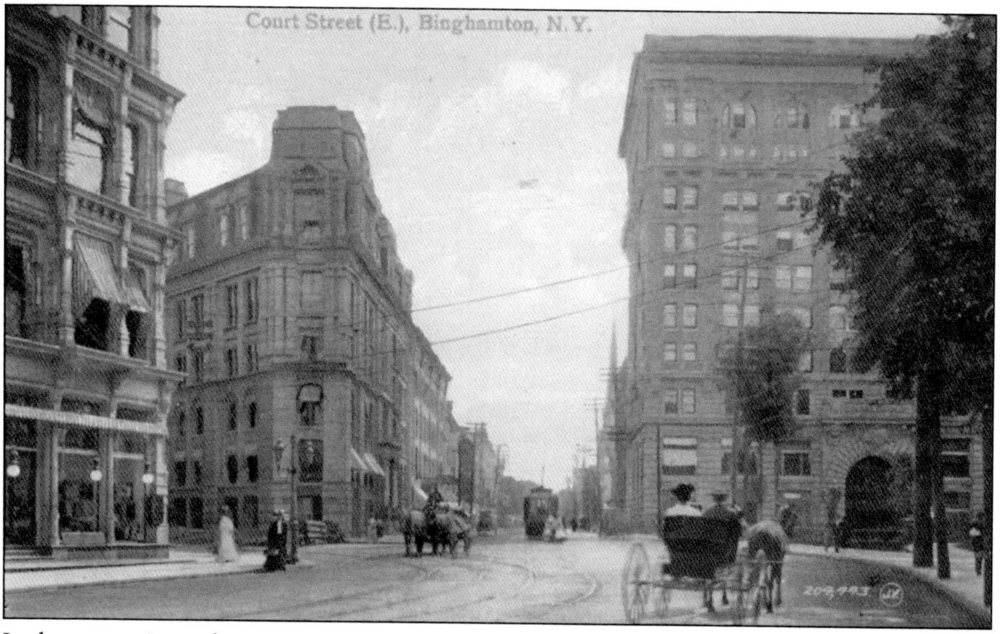

In these two views, the structures remain much the same. The old postcard was mailed in 1909, and the new one is from 1998. At the center is the Phelps Bank building, constructed in 1871. A bank has been housed on that corner for more than a century. The top floor has burned and remodeling has been done to the lower levels, but it remains an impressive historic structure. To the left is the Perry Block, a rare example of a cast-iron building. It is now on the National Historic Register. To the right is the Security Mutual Insurance building, constructed in 1903.

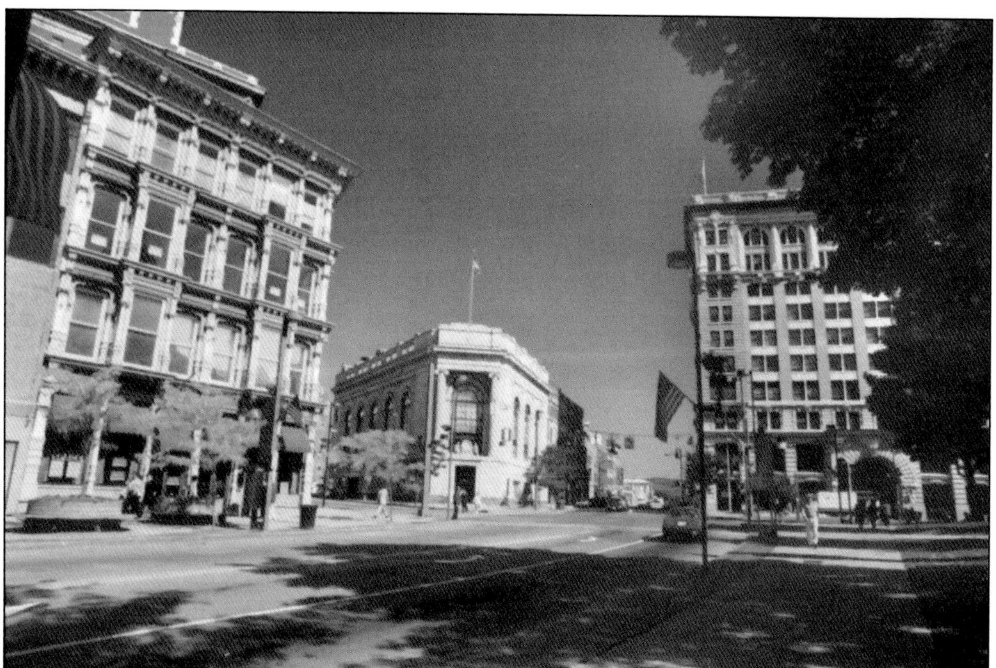

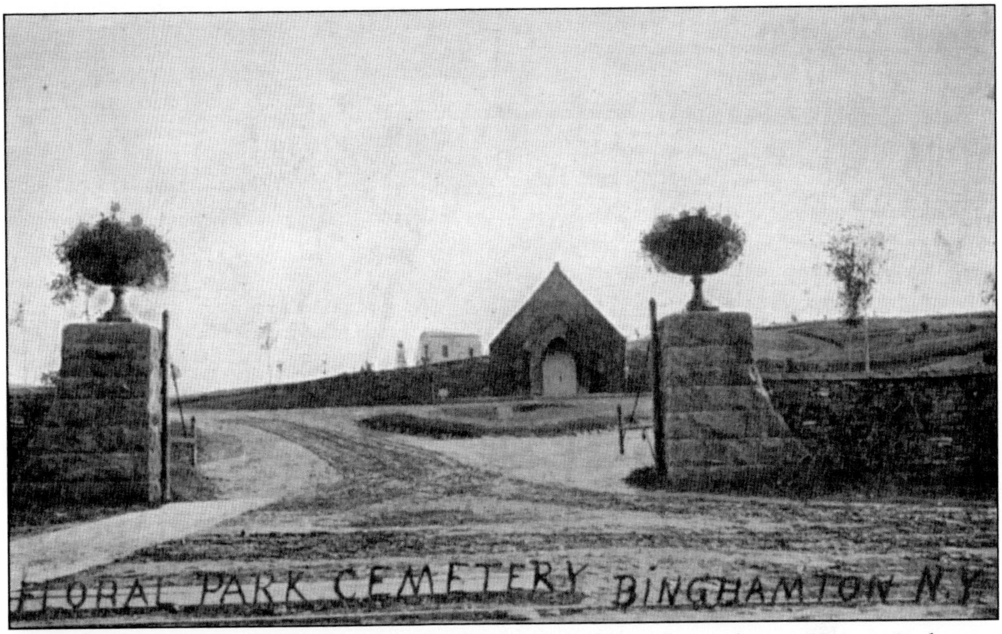

Floral Park Cemetery in Johnson City, incorporated in 1891, is located on a 50-acre site known as the Villa Park tract. It has developed into a shady retreat for the living as well as the dead. Greenery abounds throughout the well-kept paths and rows of markers. A stone chapel is a notable feature, now even more beautiful as the stone has weathered.

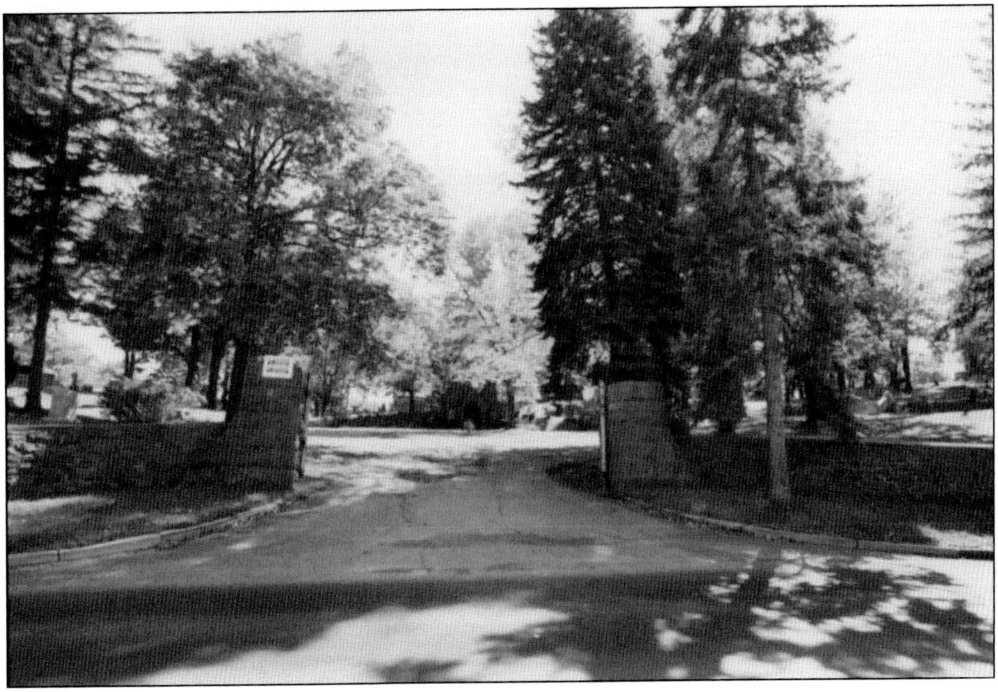

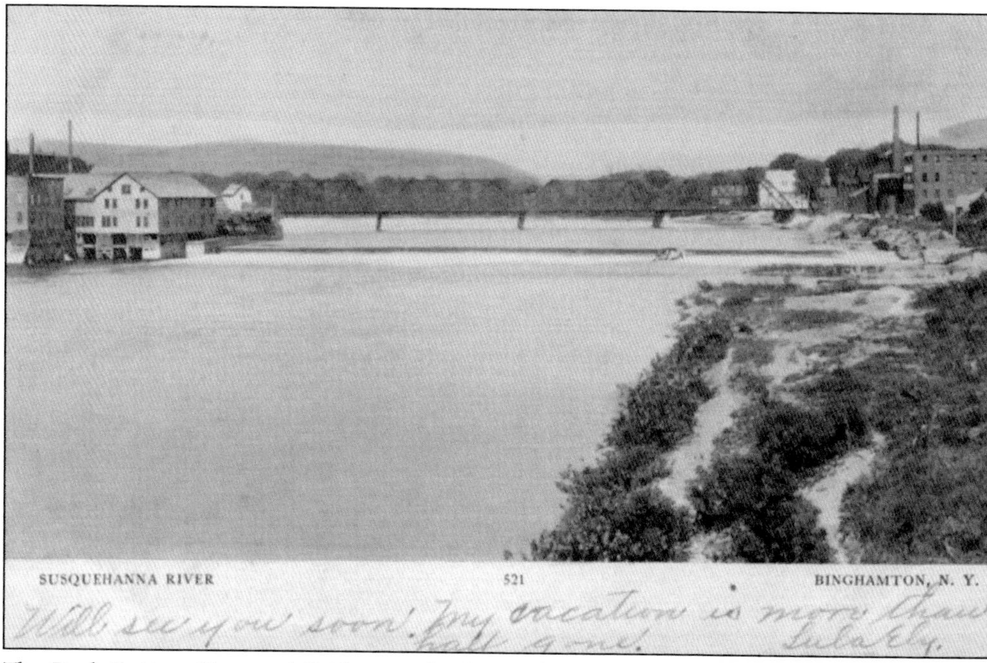

The Rock Bottom Dam and Bridge on the Susquehanna River in Binghamton has had many changes over the years. The mill on the left side of the river is completely gone, and the bridge is no longer open for any kind of traffic. Nature is claiming the iron structure as its own, with vines, trees, and wild plants covering the expanse in foliage. The Crowley Food Company on the right side of the river on Conklin Avenue is still producing quality dairy products. The Park Diner, also on Conklin Avenue, is one of the few facilities built to take advantage of the spectacular views of the Susquehanna River. It is a neighborhood institution for good food and riverside dining.

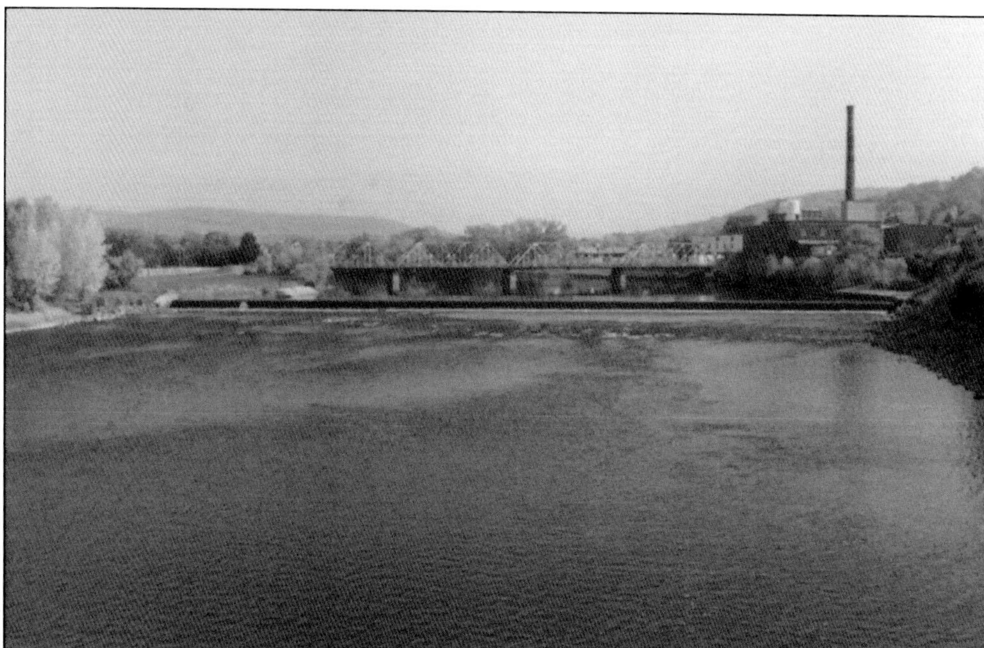

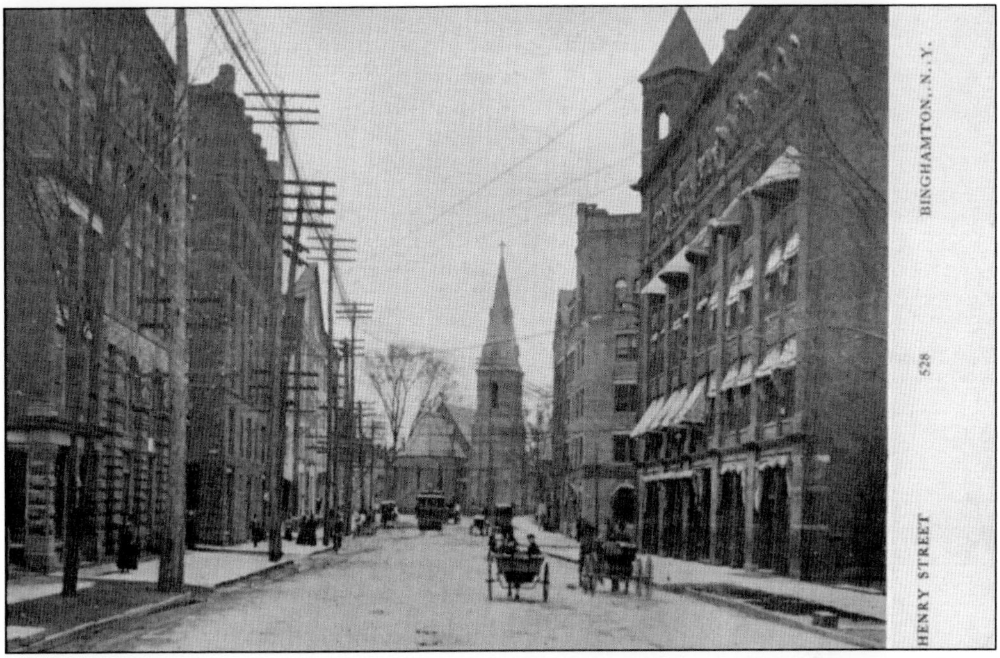

Henry Street, looking west, has undergone so many changes that it is almost unrecognizable in the earlier view. However, the spires of the landmark Christ's Church still tower above the road, which has gone from dirt to asphalt and from horses and trolley tracks to car congestion.

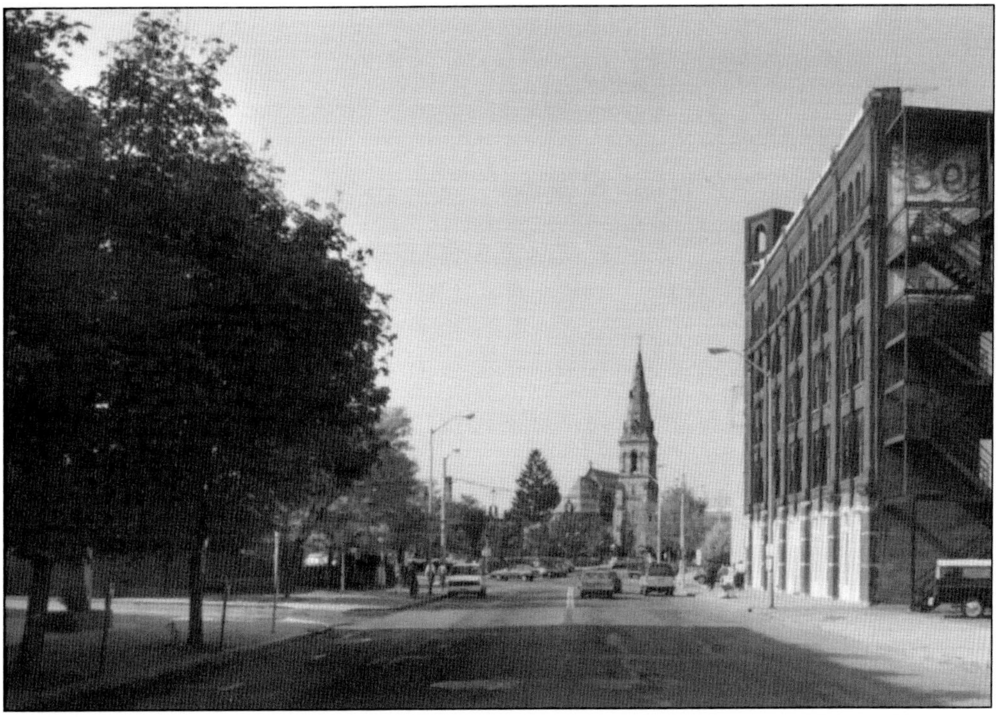

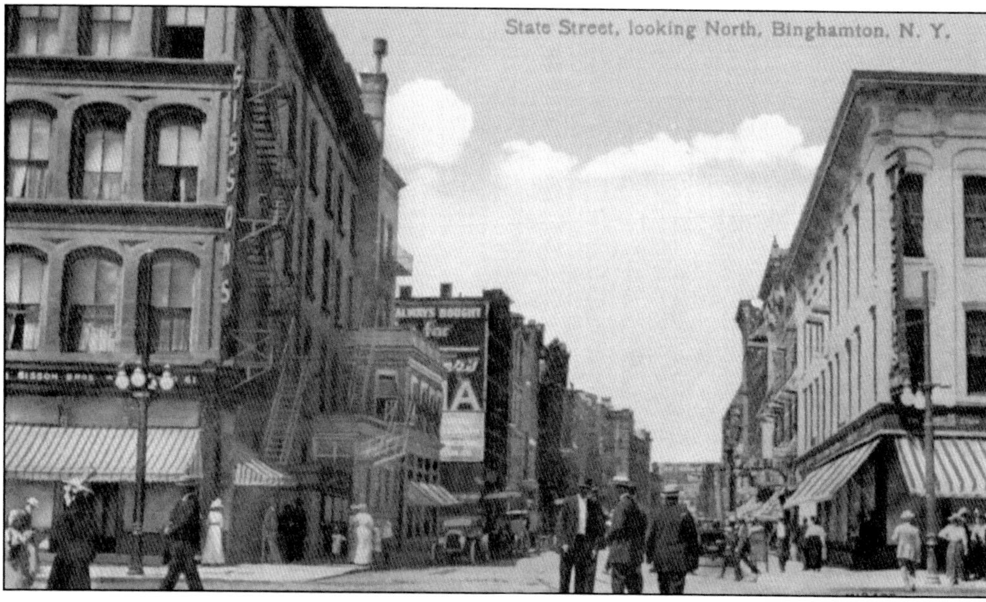

In 1842, talented cabinetmaker Benjamin Sisson and his family stopped in Binghamton on their way west and decided to stay. They opened a store in 1848, advertising "groceries and Yankee notions." The building, on the corner of Court and State Streets, replaced one of the area's earliest pioneer log cabins. Fire destroyed the business in 1862. The store was rebuilt in 1864 and although the building still exists, it and some nearby structures have been remodeled according to modern concepts to the point of being nearly unrecognizable. At one time, State Street was a canal; later, it was a dirt road; today, it is macadam and concrete. The charm, the trolley tracks, and the hordes of shoppers have moved into memory. Five radio stations are currently located in the Sisson building on the left corner.

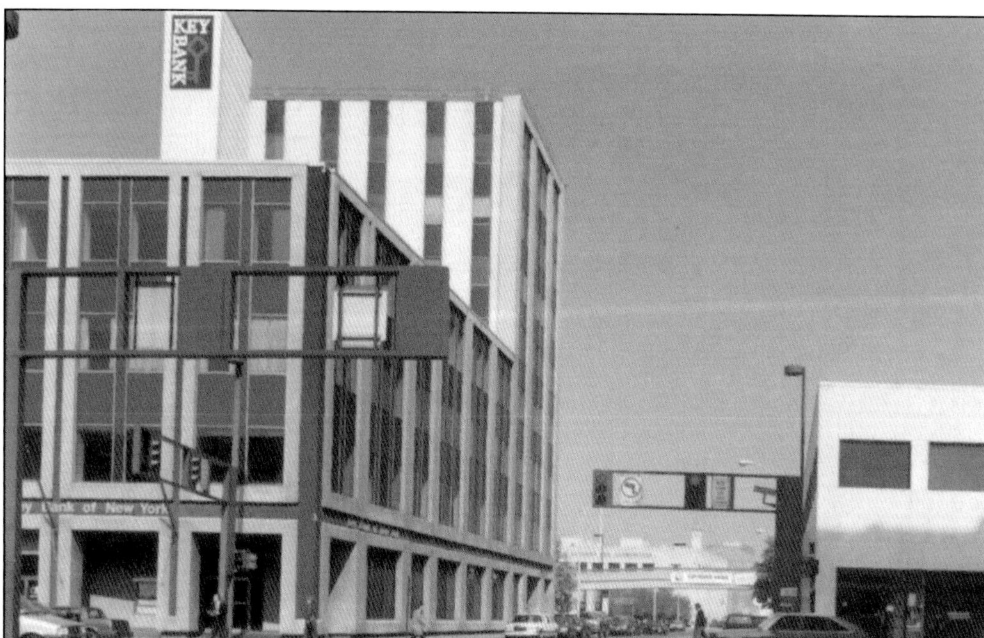

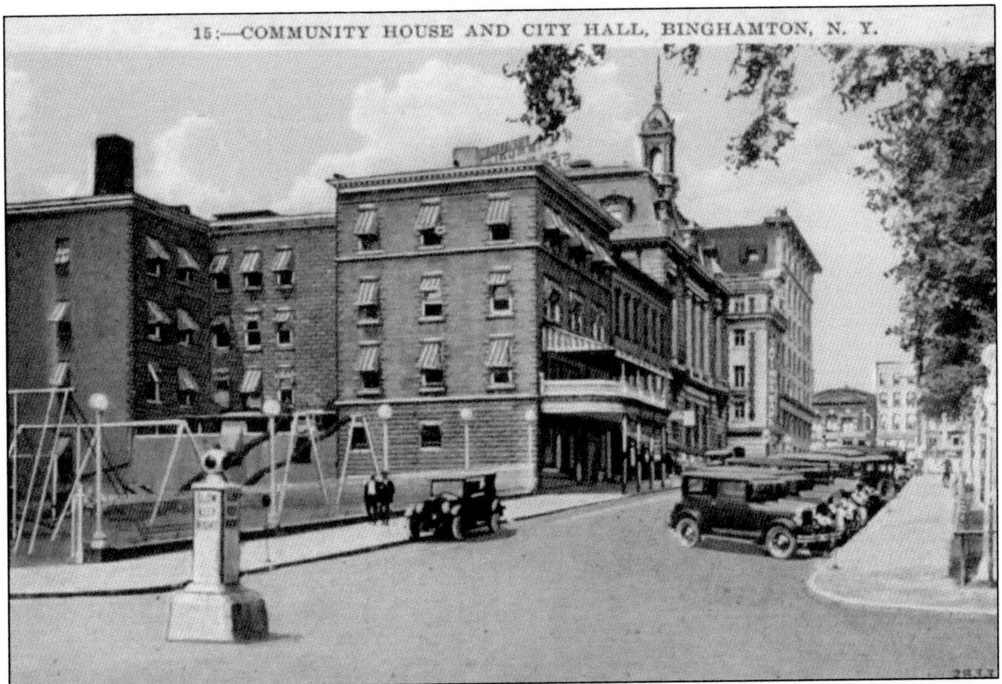

The city hall was built in the French Renaissance design in 1897. Although it is no longer used as a government site, it still exists as a hotel and restaurant. It is located in an area where progress is spelled "parking." Thus, the historic structures and the park to the left have been transformed into a multilayer ramp.

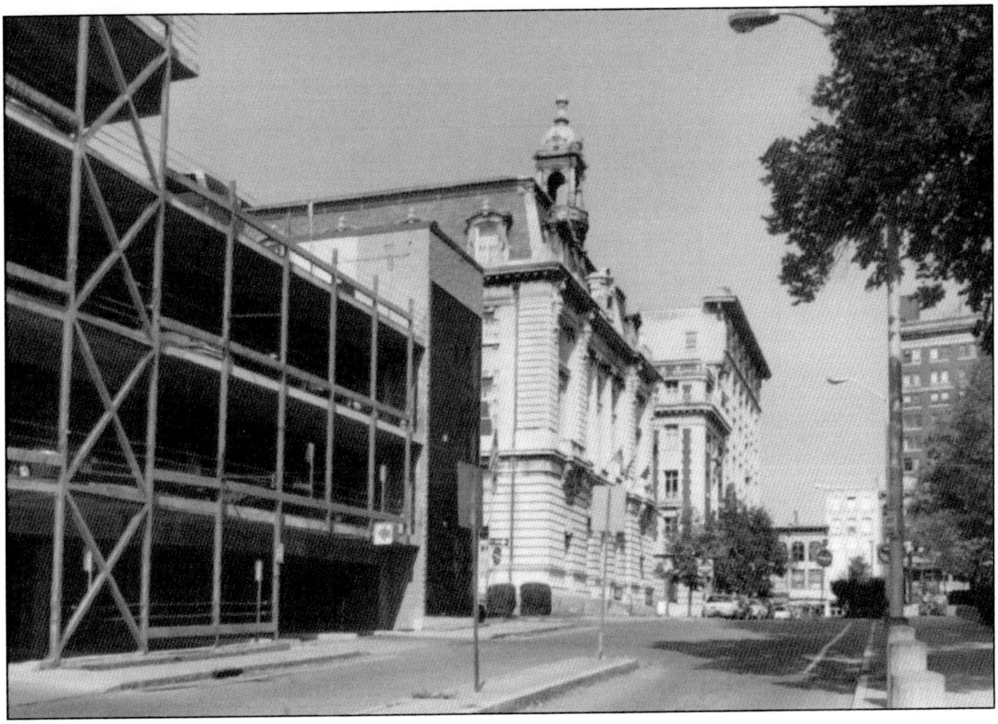

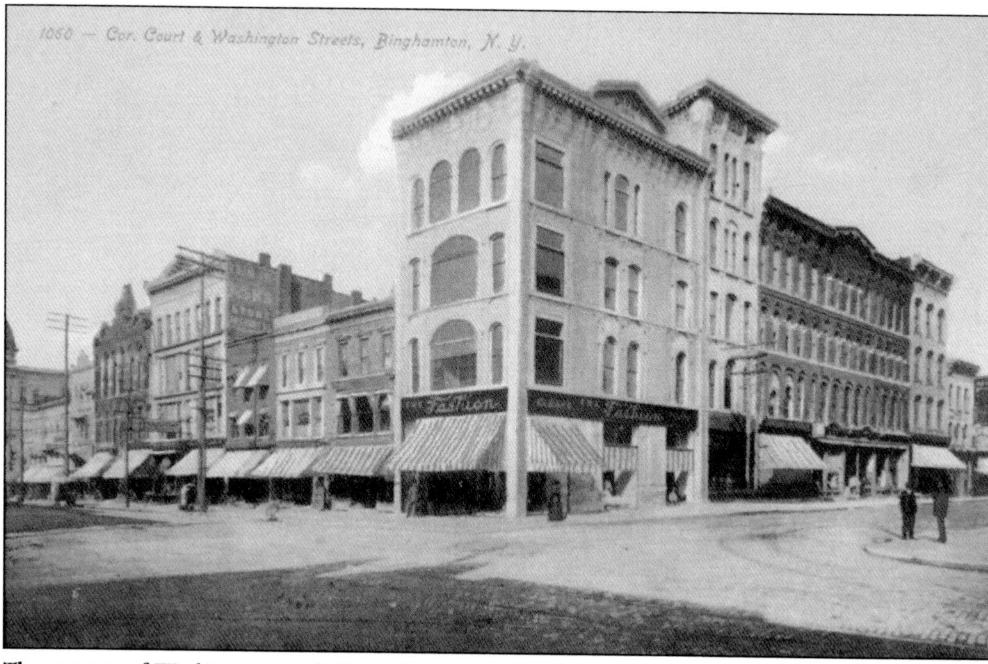

The corner of Washington and Court Streets in Binghamton shows dramatic changes. Parts of the old buildings remain, although hidden under the guise of updating. Note that the top three floors on the corner building are missing, along with the striped awnings and the character.

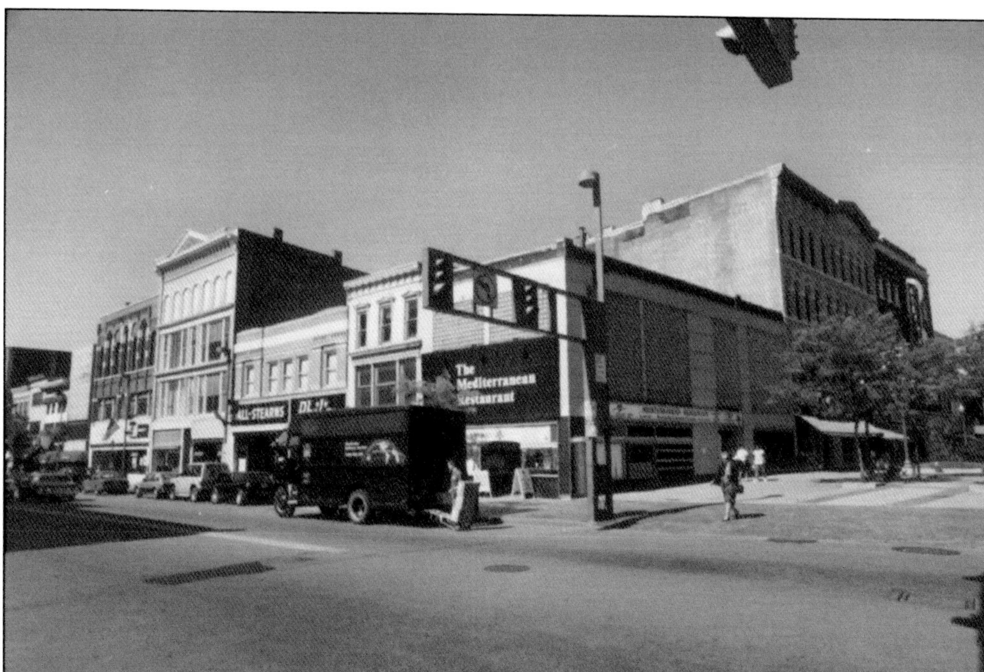

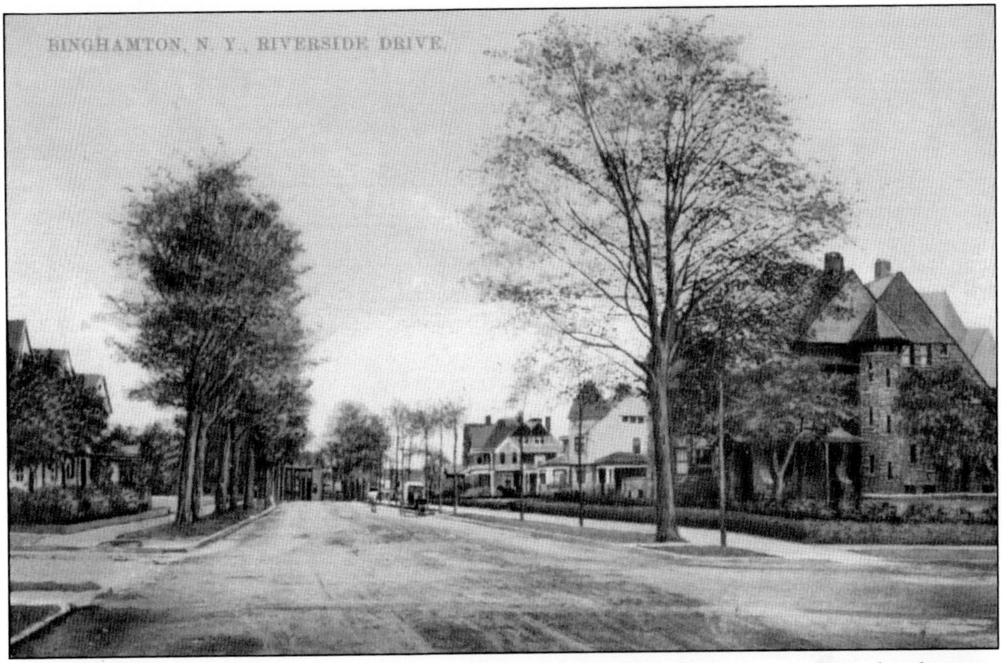

Riverside Drive at one time was a rough corduroy road made of logs. It progressed to become a neighborhood of exclusive mansions. Today, it is an area of apartment buildings, houses of worship, and professional offices. The mansion at the far end of the street has been replaced with a bridge. When Memorial Bridge was being planned, the Kilmer family was so distressed that they considered moving from their homes, believing the quiet avenue would become a noisy, busy thoroughfare. In some ways they were right, as horsepower replaced the horse and buggy. One Kilmer mansion has been preserved and is in use as a temple.

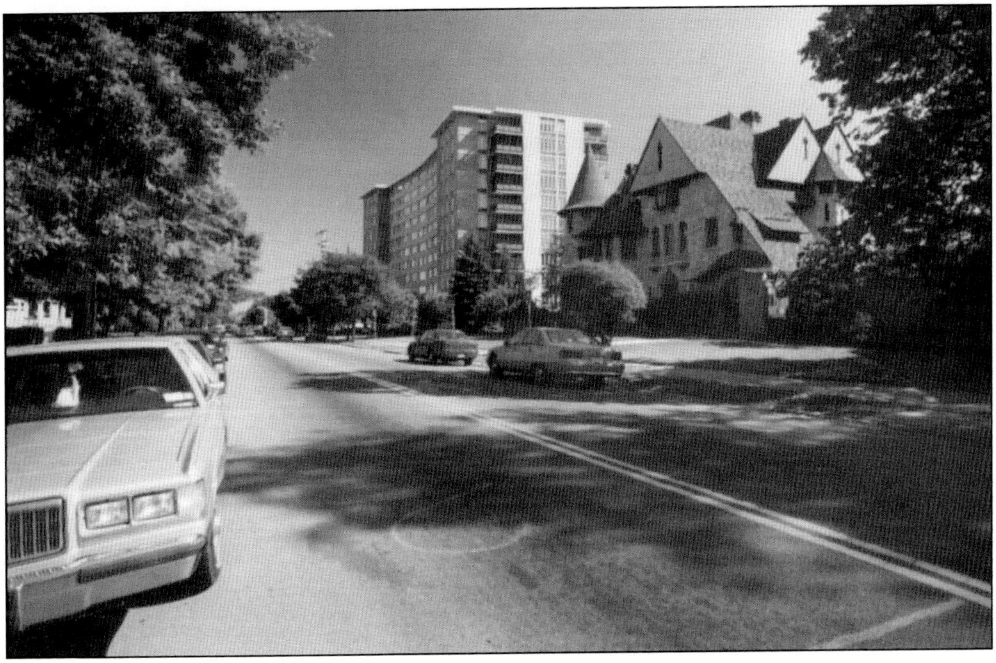

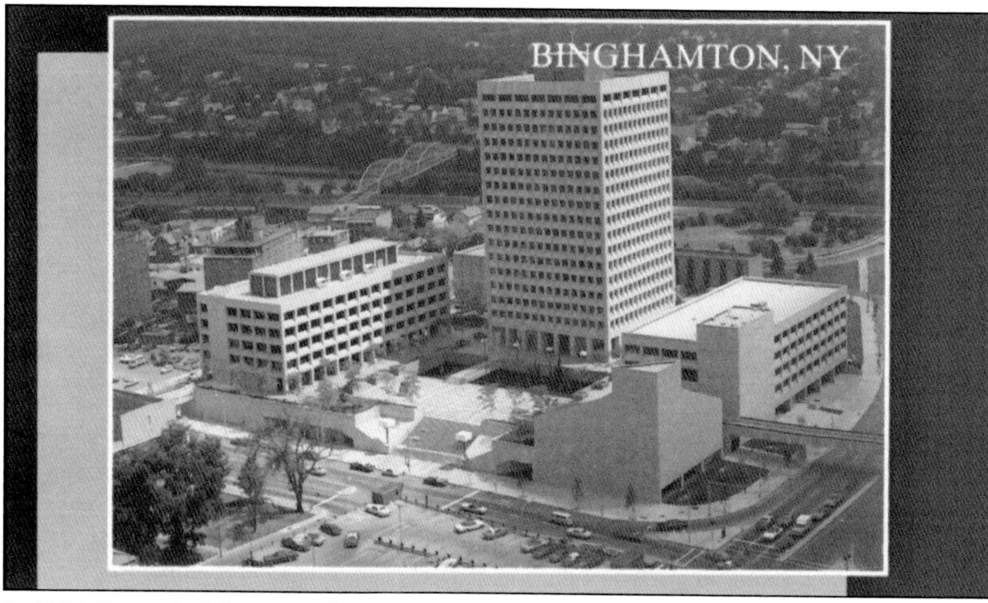

In 1981, fire again left a tragic footnote in Broome history. The 17-story New York State office building in the government plaza in Binghamton became an example of modern technology gone wrong. Flames in a transformer spread lethal PCBs and dioxins into every crevice of the entire structure. It took $40 million and 13 years of intensive cleaning, testing, and removal of deadly debris before the building could be safely reopened in 1994.

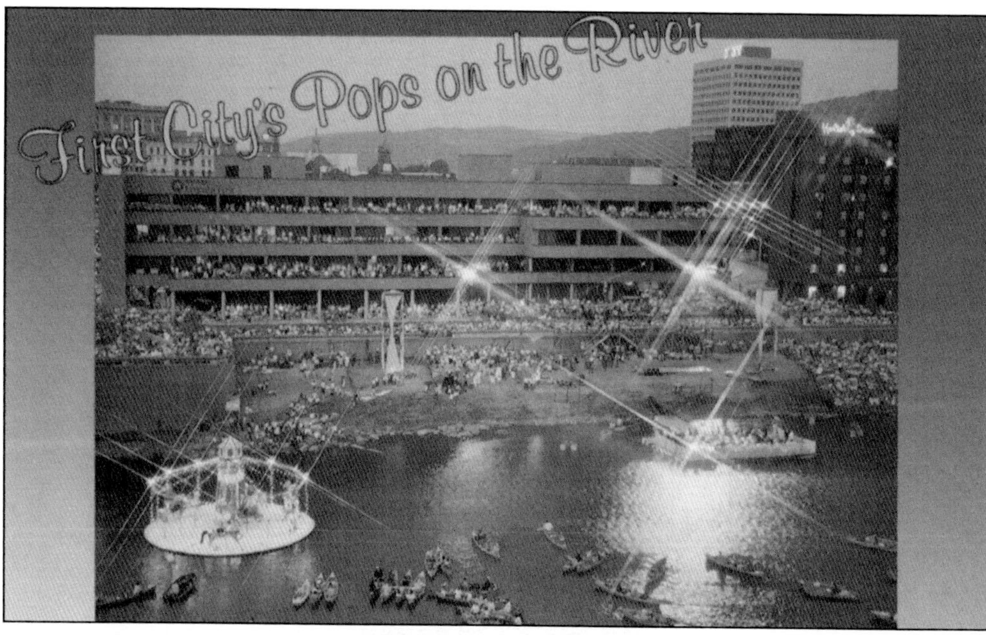

For several years, the First City National Bank sponsored a free concert, the BC (Broome County) Pops on the River. It was one of the most popular and well-attended events in Broome County. The orchestra played music on a raft anchored in the Chenango River. Each year, the performance was more spectacular than the last until production expenses became prohibitive and the event was discontinued.

The local Balloon Rally and Spiedie Festival fills the Broome County air with rainbows of color and the matchless aroma of our native delicacy. For several years, the event was held at Osteningo Park, as pictured in this photograph. Today, the activities have moved to a larger staging area at the Tri-Cities Airport in Endicott. Each summer, for a weekend, cooks vie for the title of "Best," grilling their own versions of spiedies, which consist of marinated meat or chicken. Balloonists from all over the world bring their lighter-than-air vessels here and give rides, instruct, and fill the skies with brilliantly colored airships.

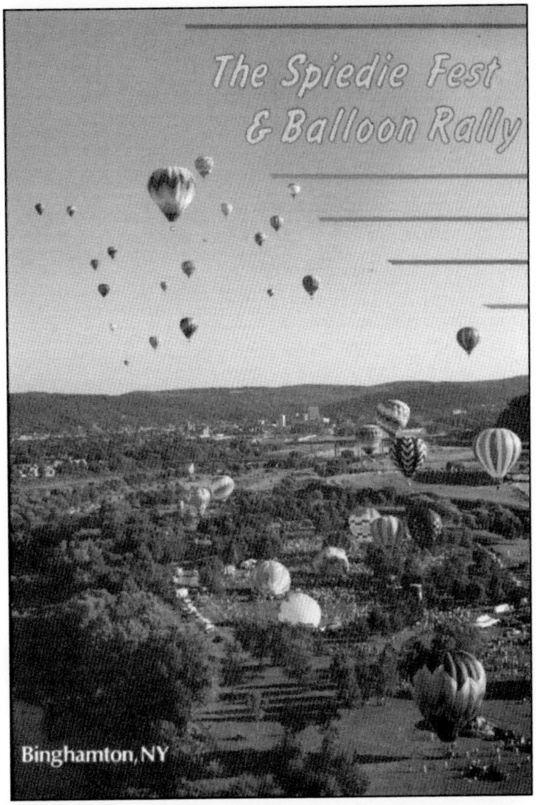

Binghamton University, part of the State University of New York, dates from 1946. It is now a large modern campus, nationally recognized for quality academic programs, a distinguished faculty, and affordable tuition. Five colleges work in concert to create an exciting and challenging university in a setting of forested hills, a 117-acre nature preserve, and a supportive community atmosphere.

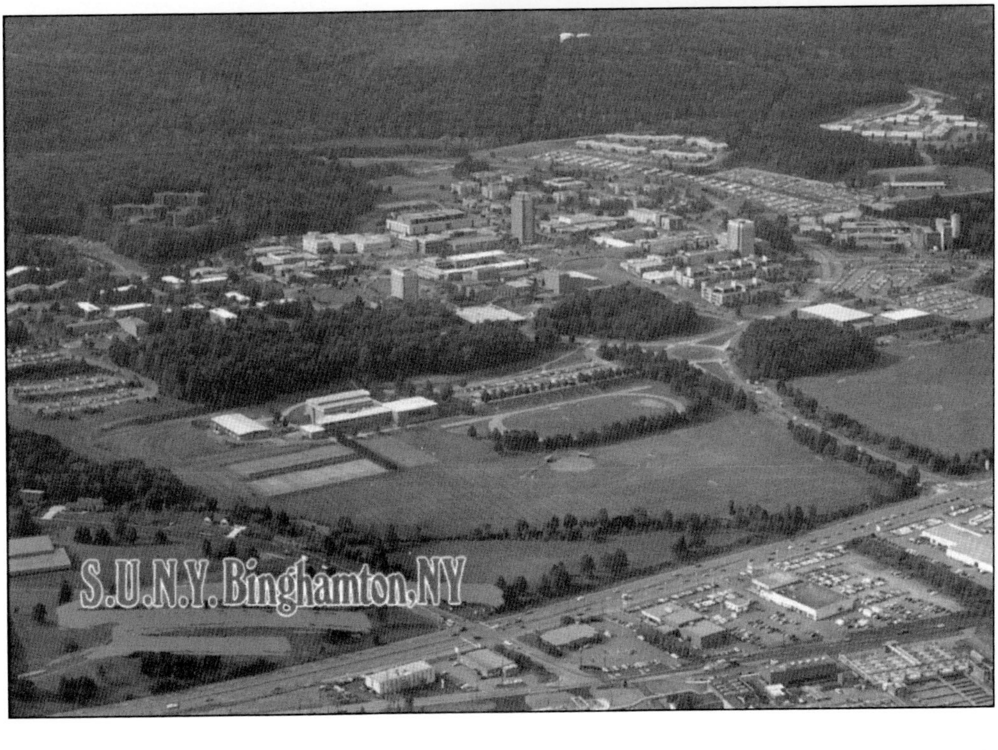

BIBLIOGRAPHY

Binghamton Centennial Souvenir Booklet, 1867–1967.

Bothwell, Lawrence. *Broome County Heritage.* Windsor Publications Inc., 1983.

Broome County Illustrated. Bellflower Press, 1895.

Everts, Ensign, and Everts. *Historical Atlas of Broome County, New York, Illustrated.* 1876.

Hinman, Marjory Barnum. *Court House Square: A Social History,* 1984.

———. *Lost Landmarks of Broome County,* 1983.

Lawyer, William S., ed. *Binghamton, Its Settlement, Growth and Development, 1800–1900.* Century Memorial Publishing Company.

Seward, W.F., ed. *Binghamton & Broome County.* Lewis Historical Society Publishing Company, 1894.

Smith, Gerald R. *The Valley of Opportunity.* The Downing Company, Publishers, 1988.

Wilkinson, J.B. *The Annals of Binghamton,* 1840.